The British World and the Five Rings

Prior to the outbreak of World War II, the British presided over the largest Empire in world history, a vast transoceanic and transcontinental realm of dominions, colonies, protectorates and mandates that covered over one-quarter of the world's land mass and comprised a population of over 450-million subjects. Spanning Europe, the Americas, Africa, Asia and Oceania, over fifty modern nations – currently recognized by the International Olympic Committee – were governed and controlled by the British crown at some stage prior to the gradual dissolution of the Empire. *The British World and the Five Rings* seeks to explore the relationship between the former British Empire and the Olympic Movement. It pays due regard to the settler dominions, but it also addresses those territories who were less willing partners in the British imperial project. In doing so, the tendency of so-called 'British World' histories to promote an apologia for Empire is rejected in favour of a critical approach to imperialism. Combining thorough research with engaging and accessible writing, *The British World and the Five Rings* is applicable to many fields of Olympic scholarship making it a central work in the growing field of sports studies.

This book was published as a special issue of *Sport in Society*.

Erik Nielsen is a Lecturer in the Department of Modern History, Politics and International Relations at Macquarie University, Australia. He is the author of *Sport and the British World, 1900–1930: Amateurism and National Identity in Australasia and Beyond* (2014).

Matthew P. Llewellyn is an Associate Professor of Kinesiology at the California State University, Fullerton, co-director of the Centre for Sociocultural Sport and Olympic Research, associate editor of the *Journal of Sport History*, and the author of numerous books and journal articles on the history of sport including *Rule Britannia: Nationalism, Identity and the Modern Olympic Games* (2012).

Sport in the Global Society – Contemporary Perspectives
Series Editor: Boria Majumdar

The social, cultural (including media) and political study of sport is an expanding area of scholarship and related research. While this area has been well served by the *Sport in the Global Society* series, the surge in quality scholarship over the last few years has necessitated the creation of *Sport in the Global Society – Contemporary Perspectives*. The series will publish the work of leading scholars in fields as diverse as sociology, cultural studies, media studies, gender studies, cultural geography and history, political science and political economy. If the social and cultural study of sport is to receive the scholarly attention and readership it warrants, a cross-disciplinary series dedicated to taking sport beyond the narrow confines of physical education and sport science academic domains is necessary. *Sport in the Global Society – Contemporary Perspectives* will answer this need.

Titles in the Series

Australian Sport
Antipodean Waves of Change
Edited by Kristine Toohey and Tracy Taylor

Australia's Asian Sporting Context
1920s and 1930s
Edited by Sean Brawley and Nick Guoth

Bearing Light: Flame Relays and the Struggle for the Olympic Movement
Edited by John J. MacAloon

Cricket, Migration and Diasporic Communities
Edited by Thomas Fletcher

'Critical Support' for Sport
Bruce Kidd

Disability in the Global Sport Arena
A Sporting Chance
Edited by Jill M. Clair

Diversity, Equity and Inclusion in Sport and Leisure
Edited by Katherine Dashper and Thomas Fletcher

Documenting the Beijing Olympics
Edited by D. P. Martinez and Kevin Latham

Ethnicity and Race in Association Football
Case Study analyses in Europe, Africa and the USA
Edited by David Hassan

Exploring the Cultural, Ideological and Economic Legacies of Euro 2012
Edited by Peter Kennedy and Christos Kassimeris

Fan Culture in European Football and the Influence of Left Wing Ideology
Edited by Peter Kennedy and David Kennedy

Football, Community and Social Inclusion
Edited by Daniel Parnell and David Richardson

Football in Asia
History, Culture and Business
Edited by Younghan Cho

Football in Southeastern Europe
From Ethnic Homogenization to
Reconciliation
Edited by John Hughson and Fiona Skillen

**Football Supporters and the
Commercialisation of Football**
Comparative Responses across Europe
*Edited by Peter Kennedy and
David Kennedy*

**Forty Years of Sport and Social Change,
1968–2008**
"To Remember is to Resist"
Edited by Russell Field and Bruce Kidd

Gender, Media, Sport
*Edited by Susanna Hedenborg and
Gertrud Pfister*

**Global Perspectives on Football in
Africa**
Visualising the Game
*Edited by Susann Baller, Giorgio Miescher
and Ciraj Rassool*

Global Sport Business
Community Impacts of Commercial Sport
Edited by Hans Westerbeek

**Governance, Citizenship and the New
European Football Championships**
The European Spectacle
*Edited by Wolfram Manzenreiter and
Georg Spitaler*

**Indigenous People, Race Relations and
Australian Sport**
*Edited by Christopher J. Hallinan and
Barry Judd*

Legacies of Great Men in World Soccer
Heroes, Icons, Legends
Edited by Kausik Bandyopadhyay

**Managing Expectations and Policy
Responses to Racism in Sport**
Codes Combined
*Edited by Keir Reeves, Megan Ponsford
and Sean Gorman*

Mediated Football
Representations and Audience Receptions
of Race/Ethnicity, Nation and Gender
Jacco van Sterkenburg and Ramón Spaaij

Modern Sports in Asia
Cultural Perspectives
*Edited by Younghan Cho and
Charles Leary*

**Moral Panic in Physical Education and
Coaching**
*Edited by Heather Piper, Dean Garratt
and Bill Taylor*

Olympic Reform Ten Years Later
*Edited by Heather Dichter and
Bruce Kidd*

**Reflections on Process Sociology and
Sport**
'Walking the Line'
Joseph Maguire

Security and Sport Mega Events
A Complex Relation
Edited by Diamantis Mastrogiannakis

Soccer in Brazil
Edited by Martin Curi

Soccer in the Middle East
Edited by Alon Raab and Issam Khalidi

South Africa and the Global Game
Football, Apartheid and Beyond
*Edited by Peter Alegi and
Chris Bolsmann*

Sport – Race, Ethnicity and Identity
Building Global Understanding
Edited by Daryl Adair

Sport and Citizenship
Edited by Matthew Guschwan

Sport and Communities
*Edited by David Hassan and
Sean Brown*

**Sport, Culture and Identity in the State
of Israel**
Edited by Yair Galily and Amir Ben-Porat

Sport in Australian National Identity
Kicking Goals
Tony Ward

Sport in the City
Cultural Connections
*Edited by Michael Sam and
John E. Hughson*

Sport, Memory and Nationhood in Japan
Remembering the Glory Days
Edited by Andreas Niehaus and
Christian Tagsold

Sport, Music, Identities
Edited by Anthony Bateman

Sport, Race and Ethnicity
The Scope of Belonging?
Edited by Katie Liston and Paddy Dolan

The British World and the Five Rings
Essays in British Imperialism and the
Modern Olympic Movement
Edited by Erik Nielsen and
Matthew P. Llewellyn

The Changing Face of Cricket
From Imperial to Global Game
Edited by Dominic Malcolm, Jon Gemmell
and Nalin Mehta

The Consumption and Representation
of Lifestyle Sports
Edited by Belinda Wheaton

The Containment of Soccer in Australia
Fencing Off the World Game
Edited by Christopher J. Hallinan and
John E. Hughson

The History of Motor Sport
A Case Study Analysis
Edited by David Hassan

The Making of Sporting Cultures
John E. Hughson

The Olympic Movement and the Sport
of Peacemaking
Edited by Ramón Spaaij and
Cindy Burleson

The Olympic Games: Meeting New
Challenges
Edited by David Hassan and Shakya Mitra

The Other Sport Mega-Event: Rugby
World Cup 2011
Edited by Steven J. Jackson

The Politics of Sport
Community, Mobility, Identity
Edited by Paul Gilchrist and
Russell Holden

The Politics of Sport in South Asia
Edited by Subhas Ranjan Chakraborty,
Shantanu Chakrabarti and
Kingshuk Chatterjee

The Social Impact of Sport
Edited by Ramón Spaaij

The Social Science of Sport
A Critical Analysis
Edited by Bo Carlsson and
Susanna Hedenborg

Towards a Social Science of Drugs
in Sport
Edited by Jason Mazanov

Twenty20 and the Future of Cricket
Edited by Chris Rumford

Who Owns Football?
The Governance and Management of the
Club Game Worldwide
Edited by David Hassan and
Sean Hamil

Why Minorities Play or Don't Play
Soccer
A Global Exploration
Edited by Kausik Bandyopadhyay

Women's Football in the UK
Continuing with Gender Analyses
Edited by Jayne Caudwell

Women's Sport in Africa
Edited by Michelle Sikes and
John Bale

The British World and the Five Rings

Edited by
Erik Nielsen and Matthew P. Llewellyn

LONDON AND NEW YORK

First published 2016
by Routledge
2 Park Square, Milton Park, Abingdon, Oxon, OX14 4RN, UK

and by Routledge
711 Third Avenue, New York, NY 10017, USA

Routledge is an imprint of the Taylor & Francis Group, an informa business

© 2016 Taylor & Francis

All rights reserved. No part of this book may be reprinted or reproduced or utilised in any form or by any electronic, mechanical, or other means, now known or hereafter invented, including photocopying and recording, or in any information storage or retrieval system, without permission in writing from the publishers.

Trademark notice: Product or corporate names may be trademarks or registered trademarks, and are used only for identification and explanation without intent to infringe.

British Library Cataloguing in Publication Data
A catalogue record for this book is available from the British Library

ISBN 13: 978-1-138-90958-8

Typeset in Times New Roman
by RefineCatch Limited, Bungay, Suffolk

Publisher's Note
The publisher accepts responsibility for any inconsistencies that may have arisen during the conversion of this book from journal articles to book chapters, namely the possible inclusion of journal terminology.

Disclaimer
Every effort has been made to contact copyright holders for their permission to reprint material in this book. The publishers would be grateful to hear from any copyright holder who is not here acknowledged and will undertake to rectify any errors or omissions in future editions of this book.

Contents

Citation Information	ix
1. Prologue: Britain, Empire and the Olympic experience *Erik Nielsen and Matthew P. Llewellyn*	1
2. For a 'United' Kingdom and a 'Greater' Britain: the British Olympic Association and the limitations and contestations of 'Britishness' *Matthew P. Llewellyn*	7
3. Flights to Empire: Australia's imperial engagement with the Olympic Games, 1900–1938 *Erik Nielsen*	25
4. (Dis)located Olympic patriots: sporting connections, administrative communications and imperial ether in interwar New Zealand *Geoffery Z. Kohe*	42
5. 'The emblem of one united body ... one great sporting Maple Leaf': The Olympic Games and Canada's quest for self-identity *Robert K. Barney and Michael H. Heine*	58
6. 'In our case, it seems obvious the British Organising Committee piped the tune': the campaign for recognition of 'Ireland' in the Olympic Movement, 1935–1956 *Tom Hunt*	77
7. Rhodesia and the Olympic Games: representations of masculinity, war and Empire, 1965–1980 *Andrew Novak*	95
8. The 'British World', other worlds, and the five rings: possibilities for trans-imperial histories and historical 'what ifs' *Mark Dyreson*	110
Index	119

Citation Information

The chapters in this book were originally published in *Sport in Society*, volume 18, issue 7 (September 2015). When citing this material, please use the original page numbering for each article, as follows:

Chapter 1
Prologue: Britain, Empire and the Olympic experience
Erik Nielsen and Matthew P. Llewellyn
Sport in Society, volume 18, issue 7 (September 2015) pp. 759–764

Chapter 2
For a 'United' Kingdom and a 'Greater' Britain: the British Olympic Association and the limitations and contestations of 'Britishness'
Matthew P. Llewellyn
Sport in Society, volume 18, issue 7 (September 2015) pp. 765–782

Chapter 3
Flights to Empire: Australia's imperial engagement with the Olympic Games, 1900–1938
Erik Nielsen
Sport in Society, volume 18, issue 7 (September 2015) pp. 783–799

Chapter 4
(Dis)located Olympic patriots: sporting connections, administrative communications and imperial ether in interwar New Zealand
Geoffery Z. Kohe
Sport in Society, volume 18, issue 7 (September 2015) pp. 800–815

Chapter 5
'The emblem of one united body ... one great sporting Maple Leaf': The Olympic Games and Canada's quest for self-identity
Robert K. Barney and Michael H. Heine
Sport in Society, volume 18, issue 7 (September 2015) pp. 816–834

Chapter 6
'In our case, it seems obvious the British Organising Committee piped the tune': the campaign for recognition of 'Ireland' in the Olympic Movement, 1935–1956
Tom Hunt
Sport in Society, volume 18, issue 7 (September 2015) pp. 835–852

CITATION INFORMATION

Chapter 7
Rhodesia and the Olympic Games: representations of masculinity, war and Empire,
1965–1980
Andrew Novak
Sport in Society, volume 18, issue 7 (September 2015) pp. 853–867

Chapter 8
The 'British World', other worlds, and the five rings: possibilities for trans-imperial
histories and historical 'what ifs'
Mark Dyreson
Sport in Society, volume 18, issue 7 (September 2015) pp. 868–875

For any permission-related enquiries please visit:
http://www.tandfonline.com/page/help/permissions

Prologue: Britain, Empire and the Olympic experience

Erik Nielsen[a] and Matthew P. Llewellyn[b]

[a]*Department of Modern History, Politics and International Relations, Macquarie University, Sydney, Australia;* [b]*Department of Kinesiology, California State University, Fullerton, CA, USA*

As the City of London successfully closed its doors to the world for the third time since Pierre de Coubertin's 1894 revival of the Olympic Movement, much attention has now turned to the growing body of scholarship focused on Britain's Olympic legacy. The end of the 2012 London Olympic Games has spawned a series of studies concerned with how vast sums of public expenditure will leave an enduring positive legacy for the people of London in particular and the UK in general (e.g. see Bernstock 2014). However, this worthy and necessary approach does run the risk of neglecting the historical context. For example, prior to the 2000 Sydney Olympics, the Centre of Olympic Studies was aligned to the School of History at the University of New South Wales (UNSW). This fruitful collaboration spawned important contributions to Australia's sporting history such as *Sport in the National Imagination* (Cashman 2002) and *Sport, Federation, Nation* (Cashman, O'Hara, and Honey 2001). This work sat well alongside preliminary considerations about the legacy of the Sydney Games. The outstanding contribution made towards understanding Sydney's legacy meant that the centre, renamed the Australian Centre for Olympic Studies, found a home at the Faculty of Business at the University of Technology Sydney despite the decision of UNSW to cease funding it (Adair 2010, 331). Here, the vital work into Sydney's legacy has continued, but the changed organizational context has seen the historical aspect deemphasized. The Australian case provides a cautionary tale for Britain in the post-London era to avoid.

The danger in avoiding the historical element is increased given the centrality of Britain to the international development of sport. It would be hard to underestimate Britain's historical influence on modern sport and the Olympic Movement. As history's largest Empire – and one fanatically devoted to sport – research has long highlighted the indelible mark that the British have left on both modern sporting and Olympic history. Yet, such focus omits a significant portion of Britain's Olympic legacy – the legacy of the Empire. Prior to the outbreak of Second World War, the British presided over the largest Empire in world history, a vast transoceanic and transcontinental realm of dominions, colonies, protectorates and mandates that covered over one-quarter of the world's land mass and comprised a population of over 450-million subjects. Spanning Europe, the Americas, Africa, Asia and Oceania, over 50 modern nations currently recognized by the International Olympic Committee (IOC) were governed and controlled by the British crown at some stage prior to the gradual dissolution of the Empire (Llewellyn 2012).

As a result, the British held an unprecedented cultural, political and sporting influence over the disparate ensemble of territories that comprised the Empire. Within the framework of the international Olympic Movement, the British oversaw the Olympic aspirations of each of its colonies. As Llewellyn (2012) has shown, the British supported the establishment of National Olympic Committees in each of its 'settler dominions' (Australia, Canada, New Zealand and South Africa), while simultaneously prohibiting the Olympic participation of all of its colonial dependencies in Africa, Asia and Central and South America. *The British World and the Five Rings: Essays in British Imperialism and the Modern Olympic Movement* seeks to explore the relationship between this vast and diverse Empire and the Olympic Movement. It pays due regard to the settler dominions, but it also addresses those territories who were less willing partners in the British imperial project. The imperial and post-imperial Olympic heritage of Ireland and Rhodesia are addressed in order to provide the opportunity for a more critical understanding of the Olympic Empire.

In addition to ensuring that the legacy of London includes a historical element, this study has several key aims. As noted above, the imperial legacy of the Olympic Games represents an important gap in the historical literature that needs to be filled. More specifically, the collection aims to explore the Olympic Movement as a site for investigating the shifting nature, meanings, complexities and limitations of 'Britishness' and British identity. The ethnic and cultural diversity within the Empire meant that 'Britishness' became a complex and layered term that was interpreted and applied differently across various parts of the Empire (Lester 2002). With its symbolic and narrative-forming properties, the Olympic Games became an important site where these meanings and limitations were played out. In addition to ethnic and cultural diversity, the meaning attributing to Britishness at the Olympic Games also altered over time. Wider historical forces, such as the development of colonial nationalisms and the later emergence of postcolonial consciousness, influenced the times at which different territories encountered imperialism. As a result, contributions to this volume are ordered in a chronological fashion.

The collection also aims to provide a wider focus rather than reasserting the centrality of the White Dominions in the imperial story through the Olympic Movement. The past 20 years have seen a growing trend towards employing a 'British World' approach to history. Historians like Buckner and Francis (2006, 6), as well as Bridge and Fedorowich (2003, 6), have suggested that the existence of a British World consists of familiar cultural values that were reinforced by 'family, cultural, commercial and professional links'. Following recent work into the relationship of sport in a wider sense (Nielsen 2014), this volume assesses ways in which the British World was negotiated in the Olympic context. Territories within the Empire beyond the UK challenged and in some cases rejected notions of Britishness, thus disrupting notions of a British World.

To address this challenge, contributions to this volume interrogate the nexus between nationalism and imperialism in a popular culture context. The relationship between imperial and national is a cornerstone of studies into imperialism, particularly with regard to the former British Empire. The Olympic Games, as a popular culture spectacle, provide the opportunity to engage with this nexus in a context that goes beyond diplomatic relations. A study of the Olympic Movement in the imperial context also has much to offer given the movement's historical development. While the founder of the modern Olympic Movement, Pierre de Coubertin, imbued the Games with an internationalist ethic, the games themselves quickly became a site where virulent nationalism could be expressed. An examination of the rising tide of nationalism within the Olympic Movement offers the opportunity to assess the relationship of cultural expressions of nationalism to political developments.

The British imperial history of the Olympic Games was also affected by the local political context. As a result, the volume also seeks to examine the way that local political forces influenced the expression of Britishness in the Olympic Movement. Despite the traditional wariness of politicians to involve themselves in sporting matters, it is clear that the local (including national and state/provincial) political context influenced the expression of Britishness within the Olympic Movement. This volume therefore seeks to interrogate the way that individuals within political systems and political events and aspirations influenced the way in which Britishness was expressed within the Olympic Movement.

These aims will be explored through four key themes. As editors, we recognize and appreciate differences in terms of methodological approach and chronological focus, and diversity is a value that we have consciously attempted to foster throughout the project. However, these themes have been developed in order to create a 'unity in diversity' and coherence within the volume. These themes reflect key debates within the wider field of British imperial studies. The first is the complex relationship between core (in this case, Great Britain in general and England in particular) and periphery (British imperial territories). Recent scholarship has preferred a fluid understanding of the relationship between core and periphery, rather than simply asserting the centrality of London (Lester 2006, 128). Contributions to this volume chart the ways in which Great Britain's dominant place within the imperial Olympic Movement was challenged by administrators, athletes and politicians across the Empire in the colonial and postcolonial era.

The relationship between imperial and national is another key theme in imperial studies that has strongly influenced this volume. The authors tell the imperial history of the Olympic Movement using territories that developed into nations. Recent scholarship has eschewed a binary distinction between imperialism and nationalism. Historians like Schreuder and Ward (2008), Curran and Ward (2010), Belich (2001, 2007) and Buckner and Francis (2005, 2006) have argued that the legacy of imperialism has continued to influence identities following independence. This volume examines the way that the interaction between imperial loyalty and the development of national consciousness was expressed through the Olympic Movement, and the effect that this interaction had on the formation of national identities. This is a process that influenced different regions of the Empire at different times, and provides further rationale for the chronological approach that the volume has employed.

Party politics, and especially the influence of the British Conservative Party, is a theme that runs through the volume. It has long been noted that British governments and politicians traditionally claimed a *laissez-faire* approach to sport in the early twentieth century, though archival research has shown a more interventionist approach when engaging with continental European governments (Johnes 2010, 452). This volume presents further evidence of a long-standing commitment on the part of British Conservatives to use sport as a forum where they could further policy goals including maintenance of British prestige abroad and the UK itself. This influenced Great Britain's relations with former Dominions as well as 'foreign' nations. British Conservative politicians that also served as Olympic administrators found it difficult to separate their political and sporting responsibilities throughout the twentieth century.

The final theme is concerned with the relationship between the wider world and a more insular 'British World' (Bridge and Fedorowich 2003; Buckner and Francis 2005, 2006). The turn of the twentieth century represents a time period when Britain's international political and economic dominance was coming under threat. The Olympic Movement represents a key site for examining the way that Britons across the world dealt with this challenge. The Games were of course founded by a Frenchman, but Coubertin was strongly influenced by British ideas about sport (Llewellyn 2012, 2). As arguably the most important sporting 'nation', Britain had to accept the presence of outsiders into the world of sport, which they had previously dominated. The way that societies under study dealt with an increasingly international Olympic Movement provides interesting insights into the general imperial response to this changing international environment.

The collection begins with Matthew P. Llewellyn's contribution concerning the definition of Britain itself in Olympic terms. Llewellyn displays that, far from a straightforward matter, 'Britain' was a fiercely contested term both within and without the UK. The 'Celtic Fringe' of Scotland, Ireland and Wales was used to separate representation in sports such as association football and rugby union and expressed discomfort and anger when faced with the prospect of combining under the English-dominated British Olympic Association (BOA). Sport was clearly and purposefully mixed with politics, as the Conservative-dominated BOA used Olympic representation as a front in the battle to preserve the Union against moves towards Irish Home Rule. Pan-British identities were reinforced and challenged through the British imperial Olympic team scheme.

Next follows two contributions on Australia and New Zealand that employ contrasting methodologies to provide fresh insights into two extremely similar and interlinked societies. Erik Nielsen's traditional approach reveals Australia's Olympic embrace of British imperialism that was at once tight, complex and long lasting. Imperialism influenced key aspects of Australia's early Olympic history, including the preparation of athletes and the construction of the Australian team, the development of the British Empire Games and the response to a changing Olympic world in the face of the rising influence of Authoritarian nations. Taking a lead from Schreuder and Ward (2008), Nielsen demonstrates that British Olympic developments were not simply repeated in Australia, but were giving an Antipodean edge. Despite this, the Australian Olympic community attempted to assert centrality within the Empire for itself.

Geoff Kohe applies what Booth (2004, 18) has termed a deconstructionist approach to demonstrate the ways in which key New Zealand Olympic Committee figures used notable expatriate New Zealanders of high social status to the benefit of the Committee. Kohe effectively demonstrates that the Olympic Movement provides an outstanding site for analysing the 'imperial associations, identities and loyalties, and transnational connections' that constitute New Zealand's relations with Britain. Like Nielsen, Kohe demonstrates that the Olympic Games were used by New Zealanders to assert their place within the international sporting landscape. The Olympic communities in both New Zealand and Australia aimed to prevent British and other international Olympic administrators from forgetting the Antipodes.

Next, Robert K. Barney and Michael Heine provide an imperial context for that iconic expression of Canadian identity, the *red* maple leaf. Barney and Heine argue that the red maple leaf came to represent a distinct Canadian culture instead of the British Union Jack, and that Canada's involvement in the 1908 Olympic Games in London played a key role in this shift. While the maple leaf was a uniquely Canadian symbol, the introduction of the symbol underlines the intertwined nature of national and imperial discourses. It was introduced to Olympic discussion by Canada's first IOC member John Hanbury-Williams, who was exported to Canada to take up a position with Governor-General Grey's staff. The maple leaf made quite an impression on and off the track in London and its later display by dual sprint gold medallist Percy Williams in 1928 at Amsterdam inspired George Francis Gillman Stanley, the designer of the current Canadian flag.

Thomas Hunt extends the nationalist theme through his examination of Ireland's fight to express its independence in the Olympic sphere. The development of Ireland into an independent state was a complex process that saw the founding of the Irish Free State, the almost immediate withdrawal of Northern Ireland back into the UK, and the later formation of an Irish republic. As a result of this process, the Irish Olympic community claimed jurisdiction over the whole island, and held steadfastly to the notion of Irish sport as representing the whole '32 counties'. In doing so, they ran into resistance from sporting figures within the UK. British members of the IOC, most notably Lord Burghley, who were also leading Conservatives (and Unionists) attempted to minimize the influence of Irish nationalism within the Olympic Movement. While other international organizations allowed the Irish republic to style itself as 'Ireland' despite Northern Ireland's status as an integral part of the UK, Burghley and his conspirators within the IOC insisted that the Irish Olympic community had no claim to the name. Burghley was able to hold this line and convince IOC leaders and officials during Sigfrid Edström's presidency to resist Irish calls. However, the Irish found a more receptive ear with the ascension of American Avery Brundage to the presidency and a resultant loss of influence of Brundage's rival Burghley. Brundage's acceptance of Irish arguments was vital in terms of keeping Ireland within the Olympic fold.

Finally, Andrew Novak engages with the ironic situation that Rhodesia found itself in during the Unilateral Declaration of Independence (UDI) era. Rhodesia was wedded to British sporting concepts, but was estranged politically. Olympic involvement is used as a lens to explore issues of race and gender that affected Rhodesian society and its relations with the outside world. While Rhodesia sent multiracial teams to the Olympic Games, the racist policies of the ruling Rhodesian Front drew the ire of the international boycott movement. The impact of the international boycott movement on Rhodesia's Olympic participation illuminates the self-proclaimed nation's relations with Britain, and the way that British governments of different persuasions dealt with Rhodesia. The shift from a hostile Labour government to a more agnostic Conservative government had clear influence on the British response to UDI, but this shift did not affect the general trend towards international isolation. Individual white Rhodesian women challenged sporting patriarchy on the field and in the administrative sphere, but were represented in gendered terms. African women did not fare as well, and gender and racial stereotypes were deployed to excuse their omission from Rhodesian teams.

This collection will hopefully provoke discussion rather than serve as the last word on the role of British imperialism and the Olympic Games. The 'British World' concept obviously does not contain the entirety of the Empire, and important stories have unfortunately been excluded from this volume. The British World approach has been criticized for 'running the risk of reasserting whiteness and Britishness' (Pickles 2011, 96). The editors and authors hope that this has been avoided here, and recognize that the imperial Olympic experience addressed here is unavoidably partial. The Olympic histories of territories such as the Indian subcontinent, British Africa, South Africa and the Caribbean amongst others have much to tell us about the interaction between British imperialism and the Olympic Movement, even if nations like Australia and Canada have traditionally boasted more impressive medal tallies. While the British World concept has been extended in this volume through the inclusion of nationalist Ireland and UDI-era Rhodesia, much more is to be done to create a truly imperial Olympic history.

Disclosure statement

No potential conflict of interest was reported by the authors.

References

Adair, Daryl. 2010. "Australia." In *Routledge Companion to Sports History*, edited by S. W. Pope and John Nauright, 330–349. Abingdon: Routledge.

Belich, James. 2001. *Paradise Reforged: A History of the New Zealanders from the 1880s to the Year 2000*. Honolulu: University of Hawai'i Press.

Belich, James. 2007. *Making Peoples: A History of the New Zealanders from Polynesian Settlement to the End of the Nineteenth Century*. Auckland: Penguin Books.

Bernstock, Penny. 2014. *Olympic Housing: A Critical Review of London 2012's Legacy*. Farnham: Ashgate.

Booth, Douglas. 2004. "Post-Olympism? Questioning Olympic Historiography." In *Post-Olympism? Questioning Sport in the Twenty-First Century*, edited by John Bale and Mette Krogh Christensen, 13–32. Oxford: Berg.

Bridge, Carl, and Kent Fedorowich, eds. 2003. "Mapping the British World." In *The British World: Diaspora, Culture and Identity*, 1–15. London: Frank Cass.

Buckner, Phillip, and R. Douglas Francis, eds. 2005. "Introduction." In *Rediscovering the British World*, 9–20. Calgary: University of Calgary Press.

Buckner, Phillip, and R. Douglas Francis, eds. 2006. "Introduction." In *Canada and the British World: Culture, Migration, and Identity*, 1–9. Vancouver: UBC Press.

Cashman, Richard. 2002. *Sport in the National Imagination: Australian Sport in the Federation Decades*. Sydney: Walla Walla Press.

Cashman, Richard, John O'Hara, and Andrew Honey. 2001. *Sport, Federation, Nation*. Sydney: Walla Walla Press.

Curran, James, and Stuart Ward. 2010. *The Unknown Nation: Australia after Empire*. Carlton: Melbourne University Press.

Johnes, Martin. 2010. "Great Britain." In *Routledge Companion to Sports History*, edited by S. W. Pope and John Nauright, 330–349. Abingdon: Routledge.

Lester, Alan. 2002. "British Settler Discourse and the Circuits of Empire." *History Workshop Journal* 54 (1): 24–48.

Lester, Alan. 2006. "Imperial Circuits and Networks: Geographies of the British Empire." *History Compass* 4 (1): 124–141.

Llewellyn, Matthew P. 2012. *Rule Britannia: Nationalism, Identity and the Modern Olympic Games*. Abingdon: Routledge.

Nielsen, Erik. 2014. *Sport and the British World, 1900–1930: Amateurism and National Identity in Australasia and beyond*. Houndmills: Palgrave Macmillan.

Pickles, Katie. 2011. "The Obvious and the Awkward: Postcolonialism and the British World." *New Zealand Journal of History* 45 (1): 85–101.

Schreuder, Deryck M., and Stuart Ward. 2008. *Australia's Empire*. Oxford: Oxford University Press.

For a 'United' Kingdom and a 'Greater' Britain: the British Olympic Association and the limitations and contestations of 'Britishness'

Matthew P. Llewellyn

Department of Kinesiology, California State University, Fullerton, USA

> During the first two decades of the twentieth century, the Home-Nations of England, Scotland, Ireland and Wales joined forces in competing in the Olympic Games under the banner of 'Great Britain' (or deviations thereof). The Olympics served as an important symbolic site for fostering and promoting a broader 'British' national identity. In practice, however, the prevalence and persistence of competing national identities and allegiances roiled early attempts to create a unified British Olympic team. These counter-prevailing forces of nationalism further served to undermine the British Olympic Association's ambitious attempt to unite the British Empire in a 'Greater Britain' team for the 1916 Berlin Olympic Games. As this work will reveal, 'Britishness' was a layered, contested and racially homogenous term that was interpreted and applied differently across various parts of the British Isles and its Empire.

Britain and British identity has been the subject of deep and sustained historiography.[1] In the past two decades alone, Liberal and Conservative scholars have debated the historical underpinning of 'Britishness', its meanings and applications both at home and abroad in an age of Empire, as well as its erosion and decline in the aftermath of World War II following an economic collapse, decolonization and the introduction of governmental multicultural policies (see, e.g., Bell 2011; Colley 1994; Davies 1998; Hitchens 2008; Marr 2000). This mainstream historiographical focus on 'Britishness' has been counterpoised by a wave of scholarship emphasizing the discourses of national identity and distinctiveness within the multinational state (Colls 2002; Davies 2007; Devine 2001; Kumar 2003). This decentring of the British nation has been predicated upon a focus on Gaelic and Celtic nationalism, regional histories, as well as an examination of the colonial push for independence and self-governance in the broader geographical realm of the British Empire (see, e.g., Bell 2011; Davies 2007; Devine 2001; Harvie 2004). Despite some noteworthy examples (Bairner 2001; Holt 1989; Holt and Mason 2000), the flourishing discipline of sport history has contributed to the decentring of a shared, civic British identity. This literature, much of which is focused on association football and rugby union, emphasizes the role of sport – and the banal national stereotypes that sport promotes – in the formation and hardening of separate and competing national identities within the Home-Nations of England, Ireland, Scotland and Wales (see, e.g., Beck 1999; Dart 2009; Johnes 2002, 2005).

In both scholarly and public discourse, contemporary Britain and 'Britishness' lay in a moribund state: as a collection of institutions with no shared foundational culture, or as an identity fixed in the past. The decline of British identity raises pertinent questions about its historical formation. Specifically, what role did international sport play in the cultivation of a shared sense of 'Britishness' among the Home-Nations? How did British sporting officials negotiate the concomitant rise of competing Irish, Scottish and Welsh claims for national distinctiveness? Did a British identity flourish on the international stage, or, alternatively, did the homogeneity of the individual nations prevail? And what were the dimensions, meanings and limitations of 'Britishness' when placed in the broader context of Empire?

The Olympic Games, the quadrennial multi-sporting global festival, provide an important symbolic site where early expressions of 'Britishness' were played out. The Olympics, similar to all international sporting events between nation-states, are occasions for competitive national self-assertion (Dyreson 1997; Keys 2006; Senn 1999). Although the Olympic Charter proclaimed that the Games are contests between individuals, not nations, the International Olympic Committee (IOC) created an institutional structure based on national representation, a decision that opened the door to frequent displays of nationalism. Pierre de Coubertin's call for peaceful internationalism was counterpoised by nations and their governments appropriating the Games as a way to both foster national identities and demonstrate national vigour. The Olympics celebrated the primacy of the nation-state. Symbols, credentials and protocol were highly charged, with athletes seen as nationalist proxies – tangible representations of their 'imagined communities' (Anderson 2006; Hobsbawm 1990; Keys 2006). Early IOC policy even encouraged this tendency by tabulating national medal performances – up to 1921. The Games provided a viable platform for inculcating national feelings and fostering an oppositional 'us' against 'them' mentality. National anthems, colours and flags were displayed as cultural artefacts to reinforce similarities and accentuate differences. The infrequency of the Olympic Games heightened anticipation and exaggerated patriotic expression (Espy 1981).

For the high-profile, politically conservative English elites who ran and controlled the British Olympic Association (BOA), the nationalistic currents enveloping the Olympics made the Games an ideal site for the construction and propagation of a shared collective sense of 'Britishness'. Between the establishment of the BOA in 1905 and the outbreak of World War I, BOA officials pursued an administrative policy designed to unite the Home-Nations of England, Ireland, Scotland and Wales into one representative British Olympic team. They also conceived of 'Britain' more holistically. As a series of sweeping imperial, political and social challenges elevated fears of national decadence and decline, BOA leaders fought to maintain Britain's global sporting position by welding the United Kingdom and its colonial possessions into a formidable Empire Olympic team. The BOA calculated that a unified 'Greater Britain' team would solidify colonial and dominion relations with the old mother country and salvage Britain's self-perceived reputation as the leader of modern sport. In practice, however, the prevalence and persistence of competing national identities and allegiances roiled attempts to create a unified British team during the early decades of international Olympic competition. An analysis of the BOA's early nation and empire building Olympic projects reveals that 'Britishness' was a layered, contested and racially homogenous term, susceptible to the counter-prevailing forces of Celtic and Dominion nationalism.

Sport, Britain and the British

The idea of 'Britain' can be tenuously traced all the way back to Roman occupation during antiquity (AD 43–410). Over the course of the next millennium, turmoil, distrust and forced occupation would gradually give way to more peaceful coexistence and interaction between the disparate cultural and ethnic groups that originally inhabited the British Isles. King Henry VIII's annexation of Wales with England in 1536 and the ascent of the Scottish King James VI to the throne England in 1603 represented the first palpable steps towards the realization of a unitary British state. In the aftermath of a bloody Civil War,

Queen Anne's passing of the Act of Union in 1707, joining the kingdoms of Scotland and England – including Wales – into a political union, followed by the addition of Ireland in 1801, ensured that the idea of 'Great Britain' became an enduring reality. Throughout the remainder of the nineteenth century, rampant commercial and colonial expansion and the acquisition of a vast overseas Empire positioned Britain and the British at the forefront of a new world order (Davies 1998; Kearney 1995; Murdoch 1998). As Linda Colley (1994, 11–18, 55) has shown, 'Britishness' was superimposed over an array of internal differences, and gradually nurtured through war – primarily against Napoleonic France – popular pageantry, empire, Protestantism, trade and mercantilism, and fear of the racial 'Other'.

The establishment of Great Britain, an Anglo-Celtic multinational state, was not an easy process. The prevalence of insular geopolitics, fuelled by competing ethnic and national identities, traditions, ideas, languages and institutions, long hampered the development of a shared sense of 'Britishness'(Hechter 1999; Robbins 1998). This is not just an historical phenomenon either, as Britain's entry into the European Union, the governmental introduction of multicultural policies, the passing of devolution in Scotland and Wales in 1997, continued civil-strife in Northern Ireland, and the resurgence of the Scottish separatist movement and a national referendum in 2014 testifies (Nairn 1981; Nairn 2000). In the United Kingdom, 'Britishness' entailed a kind of a dual identity for each of its constituent parts. For instance, the Welsh perceived, and continue to perceive themselves primarily as being 'Welsh', but in relation to foreigners they were 'British'. The same certainly remains true for both the Irish and the Scots. Unlike their Celtic neighbours who repeatedly asserted their own distinctiveness both politically and culturally, the English have traditionally identified themselves as being British. Kumar (2003, 179) argues that as the largest, wealthiest and most powerful partner in the unitary British state, the English were less inclined to trumpet their own national identity out of fear that it would threaten the 'unity and integrity' of the union.

The complexities and peculiarities of British identity hold particular pertinence in the world of international sport. Since the inception of competitive international sporting fixtures at the end of the nineteenth century, England, Ireland, Scotland and Wales proceeded to compete as individual representative nations. Sports such as association football and rugby union offered the Home-Nations, particularly the Celtic fringe of Ireland, Scotland and Wales, an avenue for reaffirming and revelling in their own distinct, submerged national identities. Sport helped to underpin the persistence of difference. Johnes (2000) contends that 'for the many people on the so-called Celtic fringes of Britain' international sport provided 'one of the few pieces of tangible evidence that their nation exists'. In Wales, participation in international rugby union can be viewed as an allegorical expression of Welsh nationhood. Victory on the rugby field was translated as a symbol of a vibrant, self-confident and independent Welsh nation, free from the orbit of English influence (Andrews 1991; Johnes 2005). Similarly, Scottish participation in association football significantly contributed to a heightened sense of national self-consciousness (Bairner 2001; Jarvie and Walker 1994). The Irish, at least the Roman Catholic dominated southerners, also harnessed the enormous nation-building potential of sport, but in a somewhat different manner. Organized under the auspices of the politically motivated Gaelic Athletic Association (GAA), the Irish revived and celebrated their own traditional sports of hurling and Gaelic football as an act of resistance against the rapacious forces of English cultural imperialism (Cronin 1999).

Paradoxically, international sport also served as a vehicle for fostering a broader 'British' national identity. In a number of sports the Home-Nations have joined forces in competing under the banner of 'Great Britain', or deviations thereof. By the late nineteenth century, the British shared a military, a parliament, a monarchy, a legal and judiciary system, an economy, political parties, a unified ruling class, and through British participation in the Olympic Games they also shared a sports team. The earliest representation of a British team, however, actually predated the 1896 Athens Olympic Games. As early as 1888 an unofficial 'British Isles' rugby union team composed of English, Scottish and Welsh players toured Australasia, laying the foundations for the future quadrennial British and Irish Lions rugby union tours to the southern hemisphere (Thomas 2005). In tennis, the creation of the Davis Cup in 1900 provided another early sporting example of solidarity and collaboration between England, Ireland, Scotland and Wales (Coombe 1949). Given the limited scope and international appeal of these events, particularly in their infancy, the Olympic Games provided the largest platform for the Home-Nations to compete under the colours of the Union Jack (Llewellyn 2012a).

Established on 24 May 1905, in a private meeting held in Committee Room Number 12 of the House of Commons, the BOA worked to unite the constituent parts of the British Isles into one official and representative Olympic team. As an institution of remarkable homogeneity, the BOA drew its members from exclusively aristocratic and upper middle-class circles, tethered together on the basis of a public school education and a strong proclivity for competitive, elite amateur sport. Given the organization's public school composition and inherently nationalistic and pro-establishment worldview, the BOA attracted high-ranking military and political English elites with strong Conservative leanings (Llewellyn 2012a, 13–16). In fact, the Conservative Party established a long-standing relationship with the British Olympic movement. Combining their work within the state structure, four Tory MP's, including Sir Howard Vincent (Sheffield Central), and Sir James Lees Knowles Bart (West Salford) attended the inaugural meeting of the BOA in the House of Commons.[2] Two of the BOA's first three Chairmen, Lord Desborough of Taplow (1905–1913) and Lord Downham of Fulham (1919–1920), and its inaugural President, the Duke of Sutherland (1923–1936), also held prominent positions within the Conservative Party (Llewellyn 2012a, 15).

The dominant presence of high-profile Conservative figures and sympathizers on the BOA reveal the organization's clear nation-building agenda. As the party of permanence, stability and tradition, the Conservatives were committed to the maintenance of monarchy, the House of Lords, the consolidation and grandeur of Empire, and the preservation of the British union – an attempt to maintain and promote a British sporting union appeared a natural extension of Conservative ideology (Coetzee 1990; Fforde 1990; Green 1996). For British Conservatives, the unification of the Home-Nations into a representative British Olympic team represented a bulwark against a powerful set of internal and external challenges. Widespread labour unrest and militant trade unionism, the rising tide of Liberal radicalism and democratization, Irish nationalist fury, the women's suffrage movement, heightened international economic competition and the aggressive tone of German naval ambition stimulated much apprehension and uncertainty during the late nineteenth and early twentieth centuries (Cannadine 1999; Reynolds 1991). Even in the sporting realm, Conservatives found markers of decadence and decline as international rivals mounted a serious challenge to Britain's historical supremacy, both perceived and real (Lowerson 1996). Perceiving an unwelcome deterioration in their country's relative position as a military, economic, imperial and sporting power, the predominantly Conservative members of the BOA naturally embraced the Olympic Games as a platform for promoting British interests both at home and abroad.

A 'United' Kingdom?

The BOA's formative nation-building efforts occurred at the precise moment when the constituent parts of the British Isles were busy fortifying, legitimizing and expressing their own distinct identities within the international sporting realm. As a testament to Britain's pioneering role in the development and diffusion of modern sport, the Home-Nations were each afforded the opportunity to compete under their own national affiliations – a privilege no longer extended to stateless nations such as the Basques and Catalonians in Spain (Bairner 2001). In association football, England, Ireland, Scotland and Wales featured competitively in the annual home international championship, which dated back to the early 1880s (Beck 1999, 26). While a deep-seated blend of isolationism and parochialism had historically deterred the Home-Nations from competing against countries outside of the British Isles, the early years of the twentieth century witnessed a gradual departure from this policy – England played a series of competitive fixtures against Austria, Hungary and Bohemia beginning in 1907–1908 (Beck 1999, 32). In rugby union, the Home-Nations were more assertive in sowing the seeds of broader international competition. Peering out from behind the comfort of their long-standing home championship, the English, Irish, Scottish and Welsh each entertained the touring New Zealand 'All Blacks' and South African 'Springboks' in 1905 and 1906–1907, respectively (Collins 2009). The Home-Nations reaffirmed their independent, equal nation status by competing as separate entities in international cross-country events, beginning in 1903 in the form of a Home Countries Championship.

The early twentieth-century British sporting landscape was a testimony to the complex relationship between nations and nation-states. Against the realities of separate national representation in association football, rugby union and cross-country, BOA officials were determined to prove that the submerged nationalities of English, Irish, Scottish and Welsh could coexist alongside a broader nationality and affiliation to a unitary British state. The 1906 Intercalated Games represented the first real participation of an organized and sizable British Olympic team (Figure 1). The Anglocentrism and elitism of the BOA naturally transferred to the Olympic arena, as evidenced by the 28 English athletes who comprised the British squad – 6 Scotsmen, 3 Irishmen and 3 Welshmen filled the remaining roster

Figure 1. The 'British' team at the 1906 Intercalated Games in Athens (Cook 1908a).

positions (Mallon 1999, 188–190). Revealing the fluid, dynamic and contested realities of 'Britishness', the inclusion of Ireland's Peter O'Connor, Con Leahy and John Daley onto a British Olympic team sparked heated opposition. Upon their arrival in the Greek capital, the three Irish athletes were reportedly surprised at the news that they had been listed in the official programme under the banner of Great Britain (McCarthy 2007). As representatives of the Irish Amateur Athletic Association (IAAA), both O'Connor and Leahy relied solely on Irish funding in order to subsidize their trip to Athens, thanks to a public subscription setup on the pages of the *Irish Field*. Ireland's third representative, John Daly, reportedly defied a GAA ban on foreign competition to compete in the marathon event in Athens at his own expense (Quinn 2004). Lacking a National Olympic Committee (NOC) of its own at this time, the Irish were officially subsumed into the Great Britain team. Incensed by the official ruling, Irish athletes arrived in Athens determined to renounce their status as British competitors by proudly asserting their own distinct Irish identities.

Irish attempts to seek full recognition as an independent athletic entity reflected the nation's broader historical struggle to achieve 'Home Rule' from Britain. Resentment towards a political union with Britain can be traced all the way back to the enacting of the Act of Union in 1801, when King George III incorporated Ireland into the greater British realm. Over the course of the next few decades, the calamity of the Great Famine and the rising forces of Anglicization fuelled heightened waves of violent and political insurrection. By the late 1800s, the Irish Parliamentary Party rose to political prominence revitalizing nationalist attempts to achieve self-government from Britain. Even with the support of Liberal Prime Minster William E. Gladstone, Irish ambitions met stern resistance from Protestant-dominated Ulster Unionists in the North, who strongly opposed Home Rule on the grounds that it would adversely affect their economic prosperity and bolster the position of the Roman Catholic Church. This stance was also shared by the Unionist's political allies in Britain, the Conservative Party. In the midst of overwhelming political opposition, the first Home Rule Bill failed to even make its way beyond the House of Commons. A second Gladstonian Bill seven years later met its demise in the Conservative dominated House of Lords. By 1906, however, the restoration of the Liberal government and their subsequent landslide victory in the general election, elevated expectations that the passage of Home Rule for Ireland was finally in sight (Boyce 1995). At the time of the Intercalated Games, however, Ireland remained a part of Great Britain in the eyes of both the international community and the IOC.

As a politically conservative organization, the BOA strongly opposed Home Rule for Ireland, as exemplified by chairman Lord Desborough's decision to switch party affiliation to the Conservatives as part of a Unionist defection in response to Liberal support for Irish independence (Llewellyn 2012a, 31). As such, the BOA lobbied the Hellenic Organizing Committee, which held jurisdiction over Olympic affairs in Athens, to reject Irish nationalist claims. Undeterred, the Irish athletes took their case to the highest authority, Prince George of Greece. After briefly considering the Irish appeal for separate representation the Crown Prince allegedly resolved, as the *Irish Independent* noted: 'When Ireland has a Parliament of its own you can hoist the flag, but not before ... Perhaps there will be an Irish Parliament by the time the next Olympian games come round' (3 May 1906, 5). As a close relative of the British royal family – King Edward VII's wife, Queen Alexandra, was his aunt – and a personal friend of high-ranking BOA officials such as Lord Desborough, Prince George's decision was not very surprising. Ruling in favour of the Irish contingent would have been widely regarded as a personal affront to King Edward VII, his uncle-in-law and a special guest of the Greek royal family during the Athens Games.

Back on Irish soil, the Crown Prince's ruling triggered a deluge of criticism. The *Irish Independent* led the charge, labelling the monarch's decision as a 'distinct injustice', especially since Britain's white dominions of Australia, Canada, New Zealand and South Africa were each granted independent status (2 May 1906, 4). Irish frustrations at their incorporation into a British sporting union manifested themselves most visibly during the course of the long jump Olympic medal ceremony. In perhaps the earliest political demonstrations in modern Olympic history, Peter O'Connor sensationally climbed the flag pole to remove the Union Jack that was cast overhead in recognition of his second place finish. While his fellow countryman Cornelius 'Con' Leahy stood guard below, an impassioned O'Connor unfurled a large green Irish flag embroidered with the words *Erin Go Bragh* (Ireland Forever), the popular maxim of the Irish Home Rule movement, and remained aloft for some considerable time waving it vigorously (Guiney 1996, 31–33; *Irish Times*, May 4, 1906, 6; *The Gaelic-American*, May 5, 1906, 4). As an unwilling member of the Great Britain Olympic team, O'Connor's actions represented an act of political defiance, a nationalistic demonstration aimed at drawing the world's attention towards Ireland's claims for political emancipation from Britain. Intruding into the debate from across the Atlantic, the *Gaelic-American* enthusiastically intoned: 'The thousands of spectators from all parts of the world know now, if they did not know it before, that Britain's blood stained banner is not respected or recognized by the Irish people' (5 May 1906, 5).

The anti-British sentiments of Irish athletes aligned with the preponderance of English athletes and officials, raises questions about the extent to which an overarching sense of Britishness prevailed among the camp. Did the British athletes share a sense of a common consciousness and a common identity despite admitted differences of region within the British Isles? Or was Britishness merely a state identity, sitting on top of more meaningful national affiliations? Unlike their Irish teammates who vociferously protested their incorporation into the British team, Scottish and Welsh athletes expressed no public disapproval of the new national combination. Nevertheless, one can only speculate as to how they felt privately about either competing under the banner of 'Great Britain' or singing the British (and English) national anthem rather than those of their respective homelands. A photograph of the British contingent in Athens appears to offer some insight, as the majority of athletes favoured their own national emblems rather than the unifying insignia of the Union Jack on their athletic jerseys (Cook 1908a). In appearance at least, there was a conflict between the acceptance of a British identity and a continuing identity as English, Irish, Scottish or Welsh.

Making the 'British' team

The BOA's nation-building efforts proved especially difficult during the early twentieth century as the Celtic nations experienced an intensive national reawakening or renaissance. Through the educational, literary, political and religious realms, the Irish, Scottish and the Welsh promoted their own distinct national and ethnic heritages, a process that distinguished them even further from the dominant people of the United Kingdom, the English. Retreating from explicitly political agitation, the Irish established the Gaelic Union (1880) to promote the Gaelic language, the Gaelic League (1893) to advance the nation's cultural heritage, and the GAA for the Preservation and Cultivation of National Pastimes (1884) to revive traditional Irish sports (Boyce 1995, 236–240). The Welsh underwent a similar cultural transformation, but with a less political anti-English overtone. Buoyed by the expansion of the South Wales coalfields that fired the British Empire, the

Welsh revived their flagging National Eisteddfod (1880), the festival of the arts in Wales, founded a national university (1893), established a Welsh Parliamentary Party and promoted their own native tongue. The cultivation and expression of a resurgent Welsh national identity was solidified even further through the creation of distinct cultural emblems such as the leek, the daffodil, the dragon of Cadwaladr and the three plumed motif of the Prince of Wales, and also through the composition of a national anthem, 'Hen Wlad Fy Nhadaw' (Morgan 1981).

Early twentieth-century Gaelic and Celtic claims for national distinctiveness have led some to question the very existence of a British *nation* or a shared national identity during this period (Bell 2011; Robbins 1998). The fractured and complex nature of 'Britishness' and British identity can be further illustrated through the example of Cornwall, a county located in the remote, agricultural southwest corner of England. The Cornish, like the Irish, Scots and the Welsh, have long championed a self-conscious and submerged identity distinct from England and the broader British realm. According to Dilwyn Porter (2014, 2), the Cornish turned to sport, notably rugby union and local forms of physical culture such as wrestling and hurling, to help 'underpin the idea that the Cornish were in some ways different from the English'. The example of Cornwall, part of a broader historiographical focus on regional British histories, serves to decentre the British nation and the notion of a collective British identity even further.

In the backdrop of a Celtic and Gaelic cultural revival, as well as the revealing of deeper, internal and regional differences, the BOA persevered in their desire to form a unified British team for the 1908 Olympic Games in London. The BOA's efforts were bolstered by the introduction of a new regulatory definition for a 'country' during the 1907 IOC session held at The Hague: 'A "Country" is any "territory having separate representation on the International Olympic Committee", or, where no such representation exists, "any territory under one and the same sovereign jurisdiction"' (Cook 1908b, 29). In effect, the Olympic Movement ruled that only nation-states represented by a seat on the IOC were coterminous with nations. For the Irish, Scottish and Welsh, this decision would hold a deep and long-lasting significance as the IOC ruling bound them to a broader British sporting union – they were unable to enjoy the legislative and representative flexibility granted to them in British-inspired sports such as association football and rugby union. Under the new guidelines, any future Celtic aspirations for independent representation were completely squashed. As non-independent governed nations without their own representatives to the IOC, Ireland, Scotland and Wales were now 'officially' subsumed into the Great Britain team.

With the jurisdictional parameters in place, the BOA adopted a more conciliatory stance in an attempt to head-off threats of Olympic withdrawal, as well as future nationalistic demonstrations. Following the visible scenes of Irish defiance in Athens, the BOA proposed a system of proportionate representation which served to guarantee a far greater presence of Irish, Scottish and Welsh athletes in London, while simultaneously curbing the predominance of English athletes within the British Olympic fold. 'While the British Isles would count as one country', BOA leaders announced, 'the Associations representing the different portions of the Kingdom would be requested to arrange with each other the athletes who should be selected to represent the county in each branch of sport'.[3] British Olympic leaders also officially adopted the geographical designation 'Great Britain and Ireland', instead of the traditional sporting labels, 'Great Britain' or the 'United Kingdom'. Plans were also put in place to produce a badge containing in each quarter the respective emblems of the Home-Nations, the Rose (England), Shamrock (Ireland), Thistle (Scotland) and Prince of Wales Feathers (Wales), for use by British athletes during the track and field portion of the Olympic programme.[4] The choice of a more representative emblem instead of the traditional unifying insignia of the Union Jack illustrates just how far BOA officials were willing to go to appease their Celtic neighbours in an effort to foster a far greater shared sense of 'Britishness'.

The BOA's conciliatory efforts masked a broader nationalistic intent. As BOA member Theodore Andrea Cook acknowledged, a stronger and committed union of English, Irish, Scottish and Welsh athletes would heighten 'British' chances of victory in London (Llewellyn 2012b). On the pages of *Baily's Magazine of Sports and Pastimes*, Cook (1908c, 116) issued a desperate plea to end political squabbling in the interests of Anglo-Celtic collaboration and victory:

> The United Kingdom must be content, for the time, to be mere geographical expressions; for it is only by the most sincere and enthusiastic union that we can hope to withstand the combined onset of the picked athletes of every other nation.

As a product of the English public school system, Cook was imbued with a Victorian and Edwardian 'games ethic' that connected competitive amateur sport with national and imperial interests (Mangan 1998). Like his colleagues on the BOA, Cook embraced the idea that struggle and competition between nation-states resided at the core of Social Darwinism, the dominant intellectual paradigm of the age and the 'secular reality' of the public schools, and revelled in Britain's natural sporting superiority (Mangan 2012, 80). Reflecting on the emergence of powerful sporting rivals such as the USA and Sweden, he feared that internal squabbling among the constituent parts of the British Isles threatened Britain's chances of Olympic success in London. Cook admonished that 'it would be something of a disgrace if we did not come up to the high standard of efficiency expected of us by the rest of the world' (1908c, 116).

The collective seven medals, including two golds, won by Irish, Scottish and Welsh competitors won in Athens, emboldened BOA officials to again unify the Home-Nations into a formidable representative British team. The Olympic Games, similar to all international sporting events between nation-states, provided a means to measure national vigour. In light of the absence of a World Cup football tournament – an initiative not introduced until 1930 – and similar major international sporting events, the most powerful nations turned to the Olympic arena as an ideal platform for trumpeting national vitality (Dyreson 1997). Victory in Olympic competition was deemed a testament to the strength and vitality of a nation, while failure was considered symptomatic of national decadence and decline. Given the transcendent power and universal appeal of international Olympic competition, coupled with the Conservative thirst for maintaining national and imperial grandeur, the BOA aimed to advance the nation's Olympic fortunes in order to project a positive image of Britain to an increasingly global audience (Llewellyn 2012a). BOA officials hypothesized that the repetitive sight of British athletes stood atop the Olympic medal podium in London, with the Union Jack cast overhead, would offer symbolic proof that the sun was far from ready to set on British power. While many in Britain vehemently dismissed the significance of Olympic defeat, issues of race, masculinity and national virility had grown inseparable in the Darwinian rhetoric of the British public schools and lay firmly entrenched in early twentieth-century Conservative political and intellectual discourse (Mangan 1998, 2012).

The BOA's attempts to unify the Home-Nations continued to flounder in the face of unwavering Celtic opposition. Rejecting pleas for reconciliation and collaboration, Irish leaders issued a renewed call for separate representation for its athletes. The political revolutionary and nationalist Sir Roger Casement emerged as the leading advocate of an independent Irish Olympic team. In the build-up to the London Games, Casement inveighed that it would be a 'disgraceful exhibition of Irish disunion or subservience' if the nation's athletes accepted BOA advances and competed under the colours of the Union Jack. 'Let the Englishman, the Scotsman, and the Welshman stand each for himself and his own land, and let the Irishman enter himself in the name of and for the fame of Ireland', he demanded (Ware 2002, 38–40). The *Munster Express* also rejected the BOA's appeals for sporting unification. 'England will never succeed in Anglicising the Gael', it decried (8 August 1908, 8). Calls for the creation of an independent Irish team betrayed an understanding of the new regulatory standard introduced at the 1907 Hague session, limiting full athletic autonomy to territories represented directly by seats on the IOC. Still lacking a NOC of their own during this period, Irish athletes found themselves integrated under the more appropriate geographical appellation, 'Great Britain and Ireland' (Mallon and Buchanan 2009, 205).[5]

Preserving the union

In the years following the 1908 London Games, the Conservatively minded elites who ran the BOA stepped up their nationalistic agenda in the face of continued Irish opposition. When Dr Michael J. Bulger of the IAAA revisited the subject of Irish sporting independence during an April 1911 Council meeting of the BOA, British officials promptly squashed his separatist ambitions. Bulger proposed the dissolution of the BOA as a necessary step to obtaining 'separate representation for England, Scotland and Ireland' on the IOC.[6] An independent voice on the IOC would entitle Ireland, under existing legal definitions of a 'nation', to register a separate team in future cycles of international Olympic competition, thus freeing themselves from the shackles of the BOA's tutelage in London. Clearly, Bulger and his countrymen considered this a far more favourable route for securing the establishment of an independent Irish Olympic team than awaiting the passage of Home-Rule (McCarthy 2010, 239–242). The BOA's continued recalcitrance to Irish separatist plans was hardly surprising, especially given their Conservative, pro-establishment world view, their overwhelmingly Anglocentric composition and their staunch opposition to previous Irish appeals.

The work of Lord Desborough outside of the BOA clearly reveals the mindset of Britain's Olympic leaders. In his concurrent position as chancellor of the Primrose League, a large-scale political movement founded in 1883 to trumpet Tory values and to 'uphold religion, the monarchy, the empire and the estates of the realm', Desborough spearheaded a Conservative campaign against the momentum of the Irish Home-Rule movement (Fforde 1990, 31–33). The 1911 passage of the Parliament Act, asserting the supremacy of the House of Commons by abolishing the legislation-blocking powers of the Tory controlled House of Lords, heightened Irish expectations that a Liberal-backed Home-Rule Bill would finally succeed. For Conservatives, particularly BOA leaders, this was a period of remarkable change and uncertainty. Following three successive general election defeats, the Conservatives were overwhelmed by the rising tide of Liberal radicalism and socialism. Extensive land and social reform, collectivism, increased governmental bureaucracy, free trade, taxation on personal wealth, anti-landlordism and the founding of the Labour Party, made Conservatives even more fearful for the future. In a sombre letter to his long-time friend, Pierre de Coubertin, the Reverend Robert S. de Courcy Laffan, the founding honorary secretary of the BOA, confirmed such trepidation, noting that a 'dangerous crisis' was afoot in Britain as the Liberals threatened to topple the propertied order, the traditional social hierarchy, and the entrenched economic system.[7] In this context, the BOA's efforts to preserve the unity of a 'British' Olympic team signified a deliberate Conservative attempt to obstruct the Liberal assault on the established order.

After supressing the latest Irish appeal for Olympic independence prior to the 1912 Stockholm Games, BOA officials launched a grand and ambitious scheme to foster a collective sense of 'Britishness': the creation of a British Empire team (Llewellyn 2012c). Plans to integrate the Empire along official and competitive lines had originated prior to the Stockholm Games, but were revived following a disappointing British showing in the Swedish capital. Clinching only 10 gold medals, a meagre medal haul illuminated by the impressive 56 golds won by 'British and Irish' athletes in London, BOA chairman Lord Desborough embraced the idea of uniting the Empire for the 1916 Berlin Games on the pages of *The Times* (2 August 1912, 4). For Desborough and his colleagues on the BOA, the rise of strong competitors, such as the USA, Germany and Scandinavian nations Sweden and Finland, made the grand imperial Olympic project an urgent necessity. The stunning success of the USA, the archetypal 'federal' sporting nation, coupled with the heightened efforts made by Britain's other imperial rivals to unify their outlying territories – Russia and Finland; Austro-Hungary and Bohemia; Germany and Bavaria – into a sporting union, made the concept of a consolidated British Empire team even more attractive.[8]

Efforts to maintain Britain's global position by welding the United Kingdom and its outlying colonial possessions into a formidable Olympic team found a political and ideological precedent in the British Conservative Party's failed late nineteenth- and early twentieth-century twin-pursuit of tariff reform and the creation of an Imperial Federation. In an era of rival territorial empires, Conservative leaders aimed to secure Britain's long-term power and prosperity by repealing free trade in favour of preferential tariff agreements with its overseas possessions and by establishing a single federal state among all territories of the British Empire. Fearful of the diminishing trend of British economic, military and cultural power, Conservative leaders urged Britain's Dominions and colonies to pool their resources, markets and political acumen in order to create an Empire-State to match and rival continental powers in size and scope (Bell 2011; Gorman 2006). Calls for the creation of a 'Greater Britain' Olympic team, like the much-maligned pursuit of tariff reform and the formation of an Imperial Federation, appeared a defensive response to the shifting international balance of power, rather than as a celebration of imperial sentiment and solidarity (Llewellyn 2012c, 403).

The advocacy of a British Empire team for the Berlin Games represented part of a broader response to the rupture in Conservative self-confidence. During the early twentieth century widespread fears that British power was eroding dangerously spawned sub-Darwinian theories about the degeneration of the so-called 'British' race. Public debates about the loss of 'national efficiency' and the circulation of social Darwinist ideas fuelled Conservative anxieties that Britain would lose its imperial pre-eminence (Searle 1989). Fears of urban degeneration – promulgated most passionately by John R. Seeley in his best-selling work *Expansion of England* (1883) – led British Conservatives to look longingly towards the settler-Dominions of Australia, New Zealand South Africa, and the prairie provinces of Canada as a pastoral, rugged alternative to the effeminacy of industrial British life (Seeley 1971). The stunning post-Boer War sporting performances of touring Australian cricketers, as well as New Zealand and South African rugby union teams, only served to solidify the masculine qualities ascribed to 'white' British subjects overseas (Nauright 1996, 121–139). In the Darwinian-charged discourse of the Edwardian era, BOA leaders naturally turned to the *hardened* and *virile* Dominion sportsman to help salvage Britain's besmirched reputation. The collective 21 medals, including 9 golds, won by Australasian, Canadian and South African sportsmen in Stockholm convinced the BOA that a strong, vibrant and unified Empire stood as the most prominent solution offered to the Conservative crisis of confidence in British sporting and national supremacy.

Britain and the British world

In the years prior to the outbreak of the Great War, the British Empire spanned 12 million miles. Straddling the globe, this vast transoceanic realm of dominions, colonies, mandates, protectorates and other territories comprised a population of over 430 million people, of whom the United Kingdom and the white self-governing Dominions made up a mere 70 million (McDevitt 2008, 66). Fuelled by an abundant reserve of human resources the British enjoyed the benefit of calling upon its 'subjects' to aid in the midst of a grave imperial crisis, as the Great War would soon fatefully demonstrate. Britain's third place overall finish at the 1912 Stockholm Games appeared, as some commentators at the time exhorted, to necessitate the full mobilization of imperial subjects from across the *entire* reaches of the British Empire. In an editorial published in the *Manchester Guardian*, Sherlock Holmes creator Sir Arthur Conan Doyle called for the establishment of a truly representative British Empire team, including 'exotic' colonials from such far-flung imperial outposts as the Caribbean, Egypt, Kenya, Singapore and the Indian sub-continent. With aspirations of a British victory in Berlin, Doyle (23 July, 1912, 16) challenged: 'Let's see whether among Ceylon and Malay swimmers, Indian runners and Sikh wrestlers we cannot find winners among the coloured races of the British Empire'. Efforts to unify this vast Empire for the 1916 Berlin Games would illustrate the degree to which BOA officials viewed both imperial subjects as fellow 'Britons' and the Empire as an extension of the British-state rather than as a collection of separate and distinct communities.

In practice, the BOA's ambitious policy to create a unified 'Greater Britain' team further revealed the prevailing conceptions and limitations of 'Britishness'. Despite plans to hoist the Empire as a visible symbol of British strength, BOA officials refused to extend an invitation to all of the nation's overseas appendages. Like all post-Enlightenment imperial powers, the British Empire had been founded, in part with evangelism and utilitarianism, upon a strict ethnocentric hierarchal structure, a racist imperialism ensconced in the enlightened and chivalrous virtues of progress and liberty (Brendon 2008; James 1997). Determined to preserve the myth of Anglo-Saxon racial and physical superiority, as well as the elaborately graded racial imperial hierarchy that sustained it, BOA leaders were only willing to position British athletes alongside their counterparts from the 'white' Dominions. The sight of the imperial *master* competing on equal terms alongside his colonial *subject* within the Olympic stadium in Berlin would shatter perceptions of the established racial and social order, sending shock waves from the metropolis to the colonial periphery and threatening the whole imperial enterprise.

The exclusion of sportsmen and sportswomen from Britain's colonial dependencies illuminated the narrow and prevailing notions of 'Britishness' (i.e. identity and citizenship). Based on the constitutional principle of *jus soli*, British subjecthood (citizenship) was granted to any individual born in any territory under the crown without distinction based on race and ethnicity (Dummett and Nicol 1990; McClelland and Rose 2006, 278–279). British subjecthood served as an imperial form of belonging, symbolically and culturally tying the disparate branches of the colonial empire to the metropole. While that was the official British stance, the actual significance of being a British subject and the meaning of subjecthood depended predominately on race. In the language of Social Darwinism, which evinced biological and anthropological racism, not all subjects under the British flag had equal rights and responsibilities (Beasley 2010). While India and the 'dark' dependencies were heralded as significant imperial possessions from an economic, military and strategic perspective, they resided in the British imagination as fundamentally *alien* (Colley 1994; Hall 2002; Said 1978). As Colley (1992) argues, 'Britishness' was an Anglo-Saxon political space, a diasporic racial community fashioned by shared norms, values and 'race' and reinforced through encounters with the exotic imperial 'Other'. The possession of a massively fragmented transoceanic empire, with a predominantly non-white, non-Christian and non-English-speaking colonial population, encouraged the 'British' to see themselves as a distinct and superior people. At the constitutional level, Bengalis, Ceylonese, Fijians, Ghurkhas, Hindus, Jamaicans, Māoris, Malayans, Punjabis and Zulus were considered British 'subjects', but they were not truly 'British'.

While 'Britishness' was underpinned by a common race (white and Anglo-Saxon), not all partners in the imperial project supported the idea of forming a British Empire Olympic team. As historian Erik Nielsen (2014) has observed, the concept threatened to sour Dominion relations with the old mother country, as the Australians, Canadians, New Zealanders and South Africans took umbrage at the concept of a 'British' team. Although late nineteenth- and early twentieth-century developments in transoceanic and transcontinental travel and communication bridged the vast geographical space between Britain and its outlying white territories of settlement, the use of the adjective 'British' to describe the Dominions was counterpoised by a burgeoning wave of non-British nationalism (Bell 2011). Binding legal, economic, constitutional and cultural ties to the old mother country still remained strong, reinforced by close sporting contacts in athletics, rugby union and cricket and through a vast literary network of sporting journals and male adventure stories (Holt 1989, 203–279). During the first quarter of the twentieth century, the Dominions, emboldened by self-government and growing in political and economic confidence, pushed for a greater degree of autonomy from the British crown – Canada was confederated in 1867, Australia became a federation in 1901, New Zealand was declared a Dominion in 1907 and the Union of South Africa was created in 1910. These new statutory nations remained overwhelmingly British in their social and cultural aspirations but actively constructed and propagated their own independent national identities complementary to, yet ultimately distinct from, the imperial metropolis. The vast multi-ethnic and polyglot populations that inhabited the Dominions, such as Aborigines and Māori in Australasia; Zulu, Xhosa and Afrikaners in South Africa; and the Indians, Inuit and French in Canada, further fuelled the emergence of a contested national identity. Dominion nationalism diverged from British imperial patriotism (Brendon 2008).

Britain's white-settler Dominions cultivated and solidified an independent national identity through participation in sport. International sport offered the Dominions an unprecedented platform for cultural propaganda, an avenue for reaffirming and revelling in their own distinct national identities and asserting equal nation status within the British imperial configuration. Victories in high-profile cricket and rugby union test matches, particularly over the old mother country, reaffirmed national superiority, while solidifying Dominion independence from the orbit of British rule. National anthems, symbols, colours and flags helped to further define the separate identity of each country (Nielsen 2014).

Unwilling to support the BOA's grand imperial project, the *Sydney Morning Herald* expressed its desire for separate Australian Olympic representation: 'Apart from all questions of loyalty to the Empire, there is a narrower local patriotism for Australia'. The Olympic Games are a 'tremendous advertisement to this continent', it objected (10 August, 1912, 15). In an interview published in the *Sydney Referee*, K.B. Keartland, the chief athletic trainer of the South African Olympic team, discredited the proposed imperial scheme further. Pointing to the growing nationalistic value of Olympic competition,

Keartland celebrated the 'advertisement' that South Africa, a nation recently unified by the joining of the Afrikaner republics of the Transvaal and the Orange Free State with the two British coastal colonies of the Cape and Natal, 'got out of its successes'. For a nation still bitterly divided racially and hampered by a faltering economy, Keartland enthused that Olympic victories 'have given South Africa the reputation for a country of stayers' (24 December 1912, 9). During a meeting of the Canadian Amateur Athletic Union, President James G. Merrick confirmed that Dominion nationalism stood as an unbridgeable impediment. 'There is the strongest feeling in support of National identity' within the Dominions, Merrick revealed, and, as a result, 'it would be hard to prove that this could be retained by the association of their athletes in a selected Empire team'.[9] Without Dominion support, and burdened by overwhelming administrative and financial complications, the BOA's imperial scheme failed even before the outbreak of World War I scuppered Berlin's hosting of the 1916 Olympic Games (Llewellyn 2012c). The Dominions were evidently not passive, but vibrant, heterogeneous and actively constructing and propagating their own national identities (Gorman 2006). Dominion nationalism weakened the imperial bonds and further undermined the tenuous existence of a shared, albeit racially homogenous 'British' identity.

The limitations and contestations of 'Britishness'

The British Isles entered World War I in 1914 as a single unitary state – 'Great Britain and Ireland' – with an empire greater in extent and larger in population than the world had ever seen. Although the Great War resembled a joint British imperial project, even to the extent of the creation of an Imperial War Cabinet, it also served as a catalyst for Celtic and Dominion nationalism. An Afrikaner revolt in South Africa, French-Canadian anti-British antagonism, Australasian criticism of British military leadership, and the 1916 declaration of an independent Irish republic, and the violent Civil War that ensued, forcefully revealed the limitations of a shared 'British' identity (Holland 1999). The rising post-war assertiveness of Britain's overseas territories, as exemplified through the 1926 signing of the *Balfour Declaration* (which laid the foundations for the Commonwealth), as well as a Raj-inspired push for Indian self-government further revealed the post-war decline of 'Britannic nationalism' (Bell 2011, 271). While the triumphalism of World War II and the defeat of Nazism spurred a temporary revival of British identity, the ensuing post-war wave of decolonization throughout the Third World and the collapse of Empire, coupled with the resurgence of the Scottish, Welsh and even English nationalist movements have led some historians to proclaim the 'Abolition' and 'Break-up' of Britain (Hitchens 2008; Marr 2000; Nairn 2000).

An analysis of Britain's early modern Olympic participation symbolically revealed the limitations and contestations of 'Britishness'. Fuelled by fears of national and imperial decline, BOA officials – particularly the high-ranking Conservative Party elites who ran the organization – worked to create a strong, vibrant and unified British Olympic team. The use of the designations 'Great Britain', 'Great Britain and Ireland', and later 'Greater Britain' for international Olympic competition, however, failed to overlay the deeper cultural differences that existed between the Home-Nations and the white-settler Dominions during the first two decades of the twentieth century. Celtic and Dominion nationalism undermined a broader allegiance and affiliation to the British-state. Throughout the inter-war years the BOA's nation-building efforts continued to falter as Irish opposition to a British sporting union remained steadfast until the realization of Home Rule and the official granting of an independent IOC status in 1920 (McCarthy

2010). While the establishment of the British Empire Games in 1930 confirmed imperial loyalties, the participation of the Home-Nations and the white-settler Dominions under their own respective flags reflected their growing autonomy from a broader British identity.

As the recent debates over the participation of a 'Great Britain and Northern Ireland' football team at the 2012 London Olympic Games testifies, 'Britishness' remains a highly contested identity (Ewen 2012). In fact, discussions over the British polity's very survival and future, now that so much of what made the Britons 'British' – religion, Empire, disaffiliation from the European Continent –has been lost, continue to dominate public and intellectual discourse. Some scholars suggest that Britain represents little more than a collection of institutions, with no shared foundational culture and fractured through the forces of twenty-first-century Welsh, Scottish and English nationalism, multiculturalism, as well as the formation of the European Union (see, e.g., Colley 1992; Marr 2000; Nairn 2000). Others present a more positivistic interpretation, viewing contemporary 'Britishness' as a mutating phenomenon: an inclusive, plural and flexible designation based on civic identity rather than a cultural one based on whiteness (Ward 2004). As battles over the meaning and future of 'Britain' and 'Britishness' continue to be debated in both the scholarly and public arenas, the Union Jack continues to fly within the Olympic stadium, at least for now!

Disclosure statement

No potential conflict of interest was reported by the author.

Notes

1. For the purposes of this work, I will be using the appellations 'United Kingdom' and 'Great Britain' interchangeably. In modern parlance, the 'United Kingdom' is a country that consists of Great Britain and Northern Ireland. Great Britain is the name of the island northwest of France and east of Ireland that consists of three somewhat autonomous regions: England, Wales and Scotland.
2. British Olympic Association, Inaugural Committee Meeting Report, 24 May 1905. Grande-Bretagne Correspondence (1892–1923), OU MO 01 14 36, IOC Archives.
3. British Olympic Association, Council Minutes, 11 March 1907, British Olympic Archives.
4. Amateur Athletic Association, General Committee Minutes, 8 February 1908, AAA/1/2/2/4, Amateur Athletic Association, University of Birmingham, Edgbaston, Birmingham, England.
5. Curiously, two notable exceptions to this policy popped up. In field hockey, the BOA granted Ireland permission to compete as a nation after their national Field Hockey Association rejected a proposal from their English counterparts to compete as a unified, Great Britain and Ireland team. As further evidence of the fluid internationalism of early Olympic competition, Ireland's polo team also compete as a separate entity – a move that whetted Irish appetites for full sporting independence.
6. British Olympic Association, Council Minutes, 25 April 1911, BOF Archives.
7. Reverend Robert S. de Courcy Laffan to Pierre de Coubertin, 15 December 1910, MBR-COURCY-CORR, 0056930 (1902–1929), IOC Archives.
8. British Olympic Association, *Aims and Objects of the Olympic Games Fund*, 14, BOA Archives.
9. Minutes, Third Annual Meeting, Amateur Athletic Union of Canada, 23 November 1912, 8–9, Amateur Athletic Union of Canada fonds, M3209, Library and Archives Canada.

References

Anderson, Benedict. 2006. *Imagined Communities: Reflections on the Origin and Spread of Nationalism*. London: Verso.

Andrews, David L. 1991. "Welsh Indigenous! And British Imperial? – Welsh Rugby, Culture, and Society 1890–1914." *Journal of Sport History* 18: 335–349.

Bairner, Alan. 2001. *Sport, Nationalism, and Globalization: European and North American Perspectives*. New York: SUNY Press.

Beasley, Edward. 2010. *The Victorian Reinvention of Race*. London: Routledge.

Beck, Peter J. 1999. *Scoring for Britain: International Football and International Politics, 1900–1939*. London: Frank Cass.

Bell, Duncan. 2011. *The Idea of Greater Britain: Empire and the Future of World Order, 1860–1900*. Princeton: Princeton University Press.

Boyce, D. George. 1995. *Nationalism in Ireland*. 3rd ed. London: Routledge Press.

Brendon, Piers. 2008. *The Decline and Fall of the British Empire, 1781–1997*. London: Alfred A. Knopf.

Cannadine, David. 1999. *The Decline and Fall of the British Aristocracy*. New York: Vintage.

Coetzee, Frans. 1990. *For Part or Country: Nationalism and the Dilemmas of Popular Conservatism in Edwardian England*. Oxford: Oxford University Press.

Colley, Linda. 1992. "Britishness and Otherness: An Argument." *Journal of British Studies* 31: 309–329.

Colley, Linda. 1994. *Britons: Forging the Nation 1707–1837*. New Haven, CT: Yale University Press.

Collins, Tony. 2009. *A Social History of English Rugby Union*. London: Routledge.

Colls, Robert. 2002. *Identity of England*. Oxford: Oxford University Press.

Cook, Theodore Andrea. 1908a. *The Cruise of the Branwen: Being a Short History of the Modern Revival of the Olympic Games, Together with an Account of the Adventures of the English Fencing Team in Athens in MCMVI*. London: Privately Published.

Cook, Theodore Andrea. 1908b. *The Fourth Olympiad: Being the Official Report of the Olympic Games of 1908 Celebrated in London under the Patronage of His Most Gracious King Edward VIII*. London: British Olympic Association.

Cook, Theodore Andrea. 1908c. "The Olympic Games in London." *Baily's Magazine of Sport and Pastimes* 150: 116.

Coombe, D. C. 1949. *A History Of The Davis Cup: Being The Story Of The International Lawn Tennis Championship 1900–48*. London: Hennel Locke.

Cronin, Mike. 1999. *Sport and Nationalism: Gaelic Games, Soccer and Irish Identity since 1884*. Dublin: Four Courts Press.

Dart, Jonathan. 2009. "Tackling a Nation's Football History." *International Journal of the History of Sport* 26 (11): 1748–1757.

Davies, John. 2007. *A History of Wales*. London: Penguin.

Davies, Norman. 1998. *The Isles: A History*. New York: Oxford University Press.

Devine, T. M. 2001. *The Scottish Nation 1700–2000*. London: Allen Lane.

Dummett, Anne, and Andrew Nicol. 1990. *Subjects, Citizens, Aliens and Others: Nationality and Immigration Law*. Evanston, IL: Northwestern University Press.

Dyreson, Mark. 1997. *Making the American Team: Sport, Culture, and the Olympic Experience*. Urbana: University of Illinois Press.

Espy, Richard. 1981. *The Politics of the Olympic Games*. Berkeley: University of California Press.

Ewen, Neil. 2012. "Team GB, or No Team GB, That Is the Question: Olympic Football and the Post-War Crisis of Britishness." *Sport in History* 32 (2): 302–324.

Fforde, Matthew. 1990. *Conservatism & Collectivism, 1886–1914*. Edinburgh: Edinburgh University Press.

Gorman, David. 2006. *Imperial Citizenship: Empire and the Question of Belonging*. Manchester: Manchester University Press.

Green, E. H. H. 1996. *The Crisis of Conservatism: The Politics, Economics and Ideology of the Conservative Party, 1880–1914*. London: Routledge.

Guiney, David. 1996. "The Olympic Council of Ireland." *Journal of Olympic History* 4: 31–33.

Hall, Catherine. 2002. *Civilizing Subjects: Metropole and Colony in the English Imagination 1830–1867*. Chicago: University of Chicago Press.

Harvie, Christopher. 2004. *Scotland and Nationalism: Scottish Society and Politics 1707 to the Present*. 4th ed. London: Routledge Press.

Hechter, Michael. 1999. *Internal Colonialism: The Celtic Fringe in British National Development*. London: Transaction.

Hitchens, Peter. 2008. *The Abolition of Britain*. London: Quartet.

Hobsbawm, E. J. 1990. *Nations and Nationalism Since 1870: Program, Myth, Reality*. Rev. ed. Cambridge: Cambridge University Press.

Holland, Robert. 1999. "The British Empire and the Great War, 1914–1918." In *The Oxford History of the British Empire: The Twentieth Century*. Vol. 4, 114–137. Oxford: Oxford University Press.

Holt, Richard. 1989. *Sport and the British: A Modern History*. Oxford: Clarendon Press.

Holt, Richard, and Tony Mason. 2000. *Sport in Britain 1945–2000*. Oxford: Blackwell.

James, Lawrence. 1997. *The Rise and Fall of the British Empire*. New York: St. Martin's Press.

Jarvie, Grant, and Graham Walker. 1994. *Scottish Sport in the Making of the Nation*. Leicester: Leicester University Press.

Johnes, Martin. 2000. "Eighty Minute Patriots? National Identity and Sport in Modern Wales." *International Journal of the History of Sport* 17 (3): 93–110.

Johnes, Martin. 2002. *Soccer and Society in South Wales, 1900–1939*. Cardiff: University of Wales Press.

Johnes, Martin. 2005. *A History of Sport in Wales*. Cardiff: University of Wales Press.

Kearney, Hugh. 1995. *The British Isles: A History of Four Nations*. 2nd ed. Cambridge: Cambridge University Press.

Keys, Barbara. 2006. *Globalizing Sport: National Rivalry and the International Communities in the 1930s*. Harvard: Harvard University Press.

Kumar, Krishan. 2003. *The Making of English National Identity*. Cambridge: Cambridge University Press.

Llewellyn, Matthew P. 2012a. *Rule Britannia: Nationalism, Identity and the Modern Olympic Games*. London: Routledge Press.

Llewellyn, Matthew P. 2012b. "Advocate or Antagonist? Sir Theodore Andrea Cook and the British Olympic Movement." *Sport in History* 32 (2): 183–203.

Llewellyn, Matthew P. 2012c. "Dominion Nationalism or Imperial Patriotism? Citizenship, Race, and the Proposed British Empire Olympic Team." *Journal of Sport History* 39 (1): 45–62.

Lowerson, John. 1996. *Sport and the English Middle-Class, 1870–1914*. Manchester: Manchester University Press.

Mallon, Bill. 1999. *The 1906 Olympic Games: Results for All Competitors in All Events, with Commentary*. Jefferson, NC: McFarland.

Mallon, Bill, and Ian Buchanan. 2009. *The 1908 Olympic Games: Results for All Competitors in All Events, with Commentary*. Jefferson, NC: McFarland.

Mangan, J. A. 1998. *The Games Ethic and Imperialism: Aspects of the Diffusion of an Ideal*. Rev. ed. London: Frank Cass.

Mangan, J. A. 2012. "Social Darwinism and Upper-Class Education in Late Victorian and Edwardian England." In *Manliness and Morality: Making Imperial Manliness, Morality and Militarism*, edited by J. A. Mangan, 78–97. London: Routledge.

Marr, Andrew. 2000. *The Day Britain Died*. London: Profile.

McCarthy, Kevin. 2007. "Irish Involvement in the Olympic Games 1896–1920, with Specific Reference to its Impact on Nationalism and National Identity." PhD diss., National University of Ireland, Cork.

McCarthy, Kevin. 2010. *Gold, Silver and Green: The Irish Olympic Journey 1896–1924*. Cork: Cork University Press.

McClelland, Keith, and Sonya O. Rose. 2006. "Citizenship and Empire, 1867–1928." In *At Home with the Empire: Metropolitan Culture and the Imperial World*, edited by Catherine Hall and Sonya O. Rose, 275–297. Cambridge: Cambridge University Press.

McDevitt, P. F. 2008. *May the Best Man Win: Sport, Masculinity, and Nationalism in Great Britain and the Empire, 1880–1935*. New York: Palgrave Macmillan.

Morgan, Kenneth O. 1981. *Rebirth of a Nation: Wales 1880–1980*. Oxford: Oxford University Press.

Murdoch, Alexander. 1998. *British History 1660–1832: National Identity and Local Culture*. London: Macmillan.

Nairn, Tom. 1981. *The Break-up of Britain*. 2nd ed. London: Verso.

Nairn, Tom. 2000. *After Britain: New Labour and the Return of Scotland*. London: Granta.

Nauright, John. 1996. "Colonial Manhood and Imperial Race Virility: British Responses to Post-Boer War Colonial Rugby Tours." In *Making Men: Rugby and Masculine Identities*, edited by John Nauright and Timothy Chandler, 121–139. London: Frank Cass.

Nielsen, Erik. 2014. *Sport and the British World, 1900–1930: Amateurism and National Identity in Australasia and Beyond*. Houndmills: Palgrave Macmillan.

Porter, Dilwyn. 2014. "Sport and the Cornish: Difference and Identity on the English Periphery in the Twentieth Century." *National Identities* 16 (4): 311–326.

Quinn, Mark. 2004. *The King of Spring: The Life and Times of Peter O'Connor*. Dublin: The Liffey Press.

Reynolds, David. 1991. *Britannia Overruled: British Policy & World Power in the 20th Century*. London: Longman.

Robbins, Keith. 1998. *Great Britain: Identities, Institutions and the Idea of Britishness*. London: Longman Press.

Said, Edward. 1978. *Orientalism*. New York: Vintage.

Searle, G. R. 1989. *The Quest for National Efficiency: A Study in British Politics and Political Thought, 1899–1914*. London: Ashfield Press.

Seeley, John Robert. (1883) 1971. *The Expansion of England: Two Courses of Lectures*. Chicago: University of Chicago Press.

Senn, Alfred. 1999. *Power, Politics, and the Olympic Games*. Champaign, IL: Human Kinetics.

Thomas, Clem. 2005. *The History of the British and Irish Lions*. 2nd ed. Edinburgh: Mainstream.

Ward, Paul. 2004. *Britishness since 1870*. London: Routledge Press.

Ware, Seamus. 2002. "Roger Casement: Traitor in England and Hero in Ireland." *Journal of Olympic History* 10: 38–40.

Flights to Empire: Australia's imperial engagement with the Olympic Games, 1900–1938

Erik Nielsen

Department of Modern History, Politics and International Relations, Macquarie University, Sydney, Australia

> Imperialism was a key concern for Australia during its early engagement with the Olympic Movement. This engagement was marked by a tension between traditional British approaches to sport and more modern approaches that could stem the tide of American superiority that had been expressed at the Olympic Games since 1896. Australia used the Olympic Games to assert its centrality within the British Empire in a sporting context. These themes are observable in three sets of circumstances: the selection of Australian teams between 1900 and 1932, Australia's engagement with the British Empire Games and Australia's response to the development of state amateurism within the Olympic Movement.

'May Britain's prosperity continue, and may Australia be adequately represented at the next Olympiad in 1912'. – Annual report of the New South Wales Amateur Athletic Association (NSWAAA), April 1909. (Alexander 1909, 7)

'… the third, and probably most important [Australian athletic team rule, Mexico 1968], under no circumstances do you ever get beaten by a Pom'. – Peter Norman, *Salute*, 2009. (Norman 2009)

Australia's relationship with Britain at the Olympic Games in the twentieth century ranged from deference to friendly antagonism. This relationship had a marked impact on how Australia engaged with the Games in general. Three sets of circumstances give us a key insight into the interaction between imperialism and Australia's engagement with the Olympic Movement: debates about the nature of the Australian team, Australia's engagement with the Empire Games and Australia's response to the development of 'state amateurism'. These are not discrete issues, and together they illuminate a key tension between dominant British approaches to amateurism and more modern approaches to sport. Australia also attempted to assert its centrality to the Empire through these issues.

These issues reflect themes that have interested historians of Australia's engagement with the Empire in general. Meaney (2001, 89) has argued that Australian history has been plagued by 'thwarted Britishness' as Australian notions of an international pan-British community were not reciprocated by their prospective British counterparts. Collins (2009, 438) has argued that Australian rugby union officials expressed a sense of thwarted Britishness, but were never willing to step outside the pale of Britishness. Schreuder and Ward (2008, 11–12) have argued that Australians played a key role in the development of the Empire, and that the agency Australia deployed meant that it avoided becoming a 'mere "repetition of England"'. In an Australasian context, Belich (2007, 304) has argued that between 1880 and 1960 New Zealand went through a period of 'recolonization'.

During this period, the conceptualization of New Zealand's place within the Empire shifted from 'Greater Britain' to one of 'Better Britain'. This reconceptualization entailed a shift from ambitions of fully independent statehood to an imperial context where New Zealand accepted an integral but subordinate place within the Empire. These ideas are all relevant to Australia's Olympic history. Through their advocacy of modern athletic methods, Australia clearly displayed agency within the imperial response to the Olympic Movement. This was always done within the confines of Empire, and Australia's Olympic administrator's claims of centrality within the Empire reflect the view that Australia was an integral part of the Empire. This idea was not always reciprocated by their British counterparts, but Australia remained wedded to the idea of a pan-imperial approach to the Olympic Games up until the years immediately prior to the Second World War.

Picking the Australian team, 1900–1932

Imperialism was an important, if controversial, aspect of the Australian approach to the early Olympic Movement (Llewellyn, 2012a, 55–56). Australian Olympic representation prior to the First World War was influenced by a clear imperialist ethic. Australians have participated at every Summer Olympic Games, although early teams were established on an ad hoc basis. Early teams were supplemented by private travellers, such as swimmer Freddie Lane (winner of two Olympic titles at Paris in 1900), and Australians resident abroad such as Edwin Flack and William Allan Stewart, a Tasmanian medical student that was commandeered from the British team in 1912 (*The Referee*, June 12, 1912, 9; July 3, 1912, 9; Gordon 1994, 1–13, 30–34). Overwhelmingly though, Australia's early Olympians had their passage paid by local community fundraising efforts constituted to send a specific athlete abroad. In spite of the discontinuous nature of the administrative efforts, a pro-imperial ethic is observable throughout the pre-First World War era.

The prime driver of the Australian Olympic Movement's pro-imperial ethic was leading Sydney track and field figure, Richard Coombes. Coombes was Australia's pre-eminent athletic journalist and administrator in the early years of the Olympic Movement. He wrote for Australia's leading sporting newspaper *The Referee*, and had helped form the NSWAAA in 1887 after migrating from England the previous year. He served as vice-president of the NSWAAA from its inception until 1893 and president from that point until his death in 1935. He was also president of the Amateur Athletic Union of Australia (AAUA) from its foundation in 1899 until his death. Coombes was invited to become a member of the International Olympic Committee (IOC) in 1905 following the resignation of New Zealander Leonard Cuff, a position he held until 1933. Although his reign was occasionally controversial, his public profile provided him with an unparalleled opportunity to influence the ideological basis for Australia's participation in the Olympic Games (Mandle 1981). Coombes' staunch imperialism has been recognized by historians of Australia's early engagement with the Olympic Movement (Henniker and Jobling 1989, 2–4; Gordon 1994, 47).

Coombes was far from a one-dimensional character, though, and he took his sporting cues from a more diverse range of influences than historians have generally been supposed. He was particularly enamoured of American approaches to sport, and embraced them earlier than Henniker and Jobling (1989, 9) have suggested. From early 1899, he warned Australians that Americans were building a team that would challenge British dominance at the English Championships and the Olympic Games to be held the next year (*The Referee*, March 5, 1899, 5). While the 'American team was clearly the strongest of those in Athens' in 1896, the English athletic establishment remained convinced of their

THE BRITISH WORLD AND THE FIVE RINGS

sporting dominance (*The Referee*, August 16, 1899, 6; Guttmann, 2002, 18). In the press, Coombes explicitly represented the passage of Sydney sprinter Stanley Rowley to the 1900 Olympic Games as a pan-imperial effort aimed at maintaining British dominance in international sport. As Rowley left in April, Coombes claimed that British athletes could challenge the Americans in most events but that it was 'in the popular events from 100yds to 880yds where the Empire needs most assistance' and that the British were particularly weak in sprinting. Coombes imagined that Britain's dearth of sprinting talent could be overcome with the help of the wider Empire. Coombes claimed that 'Australia will help the Empire' through Rowley, and 'Calcutta comes to the rescue' through Anglo-Indian sprinter Norman Pritchard (*The Referee*, April 25, 1900, 6).

Coombes' claim reflected the beginnings of what might be termed an unofficial or informal imperial Olympic team at the Olympic Games. This is best demonstrated by Rowley's participation as part of the victorious British team in the 5000-metre team event in Paris. Despite being a specialist sprinter, Rowley volunteered to compete as part of a heavily favoured five-man British team. The team was strong enough to absorb Rowley's expected last place finish, but required him to compete in order to field a team (Gordon 1994, 36–37; Guttmann 2002, 24). This experience clearly reflected Coombes' view of Australia's place within the Empire in Olympic terms. To Coombes, Australia was an integral part of the Empire and could prove its worth in the stadium. The informal imperial team was also observable at the Athens 1906 Intercalated Games, as well as the 1908 and 1912 Olympic Games. Australians were ('correctly' according to Coombes) grouped with the British team during the 1906 Games due to the fact that Australia did not provide a member of the competition jury (*The Referee*, June 20, 1906, 8). In 1908 and 1912, Australian athletes competed as part of a joint Australasian team with New Zealand. The joint team consisting of two of Britain's former colonies recently granted Dominion status added to the lustre of the Empire at the opening ceremonies of these games. The Australasian combination marched alongside teams from Great Britain as well as Canada and South Africa at both of these games (Little and Cashman 2001, 87–88, 93). As such, while these teams were nominally individual entities, they also formed a loose confederation of imperial teams. The appearance of the informal imperial team was furthered by unofficial medal tallies that included colonial successes among British victories (Little and Cashman 2001, 87–88).

The decade-long evolution of the informal imperial Olympic team provided momentum towards an official Empire team (Llewellyn 2012a, 50–57). Coombes introduced the idea at the Festival of Empire Sports held in 1911 to celebrate the coronation of King George V at a dinner hosted by the Amateur Athletic Association (AAA; *The Referee*, August 9, 1911, 9). Coombes was able to garner early support from both English and Canadian sources in the lead-up to the Stockholm Olympic Games[1] (*The Referee*, October 18, 1911, 9; January 17, 1912, 9; Llewellyn 2008, 77). However, this support evaporated after Coombes elucidated a more complicated scheme in 1913[2] (*The Sydney Morning Herald*, October 30, 1912, 11). Llewellyn (2012a, 53) suggests that Coombes would have had to relinquish his IOC membership if the Empire team plan was successfully executed. While this seems a likely result from a British perspective, it is doubtful that Coombes would have gone quietly and willingly. An Englishman by birth, Coombes held ambitions to be seen as an eminent figure in British sport regardless of his situation in the Antipodes. At the same dinner where he proposed the Empire team, he suggested a path to peace between the AAA and the National Cyclists' Union that involved himself, Lord Alverstone (AAA) and James Merrick (Amateur Athletic Union of Canada – AAUC) acting as mediators (Nielsen 2014, 117). In doing so, Coombes

27

attempted to place himself as a significant force within British athletics, matching his ambitions for Australia as a whole.

Rowley's Olympic tour was quite successful, so much so that he remains the most successful Australian male Olympic sprinter in terms of top three positions earned. He was nonetheless unable to satisfy Coombes' ambition of challenging American dominance. Coombes attributed Rowley's relative failure to a lack of proper training compared to the Americans that finished in front of him. Rather than bemoan the intrusion of professionalism through specialization, Coombes saw the potential to lift Australian performances. Following the 1900 English Championship, Coombes realized that 'until we follow the methods adopted by the American clubs and universities we cannot expect our men to beat [them] nineteen times out of twenty' (*The Referee*, July 11, 1900, 6). In his column the next week he further explained the issue and advocated for the institution of American-style athletic directors to Australia. According to Coombes, under this system '[t]here is control, management, and system from first to last. The athletic director is a mighty power in the land. His word is law'. This created an environment where the fittest survived, and only 'a veritable champion of champions' reached the standard of international competition (*The Referee*, July 18, 1900, 6). This response is a far cry from the typical British approach that decried the specialization apparent in America. However, as Llewellyn (2012a, 56) has shown, for every Rudolph Lehmann groaning about specialization, there was an Arthur Conan Doyle proselytizing on behalf of the Special Committee for the Olympic Games of Berlin formed by the British Olympic Association (BOA) following the failure of Great Britain at the Stockholm Games. This solves the paradox of Coombes embracing an approach seemingly antithetical to British approaches to sport for the express purpose of shoring up the Empire's place in sport. There was in fact a continuum of views on the matter of training and specialization within British sport, and Coombes found himself on the less proscriptive end alongside Doyle and his fellow Committeemen. To these men, providing a challenge to the Americans was more significant than maintaining the strictest conception of amateurism.

It would take time to develop a body of world-beating Australian athletes. In the meantime, Coombes and other commentators demanded managerial exactitude and argued that only athletes with a genuine chance at victory should be considered for selection. As early as 1912, Coombes was concerned that recently formed Olympic Councils in the Australian states and New Zealand would be overrun by 'nominations from comparatively moderate men [from] supporters and well meaning enthusiasts' (*The Referee*, March 6, 1912, 9). Scarce financial resources meant that Coombes greeted mere participation at the Olympics with scorn rather than idealism. This remained a tenet of the Australian approach to the Olympics into the 1920s, with fundraising remaining a concern. Following the 1924 Games, Coombes warned that 'the public will surely not respond in the same liberal manner' unless a 'drastic alteration' in selection methods was adopted. Coombes also complained that institutional knowledge was not retained, with previous manager's reports being forgotten and lessons not being heeded as a result. He repeated his claims of 1900 that American management left Australia in its wake and quoted 'ex-athlete from Melbourne' George Hume that Australian training practices were sorely lacking (*The Referee*, July 23, 1924, 9). The calls for stringent selection practices were strengthened prior to the Amsterdam Games of 1928 by the opinion of Richard Honner, who had failed to reach his potential as a 400-metre sprinter, hurdler and long jumper in Paris four years previously. Honner reiterated Coombes' argument that only 'athletes [that] possess reasonable chances of success' should represent Australia (*The Referee*, January 18, 1928, 1). He also argued for a trainer to accompany the team, and suggested that 'one or two "observers"' accompany the team to gain an insight into 'methods and systems in all departments and phases of the Games' with the object of imparting the knowledge gained to future athletes (*The Referee*, January 18, 1928, 15). Despite these interventions, Coombes was forced yet again to catalogue the same old errors following the Amsterdam Games (*The Referee*, September 5, 1928, 15; December 12, 1928, 17). Coombes possessed an ambitious plan for Australia's athletes to help provide a bulwark against American dominance, but was ultimately undermined by the community's administrative capabilities. As a result, early Australian Olympic teams have been mythologized as 'Innocents Abroad' in Gordon's (1994, 59) terms.

In addition to modernizing training and selection procedures, Coombes advocated extending the limits of 'Britishness' to include Indigenous Australians and Māori as potential Australasian Olympic representatives. Coombes was impressed by athletic successes of Native Americans (Jim Thorpe, Andrew Sockalexis and Louis Tewanima), Hawaiians (Duke Kahanamoku) and First Nations Canadians (Tom Longboat). He made repeated calls for Indigenous Australasians to be provided with training in order to develop into Olympic standard throwers: shot-put, discus and hammer in the case of Māori and javelin in the case of Indigenous Australians (*The Referee*, January 13, 1909, 10; *The Argus*, February 17, 1914, 12; *The Brisbane Courier*, February 17, 1914, 3; *The Hobart Mercury*, February 17, 1914, 5; *The Sydney Morning Herald*, February 17, 1914, 10; *The Referee*, April 15, 1914, 9). Faced with scarce resources and a limited talent pool, Coombes considered taking the step that some smaller historically white institutions in the south of the USA took in the 1960s to break the colour line in order to boost competitiveness in college sport (Martin 2010, 97). Coombes' suggestion was inconsistent with Australian racial politics of the era, with Australian politicians and sporting identities generally keen to draw a distinction between the white and coloured Empire (Nielsen 2014, 115).

This suggestion was as unsuccessful as his call for specialization among Australia's extant community of athletes. Coombes was undoubtedly hampered by the virulent racism that enveloped potential indigenous amateur athletes in Australia. In Queensland in 1903, Murri athlete Tommy Pablo was rejected as an amateur on the grounds that, as an Aboriginal, he was considered incapable of understanding the rules and core values of amateurism (Tatz 1996, 88). Coombes commented negatively on this decision within a week, but (along with fellow member of the AAUA executive E.S. Marks) ultimately decided to support the Queensland Amateur Athletic Association instead of insisting on a universal standard across Australasia (*The Referee*, March 25, 1903, 6; July 29, 1903, 6). Thus, while the NSWAAA ostensibly welcomed athletes regardless of 'social position, creed or colour', the same was not true in Queensland (*The Referee*, March 25, 1903, 6). This reflected Australian Constitutional thinking, which specifically prevented the federal government 'from making special laws for the Aboriginal people' prior to the 1960s (Irving 1997, 112). Another layer of complexity is added due to the fact that Māori were generally seen to be 'more advanced than [Australian] Aborigines' and 'were exempted from much of the extreme antagonism evinced by white colonials' (Williams 2009, 223). In an athletic context, this meant that Māori were more readily accepted as amateurs. Notable Māori amateur athletes included Australasian Pole Vaulting champions Hori Eruera (1897, at the age of 17) and James Te Paa (1899) and influential Māori activist Peter 'Te Rangihiroa' Buck, the long-jump champion of New Zealand in 1903[3] (Belich 2001, 213; Hokowhitu 2003, 208). Constructed racial hierarchies thus ensured that the hypothetical Australian indigenous Olympian had a different level of eligibility as an amateur depending on where they resided.

While the movement towards an official imperial Olympic team sputtered, remnants of the unofficial imperial team remained strong in Australasia despite the creation of separate national teams from 1920 onwards. Ryan (2001, 133) has suggested that Australasian teams in 1908 and 1912 'allowed New Zealand athletes to surmount extremely limited financial and administrative resources'. However, New Zealand gained very little in terms of financial assistance from Australia, and New Zealand was required to foot the bill to send its athletes abroad (Nielsen 2014, 161–162). Administration was a different matter, and Coombes provided New Zealand with a gateway to international Olympic politics following Cuff's resignation from the IOC. This administrative arrangement continued after New Zealand secured a place on the IOC in 1919, and Australia and New Zealand continued to collaborate in a manner befitting the era of the informal imperial Olympic team. Prior to the Antwerp Games, the New Zealand Olympic Committee (NZOC) requested information about the upcoming games from Coombes despite the fact that NZOC chairman Arthur Marryatt had been elected to the IOC.[4] In April, it was suggested to Marryatt and Arthur D. Bayfeild, who had been charged with organizing transport for the New Zealand team, that they liaise with Coombes to 'endeavour to arrange passages with the Australian Olympic team'.[5] A similar arrangement was sought prior to the 1924 Games.[6] New Zealand's competitor in the Women's 100- and 400-metre freestyle in Paris, Gwitha Shand, suffered tremendous difficulties gathering the necessary funds to compete (*New Zealand Herald*, April 11, 1924, 10). Shand's difficulties were exacerbated by the conservative social mores of the time that required young women to travel abroad with a chaperone, an expense that was beyond the swimmer (*New Zealand Herald*, February 20, 1924, 11). The NZOC attempted to mitigate this cost by asking their Australian counterparts whether the chaperone for their team could look after Shand as well. The Australians would have been better placed to agree to this request had they selected any women in their team (Gordon 1994, 480–481).[7] Interestingly, prior to the 1932 Games, the NZOC sought administrative help from Britain which they had traditionally sought from Australia. This may have been due to the failing health of Coombes, whose lack of mobility was referred to during a testimonial held in his honour on 27 April 1931.[8] Whatever the reason, in 1931, the BOA acted as an intermediary in a discussion between the NZOC and Sigfrid Edström over the eligibility at the Olympic Games of amateurs that had previously competed as professionals. The NZOC also arranged for its accommodation to be situated near the British team at the Los Angeles Olympic village.[9] In a reversal of the situation that was predominant in the 1920s, Australia expressed interest in joining this arrangement as well.[10] The imperial ethic that predominated in the early twentieth century seems to have not been disturbed by the failure of the imperial team and the institution of national teams.

The British Empire Games

The imperial ethic in Olympic-style sport was given further impetus by the development of the British Empire Games. The first Empire Games were held in 1930 and hosted by the city of Hamilton, which Gorman (2010) has described as 'a natural choice as the host city' due to its reputation as Canada's 'Empire City'. The City Council of Hamilton heavily subsidized the games, providing funds for stadia, infrastructure, travel and accommodation for international teams. The games were managed by *Hamilton Spectator* sports editor Melville Marks 'Bobby' Robinson with the assistance of a committee formed by the AAUC which included prominent business and sporting figures (Gorman 2010, 614–616). Katharine Moore argues that Robinson detected 'increasing hostility and antagonism among the participants' at the Amsterdam Olympics of 1928, where he had served as manager of the Canadian athletic team. Hence, he 'believed the family atmosphere he was promoting [at the Empire Games] would provide a more relaxed and happy environment for competition' (Moore 1989b, 244).

The manager of the Australian team to Amsterdam, Leslie Duff, claimed ownership of the idea of an Empire Sports Federation on his return to Australia in October. Echoing Coombes in 1911, Duff claimed to have made the suggestion at a banquet hosted by the AAA. In addition to controlling the Empire Games, 'the federation would speak as one voice' and overcome the allegedly poor treatment that Duff had identified in Amsterdam (*The West Australian*, October 10, 1928, 19). However, Australians were clearly antagonistic towards the idea at a conference to debate the concept. Australian IOC member James Taylor 'maintained that the plan was detrimental from an international aspect' and called for a commitment to either the Empire Games or the Olympics: 'both together would be impracticable'. Taylor was supported by both Duff and Vicary Horniman, the New South Wales Rowing Association member who had accompanied the Australian team (*The West Australian*, August 16, 1928, 17). Nevertheless, Duff was recognized as a progenitor of the Empire Games in 1930 on several occasions in the Adelaide *Advertiser* newspaper (February 21, 1930, 9; May 2, 1930, 7). Australian ambivalence towards the Empire Games was reflected in the decision by the AAUA (1930, 11) to decline the Canadian invitation on account of the 'distance and expense involved', although the union was prepared to accredit an athlete that any state association was willing to send. *The Sydney Morning Herald* (March 25, 1930, 23) suggested that the proximity of the Empire Games to the Los Angeles Olympics of 1932 also informed the decision to decline the offer to tour. Australian participation at Hamilton was eventually secured through the offer from the Canadian organizers of a $5000 (£1000 in Australian terms) subsidy towards the Australian team's passage. Announcements of the offer often suggested that the invitation was originally rejected as it was feared that fundraising efforts for Los Angeles would be unduly affected by fundraising efforts for Hamilton (*The Barrier Miner*, January 30, 1930, 4; *The Sydney Morning Herald*, February 1, 1930, 22; *The Evening News*, February 3, 1930, 2; *Townsville Daily Bulletin*, February 5, 1930, 14; *The West Australian*, February 12, 1930, 7). 'Dom' of *The West Australian* (February 12, 1930, 7) saw the Los Angeles Games as especially important for Australia: 'with the climatic conditions of California so similar to those of Australia, would provide a great opportunity for this country to do well'.

The fear that the Empire Games would overshadow the Olympic Games was reflective of a debate over the worthiness of the two events. Some observers unequivocally saw the Empire Games as a superior entity that was entitled to greater focus. In congratulating the Victorian Rowing Association for supporting the passage of Olympic Champion sculler Bobby Pearce, 'The Searcher' of the Rockhampton (Queensland) *The Morning Bulletin* observed that the Empire Games:

> [s]tand for something even higher than the Olympic Games, which have hardly stood the test of years as Australia has applied it. Breathing the spirit of Empire, the games may be made a big success with far less cost to the contesting countries. (*The Morning Bulletin*, February 12, 1930, 12)

On the other hand, New South Wales sprinter James 'Jimmy' Carlton declined to tour. While financial and career concerns were also offered as reasons for his decision, *The Sydney Morning Herald* (April 16, 1930, 17) reported that Carlton 'was also of the opinion that the British Empire tour was a secondary matter, compared with the Olympic Games'.

As a Catholic, Carlton's viewpoint may have been informed by the strength of sectarian tensions between Irish Catholics and British Protestants in Australia following the First World War (Rowe 1979; Lyons 2003). Whatever the reason, Carlton's experience reminds us that not all Australians were as enthusiastic about matters of Empire as 'The Searcher'.

The comparative worth of the Empire Games and the Olympic Games was also debated in Coombes' newspapers. *The Referee* announced the Canadian offer of assistance and also reported that the Empire Games 'should carry a more insistent and vital message to Australians than the Olympic Games'. The pro-British element of this message was left implicit as the unattributed author opined that Australia's inconsistent performance at the Olympic Games meant that 'it cannot be said that sport in this country has been uplifted, or otherwise materially benefitted by the experience' (*The Referee*, January 29, 1930, 1). On the other hand, the Empire Games represented an opportunity for Australia to prove itself internationally:

> A competition for supremacy between the kith and kin of the Empire, they are to be carried out in different centres of the Empire, each to have its turn, each to vie with the others in producing its champions and in fittingly organising within its own territory the games in happy rotation ... we shall in time see them staged in our own country, which has produced and is producing players and athletes comparable with the best anywhere. (*The Referee*, January 29, 1930, 1)

On Christmas Day 1929, Coombes himself presented a similar argument that Australia and New Zealand faced 'bigger expenses and the greater time needed by the competitors to cover these distances [to Olympic Games]'. He also elucidated a long-standing complaint held by Australians over perceived unfairness in dealings with international bodies in terms of the financing of international tours:

> While the representatives of Australia and New Zealand by their presence as competitors, while touring, financially assist the countries they visit through their drawing power at the gates, there is rarely any reciprocal attention from overseas authorities, and then only when guarantees as to expenses are forthcoming from this end. (*The Referee*, December 25, 1929, 14; for earlier debates, see *The Australasian*, January 13, 1900; April 7, 1900)

This was an anxiety that was more appropriately felt in the early twentieth century than the late 1920s. The AAUA received £112 17s. 3d. from the Victorian Amateur Athletic Association following the 1930 Australian Championship held the month following Coombes' complaint. This figure represented 10% of the profit accrued through the event, a figure that was no doubt bolstered by the presence of German Otto Peltzer and Leo Lermond of the USA (*The Argus*, January 25, 1930, 24; AAUA 1932, 19). While concepts such as 'The Imaginary Grandstand' (Davison 2002, 4–18) and 'Sportive Nationalism' (Cashman 2002, 233–237) have cast light on the benefits of international competition in terms of promoting Australian identity, it must not be forgotten that Australians participated in an international sporting landscape that for the most part denied them the opportunity of enjoying the sport first hand. Australia's greater significance within the Empire compared to the general international community held out the promise of greater access to international sport.

The discourse surrounding the Empire Games in *The Referee* reflected debates and issues that had previously related to the Olympic Games. The nature and particulars of selection again frustrated sectors of the Australian sporting community. Advocates of women's sport hoped in vain that women would join their male counterparts on the team (*The West Australian*, February 25, 1930, 4; *The Sydney Morning Herald*, March 24, 1930, 15). But the most widespread controversy over selection related to the elevation of swimmer Bill Cameron, recently arrived from New Zealand, to the six-man team. The

THE BRITISH WORLD AND THE FIVE RINGS

selection of Cameron provoked dissension from sectors of the Australian swimming community that reflects the division that did exist between territories within the Empire despite claims to imperial unity. The ex-New Zealander arrived in Sydney in early January 1930, which raised questions over his eligibility for Australian selection. Organizers of the games had determined that British subjects that had been resident in a country for six months before 1 August 1930 would be eligible to compete (Gorman 2010, 616). The Amateur Swimming Union of Australia (ASUA) and the Queensland swimming community were outraged by Cameron's selection. The ASUA had nominated Queenslander Reg Grier and New South Welshman Noel Ryan as first and second choices but were overruled by a selection committee comprising Coombes, W. Scott, Harry Alderson and B. MacDonald, much to Taylor's chagrin (*The Sydney Morning Herald*, April 5, 1930, 15). The *Courier* (Brisbane) described Cameron's selection as 'an insult to our Australian swimmers' (*The Brisbane Courier*, April 9, 1930, 7). New Zealanders were in fact quite supportive of Cameron's selection, with the *NZ Truth* attributing the disagreement to the fact that 'parochial feeling [was] all against [Cameron]' (*NZ Truth*, April 10, 1930, 17). The ASUA eventually ruled that Cameron was eligible, as the six-month residency period would elapse en route to Canada (*The Referee*, June 11, 1930, 1). While its advocates asserted that the Empire Games promised a more congenial atmosphere for friendly competition, the discourse surrounding the games was still subject to nativist responses.

This process emphasized Coombes' argument that unsatisfactory selection procedures were cruelling Australia's international sporting efforts. A front-page editorial that repeated Coombes arguments of 1912 almost verbatim appeared in *The Referee* on 26 February 1930. The editorial affirmed that '[m]en who possess no earthly chance of success of success should not be put forward [for selection]. Only those with good prospects of winning should be honoured with selection'. Echoing Coombes' arguments of 1900, it also advocated for a trainer to be sent with the team. The success of Pearce in winning the single sculls at Amsterdam was cited as evidence of the utility of training (*The Referee*, February 26, 1930, 1). Pearce had also employed the assistance of English professional sculler Ted Phelps in the lead-up to Amsterdam, but this was not publicized on this occasion. Phelps' father complained that Ted had been short-changed by the Pearces, and successfully claimed £25 from the Australian Olympic Federation (AOF) for the five weeks he spent in Holland.[11] The call for only athletes with a genuine chance at victory to be sent was repeated in another front-page editorial in *The Referee*(March 19, 1930, 1). Modern ideas about selection and athletic preparation more closely aligned to American approaches were thus seen to be a vital part of Australia's approach to the Empire Games in the 1930s, as they had been with regard to the Olympic Games.

Just as early attempts to modernize Australian approach to sport were made with an eye to improving its standing within imperial sport, *The Referee* staked Australia's claim as a significant force within the Empire Games. *The Referee* and its sister paper *The Arrow* worked assiduously on developing continuity between the 1911 Festival of Empire and the 1930 Games. In doing so, Coombes was presented as a founding father of the Empire Games movement. Coombes himself anachronistically described the 1911 event as 'the first Empire Games' in the course of a short article describing early organizational efforts (*The Referee*, February 5, 1930, 15). A similar assertion was made in a letter to Coombes from Merrick of the AAUC, who was also present in London in 1911. Merrick waxed nostalgic about 'all the glorious prospect that loomed ahead for a regular continuance of the series' that the Festival of Empire represented to its participants, that were of course not immediately realized. Merrick also offered a new explanation for the failure of the first attempt to formalize the informal imperial Olympic team prior to Stockholm, that 'the change of personnel in charge of the [Dominion] teams, who while they might know of the arrangements, could hardly be expected to carry out in the same spirit the plans which had originated with others' (*The Referee*, April 23, 1930, 15). Merrick's explanation is indicative of the gap between the proponents of the scheme and the wider sporting community. It also demonstrates that, just as administrative assistance continued to be offered among Dominion teams, the Empire Olympic team idea retained currency among its adherents, if not the wider sporting community. Merrick wistfully concluded that '[t]he idea was excellent, but the performance very difficult' (*The Referee*, April 23, 1930, 15).

Coombes himself provided readers with recapitulations of the events of 1911 on three occasions, including an insert into a full-page feature that commemorated the beginning of the Games (*The Arrow*, January 31, 1930, 13; *The Referee*, July 2, 1930, 30; August 20, 1930, 18). The full-page feature included a pictorial representation of the Empire in geographic and athletic terms. The page featured disembodied headshots of most of the members of the New Zealand and Australian teams superimposed over a world map with British territories shaded. The New Zealand team was numerically stronger than the Australian team, a fact that was both clear from the preponderance of their faces on the map and obscured by the fact that several of the team were not shown. The New Zealanders also showed greater diversity from a gender perspective as swimmer Gladys Pidgeon was included. The map provided a misleading image of imperial unity given the fact that it showed pre-Partition India, Ceylon, Malaya and Britain's West African possessions shaded despite their absence from the Games themselves (*The Referee*, August 20, 1930, 18). British East Africa was also shaded, and there was some confusion about their participation on the part of *The Referee's* writers, with the paper's 'Special Correspondent' and Coombes providing different lists of competing countries. The list of competing countries provided by Gorman (2010, 618) did not include British East Africa and conforms to the list provided by Coombes. Coombes' paternity over the Empire Games was clearly expressed even after his death in a tribute from Cuff, who asserted that '[i]t was [Coombes] who conceived the idea of the Empire Games' (*The Referee*, May 2, 1935, 13). While Coombes was certainly an enthusiastic adopter of the idea, Moore (1989a) has shown that Coombes was in fact energized by the plans of John Astley Cooper for a pan-Britannic festival most clearly enunciated in 1891. Asserting Coombes as the Games' 'father' was yet another way of claiming a place for Australia in the athletic centre of Empire.

Australia's response to authoritarian nations at the Olympic Games

The desire of the Australian Olympic Movement to prove its worthiness to the imperial and international community meant that the recurring debate within the BOA about whether the Olympic Games themselves were worthwhile was not replicated in Australia (Llewellyn 2012b). There were, however, occasional critiques over the development of the Olympic Movement – particularly as authoritarian nations came to make their mark at the Games. Conflict between nations was always a feature of the Olympic Games, and the rivalry between the USA and Great Britain had a major effect on the Olympic Movement prior to the First World War (Llewellyn 2012b, 64–86). However, 'broken-time' controversies in the late 1920s and the accusation that European countries in particular employed 'state amateurs' in their Olympic teams added a new dimension to international Olympic conflict. By the late 1920s, new forces within the Olympic Movement were

THE BRITISH WORLD AND THE FIVE RINGS

sidelining the old Anglo-American axis. In the words of Llewellyn and Gleaves (2012, 24),

> The Oxbridge, Ivy League, and hereditary European elites that comprised the original Olympic contestants in Athens in 1896, had been gradually replaced by a more socially, racially, ethnically, and geographically diverse body of participants – an impressive 2,883 athletes from 46 IOC members nations competed at the Amsterdam Games [in 1928].

With this increasing level of diversity within the Olympic Movement came even greater ideological conflict on the matter of amateurism. Amateurism had always been a matter of contention within the movement, particularly between British and Americans. However, there was at least the possibility of rapprochement between the communities due to the presence of figures such as Coombes that were favourable to aspects of the American approach. The American side also had its fair share of influential Anglophiles such as William Sloane and Caspar Whitney who vigorously advocated for a traditional, British elite approach towards amateurism (Pope 2007, 23, 30–31). The potential for dialogue was less apparent as a more diverse array of sporting cultures fought for dominance within the Olympic Movement. In 1927, the IOC came under pressure from the *Fédération Internationale de Football Association* (FIFA) to allow broken-time payment – or else it would boycott the Amsterdam Games and the lucrative football competition would be cancelled. While the IOC affirmed the traditional approach to broken-time at the Prague Congress in 1925, the threat of removing football from the schedule forced the Executive Committee of the IOC to acquiesce to the demands of FIFA. This decision drew ultimately futile counter-threats of a boycott by NOCs led by (but by no means limited to) Britain and its Dominions (Llewellyn 2012b, 174–181; Llewellyn and Gleaves 2012, 25–27). The AOF made its displeasure with the new regulations known to the IOC on two occasions: first, in August when AOF president Taylor responded to initial press reports concerning the decision and, second, in October in conjunction with missives from Britain and several other Dominions.[12] The matter was particularly sensitive for Australia as, for the first time, the Australian Soccer Association had sought to send a team to the Games (*The Argus*, October 29, 1927, 34). At a meeting of the New South Wales Olympic Council (NSWOC) in November 1927, Sydney Storey spoke in favour of broken time, putting forward the argument 'that if Australia was to be "bound to the chariot wheel of Britain", it would find itself isolated' (*The Referee*, November 16, 1927, 1). Storey's internationalist call was clearly a minority opinion within Australian Olympism.

Alderson, the vice-chairman of the AOF and general manager to the Australian team to Berlin in 1936, was particularly vexed by the issue of 'state amateurism'. According to Gordon, Alderson 'returned home disillusioned by the intrusion of nationalism and professionalism into the Olympics'. Alderson proposed in a speech back in Sydney that Australia withdraw from the Olympics and focus on the Empire Games. He claimed that the Games did not '[develop] international amity and goodwill, as was the intention of [de Coubertin]' but had turned into 'international contests in which the different nations regard the results and conduct as a serious national matter. It is only in the British Empire Games that the amateur status of the Olympic Games is genuinely recognised' (Gordon 1994, 161). While Alderson was clearly correct to notice the increasing politicization of the Games in the 1930s, his implied argument that the Olympic Games had degenerated from a pure starting point was unsustainable. National pride had been an essential part of the Olympic Games to the extent that Greek celebrations following the victory of Spiridon Louis in the 1896 marathon moved French chauvinist Charles Maurras to remark to Coubertin that 'I see that your internationalism ... does not kill national spirit – it strengthens it' (Guttmann 2002, 19). The idea that this nationalist impulse was restricted to nations outside the 'British World' was equally preposterous. Britain was a keen participant in early disputes with the USA that essentially revolved around the threat to Britain's place in the world that the USA embodied. National rivalry was certainly as much a feature at the 1908 Battle of Shepherd's Bush as it was in Berlin. As demonstrated in the previous sections, Australia's approach to the Olympic and Empire Games also subverted the strictest notions of British amateurism.

Given Australia's place as 'one of the pioneer [Olympic] nations', Taylor melodramatically considered Alderson's suggestion to discontinue Australian participation at the Games as 'a slur on our manhood'. Taylor claimed that Australia's creditable performance at Los Angeles in 1932 (three gold medals) was followed by a disappointing gold medal free performance at Berlin as 'other nations had "progressed athletically far beyond us"' (Gordon 1994, 161). Alderson and Taylor personified two poles of a tension that had gripped Australian engagement with the Olympic Games throughout the twentieth century. Participation in international competitions such as the Olympic Games was an important way for the burgeoning Australian athletic community to prove its worth to the Empire and beyond, but this required engagement with alien sporting cultures. The desire to compete and prove Australia's worth consistently won out over the desire to maintain a traditional approach to sport informed by British norms.

Australian Olympic administrators responded to the new environment by attempting to facilitate a pan-British approach to the matter of state amateurism. In doing so, they once more attempted to claim a place of leadership within the imperial Olympic Movement. At the AOF conference of delegates held in Sydney in April 1937, the Queensland Olympic Council (QOC) suggested that the Empire Games to be held in Sydney the next February offered the perfect opportunity 'to discuss Olympic matters from the Empire view point'.[13] The NSWOC made a similar resolution at a meeting held just prior to the national conference. Alderson, serving as chairman of the organization, made his fellow delegates aware that 'semi-professionalism had been allowed by certain European nations in relation to its athletes at the Berlin Games'. On hearing this information, the meeting agreed 'that the question might with advantage be discussed among the Empire officials' during the Empire Games.[14] Invoking the spirit of the 'Round Table' movement, the QOC motion suggesting that the 'meeting should take the form of a round table conference and it should be possible at such a meeting to clear up many questions that at present cause confusion between the Empire Units in matters pertaining to Olympic methods generally'. The object of Australian consternation was clear – the conflicting approach to amateurism that new athletic superpowers brought to the sport. After the submission of this item, '[a] long discussion ensued on the merits and demerits of the enforcement of the Olympic amateur law'. One delegate, a Mr Langford, suggested that the AOF write to the IOC to inform that body that several nations had won Olympic titles as a result of 'allegedly violat [ing] the Olympic amateur law of payment or reimbursement for loss of time'. Alderson stated that 'the British Commonwealth of Nations should take a firm stand to safeguard the amateur law'. The delegates present at the meeting agreed to the following motion:

> That the Executive Committee forward letters to each International Federation and the International Olympic Committee for data, and to each country of the British Empire represented at the Olympic Games.[15]

It is clear that Australian Olympic figures were feeling nostalgic for a non-existent pure age of Olympic amateurism dominated by British conceptions of amateurism. British gentlemanly amateurism had always been just one of multiple conceptions of amateurism at the Olympic Games. However, the willingness of figures like Coombes to ally American approaches to amateurism was matched in the political sphere. For example, Thompson (1998, 107) has described Australian political culture as a 'Washminster mutation' that combines British and American traditions. The new ethic behind sport in authoritarian countries was completely alien, however. The instinct of Australian Olympic administrators was to retreat to the seeming safety of the British World. They were confident not only that a pan-British response to the new athletic ethic could be developed, but also that this could hold off the forces of athletic modernization and restore British conceptions to the fore.

However, the Australian approach to this issue maintained the same tension between idealism and pragmatism that marked their response to other issues. At the same meeting, Alderson suggested that delegates 'approach their Members of Parliament with a view of ventilating the necessity of creating a Minister of Health and Sport on similar lines to that now adopted by many overseas nations'.[16] Just as British governments were wary of involving themselves in sport, the Australian Federal Government only 'provided intermittent, if limited support, for sport [from] 1920' (Stewart et al. 2004, 37; Polley 2006). Despite earlier periodic pleas for government intervention, it was not until the 1970s that the Australian Federal Government seriously invested in Olympic and other elite sports programmes (*The Referee*, February 12, 1908, 10; July 12, 1911, 9; March 16, 1927, 1). A Tourism and Recreation portfolio responsible for sport was established within Cabinet by the Whitlam Labor Government (1972–1975) following an inquiry led by physical education professor John Bloomfield (Stewart et al. 2004, 48). Bloomfield's report contained a similar lament to Alderson, although Communists were the targets rather than fascists: 'several eastern European countries have created almost full-time professional sportsmen and sportswomen simply to further the cause of nationalism in their country' (Bloomfield 1974, 15; Hutchins 2009, 200). The success of Eastern European nations, and particularly East Germany, at the Olympics influenced the Coles Report which informed the creation of the Australian Institute of Sport in 1981 and Australia's successful engagement with high performance sport (Houlihan 1997, 6; Magdalinski 2000, 317; Green and Houlihan 2005, 19, 35; Hutchins 2009, 199, 201, 208). Successful authoritarian sporting regimes either side of the Second World War eventually forced a decisive break with British amateurism that informed Australian sport since the nineteenth century (Cashman 1995, 54). This process came full circle as British sport in the 1990s came to be influenced by Australian ideas, methods, experiences and personnel as a way to improve Great Britain's Olympic performance (Green 2007, 427, 433, 435).

Conclusion

The call of the QOC to hold a conference of imperial organizations ultimately went unheeded. AOF Secretary Treasurer Eve informed the next meeting 'that he found it impossible to have the meeting called during the period of the Empire Games'. Instead, letters were sent to other imperial organizations, with a special letter sent to the BOA.[17] As was the case right through Australia's early Olympic history, there was not the administrative will to see this aim realized. Given the outbreak of the Second World War months later, it is hard to see the failure of the AOF to convene an Empire-wide meeting on amateurism Olympic style as much of a missed opportunity. From Australia's early engagement right up until the 1930s, Australia's place in the Olympic Movement was indivisible from its place as a staunch member of the British Empire. Early Australian Olympians were seen by key administrators, such as Coombes, to be part of a pan-imperial effort to stave off American dominance at the Olympic Games. This did *not* mean that Great Britain's Olympic experience was replicated in Australia though, although debates current in English sport in particular were given an Antipodean airing. Taking his cue from the most liberal strands of British amateurism, Coombes advocated for modern preparation and selection techniques as a way of maintaining British superiority over international sport. Importantly, this was also a way to assert the centrality of Australia within the Empire. Australian administrators such as Coombes opportunistically set virulent Australian racism aside and sought to boost the team by including Indigenous Australasians. Australia also contributed to an imperial Olympic ethic that could be likened to an unofficial Empire Olympic team. Even when an official Olympic team was rejected, the legacy of this ethic continued to be felt administratively. The institution of the Empire Games reinforced debates concerning imperialism that Australia expressed through the Olympic Games. Debates over selection policies continued to be expressed and Australia continued to assert its centrality to the Empire through its athletes. A final effort to assert Australia's centrality was made through an attempt to develop a pan-imperial response to the issue of state amateurism that developed as authoritarian nations began to achieve Olympic success. The concurrent suggestion to institute a Federal Minister for sport reflected a familiar tension between pan-British unity and modern athletic approaches. While the decision to employ this measure was one that ultimately severed Australia's imperial Olympic bond, the forces that led to it had a deep history.

The arguments presented here reflect the growing realization among historians that the development of national consciousness in Britain's former Dominions did not preclude the formation of a 'British World'. Australia's embrace of the Empire remained strong even in as nationally charged a forum as the Olympic Games. However, as is the case in any community, divisions between these territories abounded within this British World. Adopting a British World posture need not prevent historians from examining the tensions that were apparent within an imagined pan-Britannic community. In the case of Australia's imperially informed engagement with the Olympic Movement, diverse English responses to amateurism provided a framework for Australian athletic figures such as Coombes to challenge *dominant* English conceptions of amateurism without stepping outside the pale of Britishness. Historians must also pay heed to the fact that the British World was not hermetically sealed, and that engagement with the outside world influenced relations between communities within it. In this case, the tension between adhering to Britishness and embracing the outside world is illuminated by the struggle between the variegated British concept of amateurism and 'state amateurism' in vogue in authoritarian countries. The centrality of sporting culture to the development of the British Empire means that study of events such as the Olympic Games can play a key role in charting the formation of the British World as well as the tensions within it.

Disclosure statement

No potential conflict of interest was reported by the author.

Notes

1. Amateur Athletic Union of Canada, *Minutes of Annual Meeting: 25 November 1911*, Amateur Athletic Union of Canada fonds, M3209, Library and Archives Canada, Ottawa, Canada (AAUC fonds), 14.
2. Amateur Athletic Union of Canada, *Minutes of Annual Meeting: 23 November 1912* (AAUC fonds), 8–9.

3. Victorian Amateur Athletic Association, *Programme – Australasian Athletics Championships: 26 January 1914*, Melbourne: VAAA, 1914. Davis Sporting Collection 1, Box 6 – Amateur Athletics Association Carnivals, 1899–1931, Mitchell Library, State Library of New South Wales, Sydney, Australia, 13.
4. New Zealand Olympic Association, *Minutes of Meeting*, 27 February 1920, New Zealand Olympic Committee Records, Minute Book – October 1911 – March 1936, Olympic Studies Centre, New Zealand Olympic Committee, Wellington, New Zealand (NZOC Records, Minute Book), 38.
5. New Zealand Olympic Association, *Minutes of Meeting*, 20 April 1920, NZOC Records, Minute Book, 42.
6. New Zealand Olympic Association, *Minutes of Meeting*, 10 March 1924, NZOC Records, Minute Book, 84.
7. New Zealand Olympic Association, *Minutes of Meeting*, 10 March 1924, NZOC Records, Minute Book, 84–85.
8. New South Wales Sports Club, *The Richard Coombes Testimonial: 27 April 1931*, Sydney: NSWSC, 1931, E.S. Marks Sporting Collection, Box Q82 – Miscellaneous sports – Letters and Minute Books, Mitchell Library, State Library of New South Wales, Sydney, Australia.
9. New Zealand Olympic Association, *Minutes of Meeting*, 7 May 1931, NZOC Records, Minute Book, 175; New Zealand Olympic Association, *Minutes of Meeting*, 10 November 1931, NZOC Records, Minute Book, 180.
10. New Zealand Olympic Association, *Minutes of Meeting*, 8 March 1932, NZOC Records, Minute Book, 184.
11. Australian Olympic Federation, *Report of Executive: July 1929*, Harry Gordon Papers, A.O.F. Conference & Executive Minutes – 1928–1939, National Library of Australia, Canberra, Australian Capital Territory (Harry Gordon – Conferences), 6–7.
12. James Taylor, Telegram, 17 August 1927; James Taylor, Telegram, 31 October 1927, Grande Bretagne Correspondance 1892–1959, CIO CNO-GRABR-CORR, 9287, International Olympic Committee Archives, Lausanne, Switzerland.
13. Australian Olympic Federation, *Minutes of Conference of Delegates: 30 April 1937*, Harry Gordon – Conferences.
14. New South Wales Olympic Council, *Minutes of Biennial Meeting: 22 April 1937*, Harry Gordon Papers, Box 2C – NSW Olympic Council, National Library of Australia, Canberra, Australian Capital Territory.
15. Australian Olympic Federation, *Minutes of Conference of Delegates: 30 April 1937*, Harry Gordon – Conferences.
16. Australian Olympic Federation, *Minutes of Conference of Delegates: 30 April 1937*, Harry Gordon – Conferences.
17. Australian Olympic Federation, *Minutes of Conference of Delegates: 6 November 1938*, Harry Gordon – Conferences.

References

AAUA (Amateur Athletic Union of Australia). 1930. *Minutes of Proceedings of the Board of Control: 24 January 1930*. Melbourne: AAUA.

AAUA. 1932. *Minutes of Proceedings of the Board of Control: 15 January 1932*. Sydney: AAUA.

Alexander, W. B. 1909. *Twenty-Second Annual Report*. Sydney: New South Wales Amateur Athletic Association.

Belich, James. 2001. *Paradise Reforged: A History of the New Zealanders from the 1880s to the Year 2000*. Honolulu: University of Hawai'i Press.

Belich, James. 2007. *Making Peoples: A History of the New Zealanders from Polynesian Settlement to the End of the Nineteenth Century*. Auckland: Penguin Books.

Bloomfield, John. 1974. *The Role, Scope and Development of Recreation in Australia*. Canberra: Department of Tourism and Recreation.

Cashman, Richard. 1995. *Paradise of Sport: The Rise of Organised Sport in Australia*. South Melbourne: Oxford University Press.

Cashman, Richard. 2002. *Sport in the National Imagination: Australian Sport in the Federation Decades*. Sydney: Walla Walla Press.

Collins, Tony. 2009. "The Tyranny of Deference: Anglo-Australian Relations and Rugby Union before World War II." *Sport in History* 26 (3): 437–456.

Davison, Graeme. 2002. "The Imaginary Grandstand." *Meanjin* 61 (3): 4–18.

Gordon, Harry. 1994. *Australia and the Olympic Games*. St Lucia: University of Queensland Press.

Gorman, Daniel. 2010. "Amateurism, Imperialism, Internationalism and the First British Empire Games." *The International Journal of the History of Sport* 27 (4): 611–634.

Green, Mick. 2007. "Policy Transfer, Lesson Drawing and Perspectives on Elite Sport Development Systems." *International Journal of Sport Management and Marketing* 2 (4): 426–441.

Green, Mick, and Barrie Houlihan. 2005. *Elite Sport Development: Policy Learning and Political Priorities*. Abingdon: Routledge.

Guttmann, Allen. 2002. *The Olympics: A History of the Modern Games*. Urbana: University of Illinois Press.

Henniker, Garth, and Ian Jobling. 1989. "Richard Coombes and the Olympic Movement in Australia: Imperialism and Nationalism in Action." *Sporting Traditions* 6 (1): 2–15.

Hokowhitu, Brendan. 2003. "'Physical Beings': Stereotypes, Sport and the 'Physical Education' of New Zealand Māori." *Sport in Society* 6 (2): 192–218.

Houlihan, Barrie. 1997. *Sport, Policy and Politics: A Comparative Analysis*. Abingdon: Routledge.

Hutchins, Brett. 2009. "26 January 1981 – The Opening of the Australian Institute of Sport: The Government Takes Control of the National Pastime." In *Turning Points in Australian History*, edited by Martin Crotty and David Andrew Roberts, 198–210. Sydney: University of New South Wales Press.

Irving, Helen. 1997. *To Constitute a Nation: A Cultural History of Australia's Constitution*. Cambridge: Cambridge University Press.

Little, Charles, and Richard Cashman. 2001. "Ambiguous and Overlapping Identities: Australasia at the Olympic Games, 1896–1914." In *Sport, Federation, Nation*, edited by Richard Cashman, John O'Hara, and Andrew Honey, 81–96. Sydney: Walla Walla Press in conjunction with the Centre for Olympic Studies, UNSW.

Llewellyn, Matthew P. 2008. "A Nation Divided: Great Britain and the Pursuit of Olympic Excellence, 1912–1914." *Journal of Sport History* 35 (1): 73–97.

Llewellyn, Matthew P. 2012a. "Dominion Nationalism or Imperial Patriotism? Citizenship, Race, and the Proposed British Empire Olympic Team." *Journal of Sport History* 39 (1): 45–62.

Llewellyn, Matthew P. 2012b. *Rule Britannia: Nationalism, Identity and the Modern Olympic Games*. Abingdon: Routledge.

Llewellyn, Matthew P., and John Gleaves. 2012. "The Rise of the 'Shamateur': The International Olympic Committee and the Preservation of the Amateur Ideal." In *Problems, Possibilities, Promising Practices: Critical Dialogues on the Olympic and Paralympic Games: Eleventh International Symposium for Olympic Research*, edited by Janice Forsyth and Michael K. Heine, 23–28. London: International Centre for Olympic Studies.

Lyons, Mark. 2003. "Sectarianism." In *The Oxford Companion to Australian History* (Online Version), edited by Graeme Davison, John Hirst, and Stuart Macintyre. South Melbourne: Oxford University Press. http://www.oxfordreference.com.wwwproxy0.library.unsw.edu.au/view/10.1093/acref/9780195515039.001.0001/acref-9780195515039-e-1308?rskey=oxxI8F&result=1

Magdalinski, Tara. 2000. "The Reinvention of Australia for the 2000 Olympic Games." In *Sport in Australasian Society: Past and Present*, edited by J. A. Mangan and John Nauright, 305–322. London: Frank Cass.

Mandle, W. F. 1981. "Coombes, Richard (Dick) (1858–1935)." In *Australian Dictionary of Biography*, edited by Bede Nairn and Geoffrey Searle. Vol. 8. Melbourne: Melbourne University Press. http://adb.anu.edu.au/biography/coombes-richard-dick-5769

Martin, Charles H. 2010. *Benching Jim Crow: The Rise and Fall of the Color Line in Southern College Sports, 1890–1980*. Urbana: University of Illinois Press.

Meaney, Neville. 2001. "Britishness and Australian Identity: The Problem of Nationalism in Australian History and Historiography." *Australian Historical Studies* 32 (116): 76–90.

Moore, Katharine. 1989a. "One Voice in the Wilderness: Richard Coombes and the Promotion of the Pan-Britannic Festival Concept in Australia 1891–1911." *Sporting Traditions* 5 (2): 188–203.

Moore, Katharine. 1989b. "'The Warmth of Comradeship': The First British Empire Games and Imperial Solidarity." *The International Journal of the History of Sport* 6 (2): 242–251.

Nielsen, Erik. 2014. *Sport and the British World, 1900–1930: Amateurism and National Identity in Australasia and Beyond*. Houndmills: Palgrave Macmillan.

Norman, Matt. 2009. *Salute*, DVD. Directed by Matt Norman. Sydney: Paramount Home Entertainment (Australasia).

Polley, Martin. 2006. "The Amateur Ideal and British Sports Diplomacy, 1900–1945." *Sport in History* 26 (3): 450–467.

Pope, S. W. 2007. *Patriotic Games: Sporting Traditions in the American Imagination, 1876–1926*. Knoxville: University of Tennessee Press.

Rowe, James Brock. 1979. "Carlton, James Andrew (1909–1951)." In *Australian Dictionary of Biography*, edited by Bede Nairn and Geoffrey Searle. Melbourne: Melbourne University Press. http://adb.anu.edu.au/biography/carlton-james-andrew-5505

Ryan, Greg. 2001. "Commentary." In *Sport, Federation, Nation*, edited by Richard Cashman, John O'Hara, and Andrew Honey, 133–136. Sydney: Walla Walla Press in conjunction with the Centre for Olympic Studies, UNSW.

Schreuder, Derek M., and Stuart Ward, eds. 2008. "Introduction: What Became of Australia's Empire?" *Australia's Empire*, 1–23. Oxford: Oxford University Press.

Stewart, Bob, Matthew Nicholson, Aaron Smith, and Hans Westerbeek. 2004. *Australian Sport: Better by Design? The Evolution of Australian Sport Policy*. Abingdon: Routledge.

Tatz, Colin. 1996. *Obstacle Race: Aborigines in Sport*. Sydney: University of New South Wales Press.

Thompson, Elaine. 1998. "Political Culture." In *Americanization and Australia*, edited by Roger Bell and Philip Bell, 107–122. Sydney: UNSW Press.

Williams, Mark. 2009. "'The Finest Race of Savages the World Has Seen': How Empire Turned Out Differently in Australia and New Zealand." In *Settler and Creole Reenactment*, edited by Vanessa Agnew and Jonathon Lamb with Daniel Spoth, 223–244. Basingstoke: Palgrave Macmillan.

(Dis)located Olympic patriots: sporting connections, administrative communications and imperial ether in interwar New Zealand

Geoffery Z. Kohe

Institute of Sport & Exercise Science, University of Worcester, Worcester, UK

During the interwar period (1919–1939), protagonists of the early New Zealand Olympic Committee (NZOC) worked to renegotiate and improve the country's international sporting participation and involvement in the International Olympic Committee. To this end, NZOC effectively used its locally based administrators and well-placed expatriates in Britain to variously assert the organization's nascent autonomy, independence and political power, progress Antipodean athlete's causes and counter any potential doubt about the nation's peripheral position in imperial sporting dialogues. Adding to the corpus of scholarship on New Zealand's ties and tribulations with imperial Britain, both in and beyond sport (e.g. Beilharz and Cox, 2007, "Settler Capitalism Revisited," *Thesis Eleven* 88: 112–124; Belich, 2001, *Paradise Reforged: A History of the New Zealanders from the 1880s to the Year 2000*, Auckland: Allen Lane; Belich, 2007, *Making Peoples: A History of the New Zealanders from Polynesian Settlement to the End of the Nineteenth Century*, Auckland: The Penguin Group; Coombes, 2006, *Rethinking Settler Colonialism: History and Memory in Australia, Canada, Aotearoa New Zealand and South Africa*, Manchester: Manchester University Press; MacLean, 2010, "New Zealand (Aotearoa)," In *Routledge Companion to Sports History*, edited by Steve W. Pope and John Nauright, 510–525, London: Routledge; Phillips, 1984, "Rugby, War and the Mythology of the New Zealand Male," *The New Zealand Journal of History* 18 (1): 83–103; Phillips, 1987, *A Man's Country: The Image of the Pakeha Male*, Auckland: Penguin Books; Ryan, 2004, *The Making of New Zealand Cricket, 1832–1914*, London: Frank Cass; Ryan, 2005, *Tackling Rugby Myths: Rugby and New Zealand Society 1854–2004*, Dunedin: University of Otago Press; Ryan, 2007, "Sport in 19th-Century Aotearoa/New Zealand: Opportunities and Constraints," In *Sport in Aotearoa/New Zealand Society*, edited by Chris Collins and Steve Jackson, 96–111, Auckland: Thomson), I will examine how the political actions and strategic location of three key NZOC agents (specifically, administrator Harry Amos and expatriates Arthur Porritt and Jack Lovelock) worked in their own particular ways to assert the position of the organization within the global Olympic fraternity. I argue that the efforts of Amos, Porritt and Lovelock also concomitantly served to remind Commonwealth sporting colleagues (namely Britain and Australia) that New Zealand could not be characterized as, or relegated to being, a distal, subdued or subservient colonial sporting partner. Subsequently, I contend that NZOC's development during the interwar period, and particularly the utility of expatriate agents, can be contextualized against historiographical shifts that encourage us to rethink, reimagine and rework narratives of empire, colonization, national identity, commonwealth and belonging.

Introduction

As a former colony and Dominion of the British Empire and, at present, a Realm of the Commonwealth, New Zealand has continued a historically nuanced, politically significant, economically valuable and ideological laden relationship with its imperial colonizer (Belich 2001, 2009; Coombes 2006; Palenski 2012; Pickles 2009, 2011; Ryan 2004, 2005; Sinclair 1986). I will discuss significant aspects of this history with reference to New Zealand's national Olympic committee and its nascent presence in the developing international Olympic Movement (Henniker and Jobling 1989; Jobling 2000; Kohe 2010, 2011; Letters and Jobling 1996; Little and Cashman 2001).[1] I focus predominantly on the interwar period – demarcated by the New Zealand Olympic Committee's (NZOC) official recognition by the International Olympic Committee (IOC) in 1919, and administrative changes wrought by the onset of British Empire Games in the 1930s – as a context to examine and articulate some of the complexities and characteristics of New Zealand's imperial associations, identities and loyalties, and transnational connections.[2] During this time, the NZOC's early participation in the international sporting scene was, to an extent, largely contingent not primarily on British agents, but, instead, on a few successful and well-placed expatriate New Zealanders in Britain (namely Arthur Porritt and Jack Lovelock) who worked closely with NZOC members (particularly, Secretary-General Harry Amos) to provide a voice for New Zealand sporting concerns, and a useful conduit for transmitting information to and from Britain and the IOC.[3] Below, I detail how such expatriate agents worked with NZOC administrators to help fortify the organization, advocate for its causes within Britain, Europe and the IOC, facilitate the country's athletic competition abroad and better enable administrators to respond to athletes' 'professional' needs. In so doing, I raise questions regarding the strength and political influence of the imperial core in determining (and controlling) New Zealand's peripheral sporting participation.

New Zealand's colourful and proud Olympic history aside (for example, see Palenski and Maddaford 1983; Palenski and Romanos 2000; Romanos 2006), I argue that an examination of NZOC during the interwar period reveals much about the nation's fragmented relationship with Britain at least in the contexts of amateur athletics and the Olympic Movement. By examining Amos, Porritt and Lovelock, in particular, I suggest that New Zealand's Olympic ties during this period were rarely demonstrative of a linear power hierarchy in which direct authority is transcribed from the core to the periphery. Rather, the formative years of the NZOC's relationship with Britain and its international sporting partners could be characterized as fairly fragile, mediated precariously via a set of strategically located, socially mobile and diplomatically adept agents. As I detail below, expatriates like Porritt and Lovelock, and the communications they maintained with administrators in the Antipodes, not only positively affected New Zealand's athletic participation in the Olympic Movement and abroad but also provided the country with valuable representation in international sporting circles. In addition to political advocacy, these agents helped secure New Zealand's ongoing representation and participation in the IOC, and eventually led to a long-serving membership status that continues to be highly valued by NZOC and acknowledged as an important part of its Olympic history (Kohe 2011, 2012).

Drawing on the work of scholars like Beilharz and Cox (2007), Belich (2001, 2007), Coombes (2006), Mangan and Hickey (2000), Phillips (1984, 1987, 1990), Ryan (2004, 2005, 2007) and others – who all in their various ways encourage critique of imperialism, (sporting) nationalism and identity, empire, and colonial power and its consequences – I will examine one facet of New Zealand's early sporting relationship with Britain. This work takes as its focus the context, and political interactions therein, of transnational Olympic administration and, specifically, the actions of key agents within the initial decades of the NZOC's formation. My argument is twofold. First, I contend that the antecedents, and formative involvement, of New Zealand's participation in the Olympic

Movement reside in a close but invariably fragile and inconsistent set of relationships and communications between key administrative agents, namely expatriates Arthur Porritt and Jack Lovelock, and their resident countryman, Harry Amos. Second, I argue that by their geographical location and mobility, political representation, social status and athletic nous, New Zealand agents – at least in the case of Porritt and Lovelock – could not be considered peripheral participants in global athletics, the activities of the Olympic Movement, or the genesis and consolidation of a Commonwealth sporting fraternity. To appreciate the colonial contours and imperial intricacies of this period, I begin with a short articulation of the periodic milieu.

Fortification forces, NZOC and Olympic sport

Not unlike other sport bodies within the country, and within other parts of the British Empire, the NZOC emerged at a historical juncture punctuated globally by imperial rhetoric, international political manoeuvrings, nascent nationalistic sentiment among the colonies and developing transnational rivalries in and beyond sport. The evolution of the national committee was also contoured domestically by social and political reform, growing economic productivity, radical state liberalization, vigorous civic development and population expansion (Belich 2001; King 2003; Palenski 2012; Ryan 2004, 2005, 2007; Sinclair 1984, 1986; Sinclair and Dalziel 2000). Throughout the interwar period, these, and other, modernizing conditions – overviewed below – variously contoured New Zealand relationships with Britain, the development of its imperial and individual identities, its formative (yet fluid) conceptualization of nationhood, the structure and ethos of its sporting and particularly amateur athletic culture (Palenski 2012; Ryan 2004, 2005, 2007) and the subsequent setting in which agents in the young NZOC went about their work. The period was a definitive time for the NZOC, not only in terms of athletic successes it was able to facilitate but also for fortifying its administrative structures, maintaining its economic viability, consolidating its social and cultural importance and securing its legitimacy as one of the country's premier sporting authorities.

In the first instance, the cancellation of the 1916 Olympic Games due to World War One did not totally curtail NZOC members' activities or related sporting events for that matter or their communications with imperial allies, namely Australia and Britain. Rather, the event enabled NZOC to assess its national significance and demonstrate its support for the collective wartime cause. A consequence of the NZOC maintaining and proclaiming its associations with the Empire, and capitalizing on the (inter)nationalistic camaraderie embedded in wartime ethos, was that it could effectively engender public support for its institution and entrench its role as a key sporting agency. 'It is most pleasing', then Secretary General Arthur Marryatt noted, 'that so many athletes had volunteered for the front …'; however, the War had unfortunately 'robbed (amateur sport) of a good deal of its visual interest'.[4] Marryatt's NZOC colleagues appeared to share his sentiments. 'It is a matter of extreme gratification to the Council', one delegate proclaimed, 'that in the great conflict in which our Empire is at present engaged, so many amateur athletes are at present of active service'.[5] Sport was appropriate preparation for their defence of the Commonwealth, the delegate continued, and

> although their absence will be felt during the coming season, the Council knows that the training they received [through sport] will stand them in good stead for their arduous duties, and will prove of the greatest assistance in the share of our forces in the maintenance of British prestige. The absence of our fellow athletes on the King's service should make us the more

diligent in keeping the sport at its usual high level ... [also] ... sports meetings ...,
wherever possible, should be devoted to entirely Patriotic purposes.[6]

Similar sentiments were echoed by other NZOC members, and formed part of a wider
ideological marriage between sport and militarism that permeated other sport
organizations in New Zealand and further abroad (Richardson and Richardson 2005).[7]

War exacerbated international and political forces and had a resounding influence on
the maintenance of New Zealand's relationship with Britain as well as its developing
identity as part of a sporting commonwealth. Even though the war consumed a large
contingent of New Zealand's male population, it did not result in the cessation of sporting
activities in the country, but rather imbued the competitions and events that did continue –
including those within amateur athletics – with strong jingoistic fervour, international
camaraderie and militaristic sentiment.[8] Although the NZOC convened irregularly during
the War, agents like Marryatt worked hard to ensure the New Zealand maintained a
presence at the next international sporting table in close proximity to its wartime partners.
Consequently, the NZOC emerged after World War One, well poised to manage the
country's athletic scene and facilitate international sporting competition and, by 1919, was
effectively positioned to lobby the IOC for its separate recognition.[9]

Notwithstanding its significance, war was just one defining force of the times.
Economic and social reforms, brought about by then Prime Minister William Massey's
conservative government, attempted to stimulate post-war productivity and appeal to
developing allusion of class mobility (Belich 2001; Roche 2002). Although new-found
economic and social mobility may have been enjoyed by some, by and large class
exclusions, limitations and ideological constraints prevailed, especially in the context of
amateur athletics.[10] Echoing the composition of their contemporary sport organizations in
Britain and Australia, control of the NZOC notably still resided with an elite group of
educated, white, middle-class agents. For the NZOC's effective management and success,
this was no great issue; in fact, as will be explored below, the social status of members and
associates such as Porritt and Lovelock was ultimately a useful mechanism in their
participation in the elite echelons of British, European and IOC sporting circles.

Subsequent to the effects of the war and the economic changes experienced during the
1920s, the NZOC's imperial relationship and international sporting participation were also
shaped by the onset of the Great Depression (c.1929–early 1930s). The effects of the
global economic collapse did not, Grant (1997, 138) remarks, immediately affect New
Zealand's economy, and stockbrokers appeared 'blithely indifferent' to the catastrophe.
The inevitable outcomes of downturns in trade and consumption, rises in unemployment,
social unease, and health and welfare issues eventually came; however, the effects were
varied (Belich 2009; Molloy 2007; Olssen 1995).[11] In sport, organizations like the NZOC,
which since formation continued to be in a fiscally precarious position, appeared initially
unscathed. The NZOC persevered throughout the early 1930s in balancing their books and
protecting and preserving its small economic resources.[12] In 1931, however, NZOC
Chairman Harry Amos wrote to the IOC outlining the financial and practical constraints
the committee faced in sending a team to compete in the upcoming 1932 Los Angeles
Olympic Games.[13] In 1934, Amos wrote again, this time directly to the IOC President
Henri Baillet-Latour, lamenting about the hardships of the Depression and life in New
Zealand.[14] In particular, Amos stressed the necessity for both organizations to do what
they could to ensure the future of Olympic sport.

The Depression, along with the onset of the country's first Labour government which
took power in 1935 and promised considerable social, industrial and political reform, did

however precipitate a discernible contextual shift in New Zealand and beyond in its ties with Britain. While it is difficult to confirm the extent to which the Depression definitively influenced the NZOC's relationship with Britain, its presence as an agenda item in correspondence between agents in New Zealand and their counterparts in Britain suggests that it was a valuable cause around which they could rally collective empathy and support. Although distinct from the atrocities of War, the Depression was similarly global in its reach and consequence, and, likewise, involved international political and economic intricacies that were manipulated to varying degrees by enduring and contemporary imperial forces and ties. For the NZOC specifically, this necessitated maintaining effective working relationships with their established imperial friends and ensuring they had appropriately placed and capable spokesmen (e.g. Amos) to advocate for New Zealand's concerns in the global sporting marketplace.

Amos, the Antipodean advocate

Against this post-war backdrop of mixed parts global redirection and uncertainty and national efforts to improve productivity and instigate social change (Keys 2006; Krüger and Murray 2003), NZOC agents worked to better their organization. One of the foremost agents in this project was Amos. While not the first head of the NZOC, he was active as Chairman of the organization from 1928 until 1934 and then continued in the capacity of Secretary General from 1934 until 1950, eventually becoming one of the organization's longest serving leaders. Where previous administrators, such as Marryatt, Arthur Davies and Charles Camp, had been preoccupied with the NZOC's domestic profile, Amos actively went further to improve the tyrannies that geographical distance wrought.[15] Amos was arguably the most dedicated in developing a closer and more direct relationship with the IOC. At a time when the vestiges of the Great War still lingered and international insecurities begat increasingly politicized sporting nationalisms (Keys 2006; Krüger and Murray 2003), Amos was evidently, and importantly, outward looking.

Yet, in the mid-1920s, Amos did not necessarily inherit an organization that was well equipped to ensure its financial survival, and, with this, continue to grow the country's now historically noteworthy and nationally recognized participation in international athletic sport. Having long been involved in the country's amateur athletic scene, first as a cyclist, then as an administrator, Amos had witnessed the rapid development and modernization of the national and international sporting landscape and benefited from watching successive leaders struggle with the difficulties of the NZOC's inception and survival during its early years. Over the course of his tenure, Amos subsequently enacted a series of changes that improved the NZOC's fiscal resilience and enabled the committee to maintain its international and imperial allegiance and memberships.[16] Foremost in his actions were the decisions to seek better IOC representation. Although Marryatt had acted somewhat effectively as IOC member between 1919 and 1923, subsequent appointments had been disappointingly ineffective.[17] Amos' frustration was fairly clear. 'I really believe', Amos wrote to IOC member Bernard Freyberg, 'that it is necessary for you to consider if it would not be advisable to send in your resignation and make place for a man who could take better care of the interest of the Dominion'.[18] In his reply, Freyberg lamented that distance and military commitments had prevented him from fulfilling his IOC and NZOC obligations. 'I am very sorry', Amos appears to reply in empathy, 'that you will be very likely never be able to give more time to our Committee and there that you have considered yourself bound to send in your resignation as member of the IOC for New Zealand'.[19] Through trial and error, Amos evidently appears to have realized the need for enthusiastic, communicative, proactive associates – preferably located abroad – capable of advocating on behalf of one of the country's premier sporting authorities.

Further evidence of Amos' leadership came when he also acted as manager, and chaperone, to the 1928 Olympic Games in Amsterdam. In so doing, he was the first NZOC administrator to accompany the team abroad.[20] As manager Amos experienced first-hand the difficulties New Zealand athletes and their support crews faced in competing successfully in international sport. New Zealand's commitment to the Olympic Movement – at that point ambiguously characterized and defined largely by its internationalization and growing athletic participation – required, Amos acknowledged, dedicated domestic economic efforts that could ' . . . remove from the shoulder of the Council the very arduous task of collecting money to dispatch a team'.[21] The effects were not necessarily immediate, and Olympic teams remained relatively small for some time. Although the athletes 'did not meet with the success anticipated', Amos felt that the committee had been placed on a solid foundation.[22]

Amos' evident intentions were to improve the NZOC's ability to meet athletes' needs and their international, transnational, and eventually Commonwealth, sporting expectations and obligations are commendable. Amos' strategies included more vigorous fundraising campaigns, establishing a dedicated and reliable network of domestic sponsors, donors and patrons, soliciting mainstream press outlets to raise the NZOC's public profile, instigating a more widespread, and regular, subscription scheme, lobbying for more consistent government support, and ensuring the organization was kept abreast of Olympic (and Empire) Games plans well in advance.[23] Yet, the committee's success, at least for Amos, was contingent on establishing more permanent, and reliable agents abroad who would be cognizant of adversities faced by the country's elite athletes and be socially and politically well placed to contribute to New Zealand's Olympic profile.[24]

Exercising expatriates

To this end, two expatriates, Porritt and Lovelock, each successful athletes, scholars and medical professionals, were fortuitously placed (Colquhoun 2008; McNeish 1986, 1999; Romanos 2006, 2008). Both men were seminal figures in the nation's popular sporting imaginary and retained prestige as beloved New Zealand citizens abroad. Porritt and Lovelock also both effectively capitalized on their athletic and academic prowess to establish prominence in European sporting circles, elite British higher education systems and their respective medical professions. By virtue of their sporting knowledge, social capital, national affectations and residence in Britain, these men proved invaluable assets to the NZOC. Their early, and in Porritt's case, rather enduring *pas de deux* with the NZOC fixed in place a more resolute and reliable link between New Zealand and the global athletics and Olympic sporting community. More so than this, their respective, intertwined and nuanced involvements in the domestic and international Olympic organizations provide reason to argue more strongly for the role New Zealand agents actively played (and British agents did not) in disrupting core and periphery power hierarchies (vis-á-vis sport) in the post-colonizing context. Porritt's and Lovelock's relationships with the national committee provide some evidence to reconsider the NZOC not as a compliant, distant, partner in the linear development and burgeoning growth of Olympic (or British Empire) global sporting projects, but as an organization acutely aware of its changing international identity and capabilities to drive its own destiny. I discuss each of these men now in turn, and then consider their wider utilities within reconceptualizing New Zealand's relation with the Empire or more specifically the NZOC's associations with Britain and the Olympic Movement.

Porritt, political patronage and (ex)patriotic performances

Porritt's life has been extensively documented elsewhere (Woodfield and Romanos 2008). Born in 1900, Porritt's entrance into sporting administration was preceded by a solid educational background, first, as a boarder at the prestigious Wanganui Collegiate and , later, as medical student at the University of Otago, and vigorous sporting participation at college, national and eventually international level. Porritt's university success in New Zealand led to the award of a Rhodes scholarship to Oxford; which he took up at Magdalen College in 1924.[25] While studying medicine, Porritt actively contributed to the sporting life of Oxford's student community (Woodfield and Romanos 2008). Whether by athletic talent, previous national recognition in New Zealand, social connections with sport administrators back home or geographical position (possibly a combination of all four), Porritt earned nomination to compete at the 1924 Olympic Games in Paris as a member of the New Zealand team. At just 24, not only was Porritt nominated as an athlete, but he also assumed responsibility to captain and manage the team.[26] Porritt's athletic apex was his bronze medal in the 100-metre sprint at the 1924 Paris Olympic Games (Kebric 2014).

Beyond his sporting success, Porritt was also highly regarded. As Amos remarked when nominating Porritt for IOC membership in 1934, 'Dr Porritt is a New Zealander and is a Rhodes Scholar, he has been a good all round athlete, and is imbued with the highest ideals of sportsmanship'.[27] Olympic success notwithstanding, as a collegial and affable expatriate with a new found, yet strategically useful, knowledge of the UK's amateur athletic community, Porritt was suitably placed to assist the NZOC and aid its communication with the imperial centre. In his managerial/captaincy role, for example, he helped source training facilities, accommodation and transport prior to the New Zealand team's arrival in Britain; offered the NZOC financial contributions to assist their operations; provided medical expertise and training advice; and, even before he was made an IOC member in 1934, was active in expressing NZOC views and New Zealand concerns at Olympic congresses (Colquhoun 2008; Woodfield and Romanos 2008).[28] Between 1922 and 1934, Porritt worked with the NZOC not only improved the country's Olympic and eventual Empire Games sporting successes but also provided a more effective and reliable conduit of information from Europe to New Zealand administrators. The NZOC, in return, clearly appreciated the work Porritt did for the committee and its constituents while enjoying having a competent and successful 'national' citizen on whom they could rely.

The NZOC, or, at least, Amos as its Chairman, understood that a man of Porritt's virtue and social calibre reflected positively on its organization and its international image in IOC, British and European sporting circles. Amos' nomination was a sensible choice. Porritt served as IOC member for New Zealand for 34 years. For 16 of those years, he chaired the British Empire and Commonwealth Games Federation, and, was President of the IOC's inaugural Medical Commission. Retiring from the IOC role in 1966, Porritt returned to New Zealand for a five-year stint as Governor-General, after which he migrated back to England where he resided until his death in 1994 (Woodfield and Romanos 2008). Porritt's position in England, his lengthy service on the IOC, his professional medical and athletic knowledge, social capital and personal passion he evidently demonstrated in conducting sporting administrative affairs on New Zealand's behalf endeared him to his NZOC peers.

The imperial relationship also went the other way. Porritt's formative years spent in New Zealand and his interest in NZOC and the country's sporting community were evidently aspects to his life he valued. Porritt may have been, as Woodfield and Romanos (2008, 296) suggest, 'a remarkable man, cushioned by success in every direction'; however, he saw merit in maintaining involvement in New Zealand affairs. Yet, Porritt might be considered a peculiar agent. Residing for the majority of his life in England, and by not being an official NZOC member, it would be easy to relegate Porritt to the margins of New Zealand's early history in the Olympic Movement. Yet, by analysing Porritt's sustained interest in his 'home' country, it is possible to understand that while the NZOC evidently benefited from having someone of Porritt's ability to effect political participation at a global and imperial level, concomitantly the organization gave Porritt a clear link back to the Antipodes. In addition, with its emphasis on premier sporting achievement, the NZOC also provided a distinct patriotic and nationalistic cause that Porritt could identify with. The IOC membership also afforded opportunities to fraternize with the upper echelons of the global sporting community and enjoy the convivial camaraderie of his Commonwealth companions (Woodfield and Romanos 2008).

Porritt was, however, just one mechanism in a set of broader transnational processes and networks of people and information that produced, reproduced and disrupted imperial relations. Taking cues from authors who urge us to destabilize and problematize notions of the 'core' and 'periphery' dichotomy in imperial debates (Belich 2001, 2009; Gibbons 2003; Phillips 1987; Pickles 2009, 2011; Thompson and Fedorowich 2013) – it is possible to see Porritt anew. Echoing Pickles' (2011) sentiments about reconfiguring parochial intentions embedded within colonial histories, Porritt should be conceived of as more than just an individual New Zealand agent operating abroad. His contributions were not simply about advancing the Olympic Movement within New Zealand per se but also to support and fortify New Zealand's nascent post-colonial identity, imperial allegiances and place in the Olympic Movement through representation and participation at the highest levels of international sport. Porritt's emergent quasi-cosmopolitan identity, personal affections for the antipodes and colleagues therein, participation in global sport politics and expatriate desire to sustain connections to 'home', for instance, effectively highlight some of the ways in which the NZOC's early development and Britain's bond with its colonies and Dominions are potentially more nuanced, complex and nationally transcendent than might be imagined.

Lovelock links

Porritt was not, however, the only active agent abroad. One of his contemporaries, and friends, Lovelock, was also instrumental in developing the national organization's transnational relationships, profile and successes and related imperial connections. Albeit 10 years Porritt's junior, Lovelock, was comparably invested in New Zealand sport and helping the NZOC improve its practices to ensure future international success. Like Porritt, Lovelock's life has drawn significant attention elsewhere (Colquhoun 2008; McNeish 1986, 1999; Romanos 2006, 2008; Woodfield 2007). From an early age, Lovelock demonstrated a high level of sporting and educational prowess. His studies took him to the University of Otago, Dunedin, where he studied medicine and ran competitively at the national amateur athletic level. In 1931, he was awarded a Rhodes scholarship to Oxford which he took up at Exeter College. While at Oxford Lovelock was quickly introduced to the British and international amateur athletic scene. His successes and records over the 1-mile and 1500-metre distances gained him recognition and subsequent selection for the 1932 Olympic Games in Los Angeles, the 1934 British Empire Games in London and the 1936 Olympic Games in Berlin. At the Berlin Olympic Games, he reached his athletic peak, winning gold in the 1500-metre event (Colquhoun 2008; Woodfield 2007). The event, unsurprisingly, endeared him to New Zealand fans back home.[29]

Lovelock's win in 1936 was particularly profound. 'Lovelock did more than win an Olympic title', one media correspondent remarked, 'he won the admiration of the sporting world for his attitude to sport' (Ingram 1937, 55). For administrators back in New Zealand, Lovelock's victory could not be ignored. The NZOC quickly went to work to lobby the government for funds to support Lovelock's tour of New Zealand. Their efforts were significantly enhanced by the fact that one of their members, Joseph Heenan, was Secretary of the Department of Internal Affairs. 'If this were a simply a matter of giving an athlete a free trip I would unhesitatingly recommend against it', Heenan remarked, 'but, Lovelock is more than merely the greatest mile runner the world has yet produced. I feel sure he is of great physical and education value, for Lovelock has made a really scientific study of sport' (Woodfield 2007, 94). The New Zealand Government responded positively. Over the southern hemisphere summer of 1936/1937, Lovelock was provided with passage 'home' and treated to lavish hospitality around the country that included banquets, state occasions, gifts and public accolades (NZOC, 1933–1934; Woodfield 2007). In addition to competing in several invitational and exhibition running events, Lovelock toured the country offering his athletic and medical expertise to fellow athletes and scientists and educationalists (Ingram 1937, 55). 'Large, enthusiastic crowds', Woodfield (2007, 97) notes, 'welcomed him where ever he went'. Reflecting on Lovelock's visit after his departure, Ingram noted fondly, 'he gave we New Zealanders much good advice' (*sic*) (Ingram 1937, 54). Following the tour, Lovelock returned to England. He later served in the Royal Army Medical Corp during World War Two, and shortly thereafter moved to New York where he continued to practise medicine up until his untimely death in 1949 (Colquhoun 2008; Woodfield 2007).

In understanding the utility of these men within the imperial sporting context it is difficult to deny their specific corporeal politics. Lovelock and Porritt were not only reflections of the NZOC's proficiency as a competent national sporting body, but also physical embodiments of colonial dominance. Both men, for example, were archetypes of a hegemonic conceptualization of a fairly nascent 'New Zealand' identity in that they simultaneously epitomized the 'success' of empire, the vitality of the nation and the masculine – yet gentlemanly – vigour of its sporting culture (Phillips 1987; Palenski 2012). Despite the country's political autonomy and some of the emergent iconographical markers of identity (e.g. flag, anthem, silver fern, black singlet, etc.) that had emerged prior to and during World War One,[30] distinctions about who New Zealanders were and who they were not mattered. Against the interwar and post-Depression backdrop, Lovelock's success and subsequent visit clearly offered the nation a visible conduit through which to channel shared sentiments about (a domineering white, athletic, pioneering, forthright, collective version of) 'New Zealand' identity (Belich 2001, 2009; King 2003; Phillips 1984, 1987; Sinclair 1986; Sinclair and Dalziel 2000).

Given the fact that Lovelock had been living abroad since 1931 and only ever returned for this one visit, the veneration he received as 'national' figure and sporting patriot might certainly be considered perplexing. Yet, evident in the public attention he was given, the hospitality he was afforded and commentary he drew in popular press were the idea that here was not just a world-class athlete, but also a world-class New Zealander, a man who, in his athletic prowess and gentle-manner, exhibited simultaneously the best of nation's 'home-grown' talent, but concurrently embodied a fine, polished-abroad, specimen of the imperial stock. Lovelock was, as Amos remarked to his NZOC colleague, 'a very distinguished son' of whom the country and organization could be rightly proud.[31] Lovelock, in response, played his part by maintaining fairly regular, detailed and scientifically progressive communications with administrators in New Zealand, fulfilling informal ambassadorial roles in supporting New Zealand athletes abroad, and, notably, by offering the NZOC an ongoing critical friendship from afar.[32]

Colonial contemplations and the 'cultural cringe'

The examination of a few key figures in the early history of the Olympic Movement in New Zealand is useful in articulating some of the ways in which the country negotiated its participation in international sport and imperial identities and allegiances during the interwar period. While this might be important sport history, such a study assumes an additional salience when contextualized against disciplinary shifts in imperial and national historiography that have occurred within and beyond New Zealand's shores. Some of the changes have been alluded to at the outset of this paper (recall Pickles 2009, 2011), yet they are worth detailing further. For the last 40 odd years, New Zealand historians, and those elsewhere, have strongly contested the post-colonial(-esque) paradigm alteration in imperial scholarship (e.g. Fairburn 1989; Fergusson 2008; Munz 1971, 1984).[33] Disciplinary movement has been heralded by other historians in the hope that it might provide a counterpoint to, and a displacement and disruption of, dominant nationalistic narratives (e.g. Belich 2009; Burton 2003; Gibbons 2003; Lambert and Lester 2006; Pocock 1974; Thompson and Fedorowich 2013). Essentially, the intention is to take us from, what Pickles (2011, 87) laments as 'the spotlight on British settlers and their colonial legacy', towards new modes of transnationally intricate inquiry that might remap and remake current ideas about geopolitical and ideological allegiance and identity. A key tenet of this debated scholarly shift is the rejection of narratives overemphasizing the role of the Empire (in this case the British version thereof) within processes and consequences of colonization and, subsequent, post-colonial identity formation and belonging (Beilharz and Cox 2007; Pickles 2009, 2011). Explicit within this rejection, Pickles argues, is the related need to debunk, and transcend, the 'cultural cringe' aspect inherent within nation-based colonial history projects; characterized namely by excessive and needless comparisons with Britain/British schools of thought, parochial constructions of historical agency centred on an imperial core and misplaced assumptions about inferiority and power relations.[34]

Bearing in mind the arguments above, the crux of this work is, essentially, that New Zealand agents were not passive participants in the country's imperial and transnational relations during the interwar years. Rather, connections forged first by people like Amos, and then more directly by expatriates such as Porritt and Lovelock, were instrumental in establishing New Zealand sport administrators as active contributors to global athletic sport. Taking account of Pickles' comments, Amos, Porritt and Lovelock were not merely reactive agents responding to circumstances that lay beyond their immediate control or influence. Nor, for that matter, did they accept their political membership being mediated through British counterparts. Their most significant contributions – certainly in the framework of contemporary trends in imperial historiography, to which this collection contributes – were the parts each played in reaffirming New Zealand's nascent sporting identity and contesting a sense of the country's peripheral, and by default subordinate, status within international sporting fraternities. Through their achievements, roles, status and administrative prowess, figures such as Amos, Porritt and Lovelock, along with other contemporaries in other key sporting institutions, contributed to the vitality of New Zealand's sporting culture and the professionalism of its Olympic administration. Concomitantly, however, as 'expats' the latter two men were also emblematic of the 'success' of sporting and educational colonialism, and, as such, were positive reflections and ambassadors for Britain and the empire. Although Porritt and Lovelock were valuable to the NZOC and its imperial relationships, I argue that their utility needs to be situated within critical historiographical assessments that explore the country's increasingly stronger national sentiment, sense of collective national purpose and political quest for greater autonomy and respect for the historical significance of imperial membership (e.g. Byrnes 2009; MacLean 2010; Palenski 2012).[35]

Operating largely from abroad, these men – I recognize that there were others with whom they worked – effected change in the ways the NZOC went about its work, namely by providing an information channel and more resounding voice for New Zealand sporting concerns at an international level. Amos, Porritt and Lovelock's agency provides reason to query New Zealand's peripheral place within conceptions of Empire and discussions about imperial allegiance. Porritt and Lovelock, in particular, demonstrated that New Zealand, or more precisely the NZOC, did not have to be reliant on their British counterparts to mediate their participation on the world stage. For Amos, the historic imperial links with Britain, though not inherently problematic, begat frustrating pragmatic concerns (e.g. impeded information flows, ideological challenges over the specificities and peculiarities of amateurism and the inability to implement effective long-term financial planning) that curtailed New Zealand's Olympic participation and eventual success. Amos' approach to the internationalization of NZOC, at least in terms of Olympic participation, is partial evidence of an attempt to redefine the historic power relations – and imbedded administrative subservience therein – within colonial and imperial sporting ties. Although part of the reliance on Australia and Britain had been borne out of historic, pragmatic and/or economic necessities, during this interwar period, NZOC used its own members, and their political acumen, to announce and consolidate their independence, autonomy and identity. Affiliations with the Empire may have mattered to a degree,[36] yet such associations were effectively secondary to the desire for the NZOC to be truly and fully an active constituent of transnational sporting affairs.

The arguments about imperial connections rehearsed here only go part of the way towards changing our disciplinary visions of imperial relations. I also recognize my interpretations here are limited. I have, for instance, only focused on a few key agents at one specific historical moment. Moreover, there is still much we do not know about the articulation of empire within particular sporting contexts during this period. Nonetheless, by foregrounding some of the distinct roles particular New Zealanders played in determining the NZOC's international and imperial sport participation, it is possible to appreciate some of the ways in which the country was negotiating its relationship with Britain at a key historical juncture. Amos, for example, took a lead role in ensuring the NZOC retained a visible presence in the Olympic Games and that its role in the movement writ large could be assured irrespective and independent of its imperial relationships. To recall Pickles contentions here about rethinking core/peripheral dynamics (Pickles 2011), the ways in which Amos operated and undertook affairs on behalf of the NZOC was not, it need be said, an attempt to wrestle more authority, control or autonomy from the core to the periphery. Rather, here was an example of an outlying, though historically noteworthy, member of the Empire strategically seeking opportunities to better communicate with the global sporting fraternity.[37]

THE BRITISH WORLD AND THE FIVE RINGS

Colleagues such as Porritt and Lovelock worked in their own particular ways to help Amos achieve some of these goals. To their credit, and notwithstanding the influence of structural forces and/or individual protagonists, all three men worked to challenge and change the country's sporting profile and its political participation abroad and punctuate imperial athletic conversations with a distinct Kiwi twang. Where Lovelock aided the NZOC's public profile in the short term, Porritt exhibited a more enduring commitment to the organization. The efforts of England-based expatriates such as Porritt and Lovelock, too, help reveal that New Zealand's evolution in the Olympic Movement was not just mediated from afar but was contingent on strategically (dis-)located, white, educated, upper middle-class agents who were best placed to affect and advocate for its causes. Such was their influence and success that they helped set the NZOC on a trajectory where they would no longer be considered a peripheral participant in global athletics or the activities of the Olympic Movement, but rather a key member of an international sporting fraternity.

Disclosure statement

No potential conflict of interest was reported by the author.

Notes

1. New Zealand's associations with the Olympic Movement tentatively began in 1892 when there was a brief, and much mythologized, interaction in Paris between leading New Zealand amateur athletics administrator Leonard Cuff and eventual renovator of the modern Olympic Movement Baron Pierre de Coubertin. An eventual consequence of this meeting was Cuff's co-option onto the inaugural IOC. Yet, the co-option did not give immediate rise to the New Zealand Olympic Committee (NZOC). See, variously, Henniker and Jobling (1989), Jobling (2000), Kohe (2010), Little and Cashman (2001) and Letters and Jobling (1996). To note also, the Committee originally began as the Olympic Council of New Zealand. Over the course of its existence, however, NZOC has undergone a number of name changes to reflect the authority and remit of the organization, and its associations with various British Empire sporting competitions. Today, the organization still retains its title as the NZOC and reference initials NZOC. See Kohe (2011) for a chronology of these changes.
2. Although formally established on 18 October 1911, the effective cessation of most national and international Olympic business during World War One meant that the IOC did not officially get around to recognizing NZOC, and accepting its important separation from the Australasian union, until 1919. Nevertheless, three New Zealand athletes had competed as part of an Australasian team at the 1908 Olympic Games (in which Harry Kerr become the country's first Olympic medallist winning bronze in the 3500-metre walk). Three New Zealanders competed again for Australasia in the 1912 Olympic Games. One of the members of this latter team was the national, Australasian and Wimbledon tennis champion Anthony Wilding. Between 1907 and 1914, Wilding's athletic success abroad had helped raise the country's sporting profile and reaffirm imperial ties between Britain, New Zealand and Australia. See Kohe (2010), Palenski and Maddaford (1983), Palenski and Romanos (2000), Romanos (2006, 2008) and Richardson and Richardson (2005) for further details.
3. Such exchanges, of course, involved not only amateur athletics, but also other sports, including rugby union and league, and cricket. See Palenski (2012) and Ryan (2004, 2005, 2007).
4. New Zealand Amateur Athletics Association (NZAAA), *Official Minute Book (vol. 2)* (Hereafter *NZAAA Minute Book*), 11 September 1914, Athletics New Zealand Collection, Alexander Turnbull Library, Wellington, New Zealand, 43.
5. NZAAA, *NZAAA Minute Book*, 23 November 1914, 50.
6. NZAAA, *NZAAA Minute Book*, 23 November 1914, 50.
7. Richardson and Richardson's (2005) work on the multi-Wimbledon Champion Anthony Wilding (who incidentally was killed at the battle of Ypres) provides a particularly good overview of the context and consequences for the nation's athletes during this period.

53

THE BRITISH WORLD AND THE FIVE RINGS

8. NZOC, and its allied association the NZAAA, for example, maintained an active calendar of sport events throughout the country, and, in particular, were diligent in demonstrating support for Australian and American (and occasional British) allies by fostering sporting competition and participating in military athletic championships within the country. NZOC, *Official minute book, 1912–1932* (hereafter *NZOC Minute Book 1912–1932*), NZOC Olympic Studies Centre, Wellington, New Zealand.

9. This was largely due to Chairman Arthur Marryatt maintaining correspondence with Australian IOC member and amateur athletic administrator Richard Coombes, and IOC members in Britain and Europe during the War. Support for the war was also a good public advertisement for NZOC in particular as their official minutes were regularly published in mainstream press.

10. For example, although NZOC and the NZAAA had made some changes to amateur sport policies (e.g. there were exemptions for physical education teachers, coaches and blue-collar business sport teams).

11. Notwithstanding Grant's assessment, it need to be recognized that at the time the country's financial sector was comparably weaker than other areas of the country's economy. However, eventually, as a consequence of countries shifting investments to the Britain – one of the only available free markets – New Zealand's primary export industry revenues (namely in dairy and agriculture) did plummet (Belich 2001; Grant 1997, 138; Molloy 2007; Olssen 1995).

12. NZOC, *NZOC Minute Book 1912–1932*.

13. New Zealand Olympic Committee, *Communication to the International Olympic Committee*, Lausanne, 13 July 1931.

14. New Zealand Olympic Commitee, *Personal communication Baillet-Latour*, Wellington: NZOC, 19 February 1934.

15. NZOC, *NZOC Minute Book 1912–1932*.

16. NZOC, *NZOC Minute Book 1912–1932*.

17. To summarize, Marryatt was initially replaced by local educationalist Joseph Firth (tenure 1923–1927), then respected military hero Bernard Freyberg (tenure 1928–1930), and later, lawyer and expatriate, Cecil Wray (tenure 1931–1934). Despite possibly the best intentions of assisting NZOC with some of the tyrannies of distance it faced, and maintaining the visible profile of New Zealand in transnational sporting discussions, all three of these appointments were ineffectual.

18. Harry Amos, *Personal Correspondence to Freyberg*, 22 March 1930, Lausanne, IOC files.

19. Harry Amos, *Personal Correspondence to Freyberg*, 6 April 1930, Lausanne, IOC files. NZOC also exchanged similar dialogue with fellow IOC members Joseph Firth and Cecil Wray. In addition, and perhaps recognizing the benefits of soliciting expatriates, Amos and his colleagues had initially viewed Wray as 'a very suitable man' who 'would do full justice to the position' (NZOC, *NZOC Minute Book 1912–1932*, 30 August 1930, 164). Yet, Wray lasted just three years, during which time his influence on the IOC and NZOC was negligible.

20. Previously the role had been taken up by associated in Australian and/or Britain, or coaches and chaperones. NZOC, *NZOC Minute Book 1912–1932*. As was customary at the time, Amos' wife's role was to serve as chaperone to the team's female member.

21. NZOC, *NZOC Minute Book 1912–1932*, 26 June 1929, 154.

22. The organization's balance at the time was approximately £1245. As such, Amos also worked hard to ensure NZOC's meagre economic resources remained financial stable. Such stability was vital not only the continued participation of New Zealand athletes abroad, but necessary to demonstrate the organization's professional capabilities. NZOC, *NZOC Minute Book 1912–1932*, 26 June, 1929, 154.

23. NZOC, *NZOC Minute Book 1912–1932*; NZOC, *Official Minute Book, 1933–1964* (hereafter *NZOC Minute Book 1933–1964*); NZOC Olympic Studies Centre, Wellington, New Zealand.

24. As a reflection of his tireless work for the organization in 1952 the IOC awarded Amos a prestigious Olympic diploma in recognition for both his administrative nous and enduring support for amateurism. http://library.la84.org/OlympicInformationCenter/OlympicReview/1952/BDCE34/BDCE34d.pdf, accessed September 19, 2014.

25. At the time, Porritt was only the second New Zealand Rhodes recipient.

26. Porritt went on to repeat this role at the 1928 and 1936 Olympic Games and 1934 British Empire Games.

27. Harry Amos, *Personal Correspondence to IOC President Comte Henri de Baillet-Latour*, 19 February 1934, Lausanne, IOC files.

28. NZOC, *NZOC Minute Book 1912–1932.*
29. NZOC, *NZOC Minute Book 1933–1964.*
30. See Daley (2012) for an insightful discussion of the complicated cultural nuances and historical significance of one of these icons and a broader critique of the construction of the national imagination.
31. NZOC, *NZOC Minute Book 1933–1964*, 3 October 1936, 168.
32. NZOC, *NZOC Minute Book 1912–1932.*
33. For some of the most interesting examples, see Ballantyne (2012), Belich (2009), Burton (2003), Gibbons (2003), Lambert and Lester (2006) and Thompson and Fedorowich (2013). In important contradistinction, however, are resistant stances to the paradigm shift that have been variously offered by respected New Zealand scholars such as Fairburn (1989) and the late Munz (1971, 1984). To this can be added Fergusson's (2008) broader sweeping and controversial neocolonial work *Empire: How Britain Made the Modern World* that holds fast to the central authority of Imperial forces within transnational and global historiography.
34. However, Beilharz and Cox provide useful assessments of assumptions about settler capitalism in Antipodean colonies, and the need to be critical of some of the characteristics of the dialectical relationship between New Zealand and its colonizer.
35. Palenski (2012) offers further examination of the ways in which aspects of this identity were forged in other sporting, and non-sport, contexts. For extended discussion, see the range of perspectives and debates presented in Byrnes' (2009) edited book *The New Oxford History of New Zealand*. Byrnes' introduction and several other chapters therein attend to the argument that the country's historiographical trends need to better consider post-national approaches. The point has been articulated further within the sport context by Maclean (2010) in his piece on sport history/historiography in New Zealand. In keeping with the desire to rethink the country's position within Imperial scholarship, Maclean asserts that in a quest for meaning and legitimacy New Zealand sport and its histories have been concomitantly inwardly and outwardly looking.
36. Consider, for example, traditional allegiance/alliances, and positioning and politicizing the country's Commonwealth and sporting identities externally and internally.
37. With the onset of the Empire Games in 1930, and the consequential administrative restructuring of NZOC, Amos' work in redefining the organizations working relationships with its colonial forebears and partners would become even more valuable.

References

Ballantyne, Tony. 2012. *Webs of Empire: Locating New Zealand's Colonial Past*. Vancouver: University of British Columbia Press.
Beilharz, Peter, and Lloyd Cox. 2007. "Settler Capitalism Revisited." *Thesis Eleven* 88: 112–124.
Belich, James. 2001. *Paradise Reforged: A History of the New Zealanders from the 1880s to the Year 2000*. Auckland: Allen Lane.
Belich, James. 2007. *Making Peoples: A History of the New Zealanders from Polynesian Settlement to the End of the Nineteenth Century*. Auckland: The Penguin Group.
Belich, James. 2009. *Replenishing the Earth: The Settler Revolution and the Rise of the Anglo-World, 1783–1939*. Oxford: Oxford University Press.
Burton, Antoinette, ed. 2003. *After the Imperial Turn: Thinking with and through the Nation*. Durham, NC: Duke University Press.
Byrnes, Giselle, ed. 2009. *The New Oxford History of New Zealand*. South Melbourne: Oxford University Press.
Colquhoun, David. 2008. *As If Running on Air: The Journals of Jack Lovelock*. Nelson: Craig Potton.
Coombes, Annie E. 2006. *Rethinking Settler Colonialism: History and Memory in Australia, Canada, Aotearoa New Zealand and South Africa*. Manchester: Manchester University Press.
Daley, Caroline. 2012. "Taking Off the Black Singlet." *The New Zealand Journal of History* 46 (2): 113–128.
Fairburn, Miles. 1989. *The Ideal Society and Its Enemies: The Foundations of Modern New Zealand Society, 1950–1900*. Auckland: Auckland University Press.
Fergusson, Niall. 2008. *Empire: How Britain Made the Modern World*. London: Penguin Books.
Gibbons, Peter. 2003. "The Far Side of the Search for Identity." *The New Zealand Journal of History* 37 (1): 38–49.

Grant, David. 1997. *Bulls, Bears, and Elephants: A History of the New Zealand Stock Exchange.* Wellington: Victoria University Press.

Henniker, Gary, and Ian Jobling. 1989. "Richard Coombes and the Olympic Movement in Australia: Imperialism and Nationalism in Action." *Sporting Traditions* 6 (2): 2–15.

Ingram, W. F. 1937. "Panorama of the Playground: Physical Fitness and the Daily Dozen." *New Zealand Railways Magazine* 11 (10): 54–55.

Jobling, Ian. 2000. "In Pursuit of Status, Respectability and Idealism: Pioneers of the Olympic Movement in Australasia." *International Journal for the History of Sport* 21 (4): 142–163.

Kebric, Robert B. 2014. "London 2012, *Chariots of Fire* Resurrected and Colombes Stadium Today: Hype, History and Olympic Realities." *Sport in Society* 17 (5): 656–673.

Keys, Barbara. 2006. *Globalizing Sport: National Rivalry and International Community in the 1930s.* Cambridge, MA: Harvard University Press.

King, Michael. 2003. *The Penguin History of New Zealand.* Auckland: Penguin Books.

Kohe, Geoffery Z. 2010. "The Unexceptional: New Zealand's Very Ordinary Olympic History." *Sport History Review* 14 (2): 146–163.

Kohe, Geoffery Z. 2011. *At the Heart of Sport: The New Zealand Olympic Committee and the History of the Olympic Movement in New Zealand.* Wellington: NZOC.

Kohe, Geoffery Z. 2012. "Reflexivity in the Apologetic Aeon: NZOC's Return to Moscow." *Museum & Society* 10 (2): 121–140.

Krüger, Arnd, and William J. Murray. 2003. *The Nazi Olympics: Sport, Politics and Appeasement in the 1930s.* Urbana: University of Illinois Press.

Lambert, David, and Alan Lester, eds. 2006. *Colonial Lives across the British Empire: Imperial Careering in the Long Nineteenth Century.* Cambridge: Cambridge University Press.

Letters, Michael, and Ian Jobling. 1996. "Forgotten Links: Leonard Cuff and the Olympic Movement in Australia, 1894–1905." *Olympika: International Journal of Olympic Studies* 5: 91–110.

Little, Charles, and Richard Cashman. 2001. "Ambiguous and Overlapping Identities: Australasia at the Olympic Games, 1896–1914." In *Sport, Federation, Nation,* edited by Richard Cashman, John O'Hara, and Andrew Honey, 81–96. Sydney: Walla Walla Press.

MacLean, Malcolm. 2010. "New Zealand (Aotearoa)." In *Routledge Companion to Sports History,* edited by Steve W. Pope and John Nauright, 510–525. London: Routledge.

Mangan, James A., and Colin Hickey. 2000. "Pioneer of the Proleteriat: Herbert Milnes and the Games cult in New Zealand." In *Sport in Australasian Society,* edited by James A. Mangan and John Nauright, 31–48. London: Frank Cass.

McNeish, James. 1986. *Lovelock: A Novel.* Auckland: Hodder & Stoughton.

McNeish, James. 1999. "Death of a Dream: The Fact and Fictions of Jack Lovelock." In *Sport, Society and Culture in New Zealand,* edited by Brad Patterson, 31–37. Wellington: Stout Research Centre.

Molloy, Maureen. 2007. "Citizenship, Property and Bodies: Discourses on Gender and the Inter-War Labour Government in New Zealand." *Gender & History* 4 (3): 293–330.

Munz, Peter. 1971. "The Purity of the Historical Method." *The New Zealand Journal of History* 5: 1–18.

Munz, Peter. 1984. "The Two Worlds of Anne Salmond in Postmodern Fancy-Dress." *The New Zealand Journal of History* 28: 60–75.

Olssen, Eric. 1995. "Towards a New Society." In *The Oxford History of New Zealand,* edited by Geoffrey Rice. 2nd ed., 254–284. Auckland: Oxford University Press.

Palenski, Ron. 2012. *The Making of New Zealanders.* Auckland: Auckland University Press.

Palenski, Ron, and Joseph Romanos. 2000. *Champions: New Zealand Sports Greats of the 20th Century.* Auckland: Hodder Moa Beckett.

Palenski, Ron, and Terry Maddaford. 1983. *The Games.* Auckland: Moa.

Phillips, John O. C. 1984. "Rugby, War and the Mythology of the New Zealand Male." *The New Zealand Journal of History* 18 (1): 83–103.

Phillips, John O. C. 1987. *A Man's Country: The Image of the Pakeha Male.* Auckland: Penguin Books.

Phillips, John O. C. 1990. "Of Verandahs and Fish and Chips and Footie on Saturday Afternoon: Reflections of 100 Years of New Zealand Historiography." *The New Zealand Journal of History* 24 (2): 118–134.

Pickles, Katie. 2009. "Transnational Intentions and Cultural Cringe: History beyond National Boundaries." In *Contesting Clio's Craft: New Directions and Debates in Canadian History,* edited by Christopher Dummitt and Michael Dawson, 141–161. London: Institute for the Study of the Americas.

Pickles, Katie. 2011. "The Obvious and the Awkward: Postcolonialism and the British World." *The New Zealand Journal of History* 45 (1): 85–101.

Pocock, John G. A. 1974. "British History: The Plea for a New Subject." *The New Zealand Journal of History* 8 (11): 3–21.

Richardson, Len, and Shelley Richardson. 2005. *Anthony Wilding: A Sporting Life*. Christchurch: University of Canterbury Press.

Roche, Michael. 2002. "Soldier Settlement in New Zealand after World War 1: Two Case Studies." *New Zealand Geographer* 58 (1): 23–32.

Romanos, Joseph. 2006. *New Zealand's Top 100 Sports History-Makers*. Wellington: Trio Books.

Romanos, Joseph. 2008. *Our Olympic Century*. Wellington: Trio Books.

Ryan, Greg. 2004. *The Making of New Zealand Cricket, 1832–1914*. London: Frank Cass.

Ryan, Greg. 2005. *Tackling Rugby Myths: Rugby and New Zealand Society 1854–2004*. Dunedin: University of Otago Press.

Ryan, Greg. 2007. "Sport in 19th-Century Aotearoa/New Zealand: Opportunities and Constraints." In *Sport in Aotearoa/New Zealand Society*, edited by Chris Collins and Steve Jackson, 96–111. Auckland: Thomson.

Sinclair, Keith. 1984. *A History of New Zealand*. Auckland: Penguin Books.

Sinclair, Keith. 1986. *A Destiny Apart: New Zealand's Search for National Identity*. Wellington: Allen & Unwin.

Sinclair, Keith, and Raewyn Dalziel. 2000. *A History of New Zealand*. Revised ed. Auckland: Penguin Books.

Thompson, Andrew S., and Kent Fedorowich, eds. 2013. *Empire, Identity and Migration in the British World*. Manchester: Manchester University Press.

Woodfield, Graeme. 2007. *Lovelock: Athlete and Doctor*. Wellington: Trio Books.

Woodfield, Graeme, and Joseph Romanos. 2008. *No Ordinary Man: The Remarkable Life of Sir Arthur Porritt*. Wellington: Trio Books.

'The emblem of one united body ... one great sporting Maple Leaf': The Olympic Games and Canada's quest for self-identity

Robert K. Barney and Michael H. Heine

School of Kinesiology, Western University, London, Canada

> For Canadians, the enduring late nineteenth- and early twentieth-century debate between adherents of sustained British imperialism and those champions of Canadian sovereignty closed in December 1964 by dint of a Canadian Parliamentary act establishing a new national symbol, one that henceforth removed the British ensign from national flag and federal governmental identifications and replaced it with a simple red maple leaf embossed on a white background between two panels of red. This is the primary identification symbol, the logo, indeed the brand, by which Canada is now recognized throughout the world. The birth of the red maple leaf logo's legitimization in both national and international context points to a role played by the Canadian Olympic Committee, the embryo saga of which was superimposed on the initiatives of the nation's first Olympic team, the aggregation of male athletes that competed in the London Games of 1908. This work argues that the introduction of the red maple leaf as a national symbol of Canada, with respect to the logo's initial international debut at the Games of the Fourth Olympiad celebrated in London in 1908, provided the first in a series of succeeding international Olympic occurrences that lent sustenance to a greater Canadian movement towards neoliberal promoted national self-identity and a commensurate beginning of the erosion of what most Canadians would refer to as 'Britishness'.

Introduction

In February 2010, Vancouver celebrated its hosting of Canada's second Olympic Winter Games. It proved to be a sustained celebration of Canadian culture and identity, one underscored by striking national and international television ratings. Front and centre in the festive atmosphere of the Vancouver celebrations were Canada's national symbol, the red maple leaf. It was everywhere in the city's public space: on the omnipresent flags flying throughout the city, imprinted on the hundreds of licensed articles on sale in stores and kiosks, painted on the faces of thousands of Canadian Olympic visitors and embellished on the uniform paraphernalia of every Canadian Olympic athlete. That the ubiquitous nature of the red maple leaf as the symbolic expression of Canadian national identity owed a formative Olympic precedent that reached back over a century was most certainly unknown to Vancouver's Olympic revellers. Perhaps that fact alone provides an incentive for a mission of discovery, one pursued on the following pages. Thus, it is the intent of this essay to pursue the argument that the introduction of the red maple leaf as a national symbol of Canada, with respect to the logo's initial international debut, the Games of the Fourth Olympiad celebrated in London, England, in 1908, provided the first in a series of succeeding international Olympic occurrences that lent sustenance to a greater Canadian movement towards national self-identity and commensurate erosion of sympathy for and influence of British 'Imperial' dispositions.

There is little argument over the fact that Canada, to a great extent, had been both influenced and shaped by its enduring membership in the British Empire and its exceedingly close relationship with the affairs of Great Britain. This was quite natural considering the English military conquest of that which was originally French prior to the mid-eighteenth century, and the subsequent imposition of British military garrisons, the arrival of Loyalists from the consequences of the American Revolution, followed by the forces of English immigration and the establishment of entrepreneurial initiatives, including, not in the least, the great mercantile firms known as the MacIntosh and Hudson's Bay Trading Companies. Great urban centres arose, permeated with social and economic atmospheres linked to British interests and heritage. With all this came identification with British symbols: the world-renowned ensign (Union Jack), various editions of coats of arms and the omnipresent Royal golden lion. By 1907, Canada, along with its British Empire fellow brethren, Australia, New Zealand, South Africa and Newfoundland, could be legitimately described as 'Dominions'. Indeed, there was great enthusiasm across Canada for 'imperial union', in which the 'mother dominion' (England) would provide 'security against the proclaimed Manifest Destiny of the United States to embrace all of North America' (Thompson 2013, 8–9). Writing in 1935, the distinguished early twentieth-century Canadian journalist Arthur Beverley Baxter reminisced: 'The Imperial connection was neither a doctrine nor a sentiment. It was part of the very texture of our being ... It was the expression of a people ... Like all things great it had the quality of inevitability' (1935, 49).

But, as can be seen indelibly in countless histories of settlement and cultural development in new lands, irrespective of the dominance of the original group and its intention to steadfastly retain 'transplanted' institutions, succeeding generations of 'native born', in increasing intensity, tended to question, then challenge, and finally strive for change befitting the circumstances of their rapidly evolving contemporary sociocultural environment. Similarly, such a phenomenon occurred in Canada, from the middle of the nineteenth century till slightly more than a century later, at which time the British Imperialistic notions in Canada had, in large measure, been laid to rest (Thompson 2013, 357–358). Embedded in the middle of this century-long saga was the question of a national symbol and, indeed, a national flag.

Canadian identity and the maple leaf symbol

The emergence of the specifically 'Canadian' identity that the maple leaf emblem came to express was itself partially contingent on the concurrent containment of an identity position based in the cultural and political influences of Imperial Britain, then visible in the space of sports through the dominance of the ubiquitous Union Jack, or British ensign. It is thus necessary briefly to explore the increasing incidence with which the maple leaf emblem came to be used as an expression of a Canadian identity, sometimes explicitly constructed in contradistinction to identity positions referencing the ties with the British Empire.

The initial use of the maple leaf emblem as a symbol of Canadian national identity becomes noticeable during the first half of the nineteenth century. A well-known early reference is attributed to Jacques Viger, the first mayor of Montreal, who in 1834 referred to the maple leaf as 'king of the forest, the symbol of the Canadian people' (Montreal, *Le Canadien*, undated). In addition, in 1858, the badge for the newly organized Prince of Wales' Royal Canadian Regiment Foot 100th included a maple leaf. Only two years later, the strategic use of the symbol by political groups in Canada emerged during the 1860 state visit by the Prince of Wales. A meeting was held in Toronto's St. Lawrence Hall on the evening of 21 August, shortly before the Prince was scheduled to visit the Queen City on his tour of the Dominion, a meeting at which representatives of the 'Committee on Programme for Reception of the Royal Highness' debated a motion put before them by a large and enthusiastic group of native-born Canadians intent on joining the contingents of political and ethnic representatives organized to welcome the Prince. To express their distinct and inherently Canadian identity, the group, it was suggested, should wear 'the Maple Leaf to show that they were Native Canadians – to be known to the world as such …' (*The Daily Globe – Canada West*, August 22, 1860). The motion was approved unanimously and when the time came, the 'native Canadians' marched forward with maple leaf patches sewn to the breasts of their jackets. By displaying 'the emblem of the land of their birth', native-born Canadians presented a new symbol of identity, one rivalling and eventually replacing the thistle of Scotland, the rose of England and the shamrock of Ireland, symbols of British influence in Canadian cultural affairs, of which sport in general and the Olympics in particular became distinct elements.

Between 1876 and 1901, the maple leaf figured in the mint design of the Canadian penny. By the end of the nineteenth century, the heraldic coats of arms appearing on the flags of both Quebec (Lower Canada) and Ontario (Upper Canada) featured the maple leaf. Likewise, by the time of the second Boer War, commencing in 1899, Canadian troops appeared in South Africa clad in military uniforms featuring a 'collar brass' design that included a maple leaf. This collar design was replicated for Canadian military uniforms in the Great War (1914–1918). Beyond such early examples of the maple leaf in Canadian context, there is little doubt that the celebrated song, *The Maple Leaf Forever*, composed by Alexander Muir in 1867 to celebrate the Confederation of Canada, did much to inspire the maple leaf as a Canadian symbol of national identity. A childhood emigrant from Scotland to Canada in the 1830s, Muir grew up in Toronto, attending Queen's College in Kingston, from which he graduated in 1851. His career was devoted to education, first as a public school teacher and later as a principal, but it was his hobby as an amateur poet and songwriter that ultimately and indelibly recorded his name in enduring national context. His song, *The Maple Leaf Forever*, submitted to a panel of judges presiding over a contest to identify a musical work best fitting the national confederation celebration, was heavily influenced by 'flower coats-of-arms standards' representative of Great Britain (the rose of England, thistle of Scotland, shamrock of Ireland and the lily [*fleur d' lis*] of New France). But above such 'ethnic allusions' loomed Muir's maple leaf, 'a modern symbol representing a cohesive new land, full of hope and promise, beauty and awe', as Muir rhapsodized in the song's chorus: 'The Maple Leaf, our emblem dear, The Maple Leaf Forever! God save our Queen and Heaven Bless, the Maple Leaf Forever'. Muir's song did not win the competition; he was accorded second place. But, *The Maple Leaf Forever* rapidly captured national attention and was often sung as an unofficial 'de-facto' national anthem.

Though the maple leaf received notable attention as an iconographic Canadian symbol long before it was presented in red on the national flag in 1965, its earliest depictions in Canadian heraldry were in the colour green. The first example of the maple leaf replicated on a flag of any kind dates to the Patriot Battle Flag of the early 1850s (preserved at the Musée Château Ramezay in Montréal). The maple leaf's first appearance on a coat of arms is that of Louis-Hippolyte Lafontaine, granted to him by Garter King of Arms in 1854 (Beddoe 1981, 51). There are other examples of the maple leaf appearing in green and other colours (but not in red) in nineteenth-century iconography, such as the 1868 Royal Warrant granting coats of arms to the four original Canadian provinces, where, in the cases of Ontario and Quebec, the maple leaf was depicted in gold and green, respectively. Nineteenth-century forms of what served as the national flag ranged from British-oriented designs to those balanced against a growing nation of newly established provinces. The first Canadian flag was known as the Flag of the Governor-General, or Royal Union Flag. In 1868, this took the form of its upper left quarter presenting the well-known and thoroughly familiar British ensign (Union Jack). Centred in the middle of the right half of the flag were arranged the quartered coats of arms of the four Canadian provinces existing at the time – Nova Scotia, New Brunswick, Quebec and Ontario.

The maple leaf as symbolic identifier in sporting contexts

Beyond the maple leaf's appearance on coins, military brass, stamps, coats of arms, and in poems and song, it was also presented as a theme adopted by various sporting aggregations in both nineteenth- and early twentieth-century contexts. The earliest known, as well as the most prominently recognized presentation of the maple leaf logo in sporting context, concerned the baseball uniform shirts of the Guelph Maple Leafs, distinguished in Canadian sport history as the Dominion's first championship team (1870), and, indeed, immediately following that achievement, the organization that ushered in the earliest era of professional baseball in Canada (Lang 2002). Closely succeeding the Guelph Maple Leafs' popularization of the symbol as a sporting logo, a lacrosse team's tour of Britain and Ireland in 1883 provides an early example of the symbol's use in international sporting competitions. Composed of players from the Montreal and Toronto Lacrosse Clubs, the team's white uniform jerseys were adorned with a maple leaf – of unknown colour, possibly blue – the interior of which bore a white letter 'C' (Morrow and Wamsley 2010, 88–89).

As amateur sport grew and flourished in Canada, especially in two distinct areas of organization, private and community sporting clubs and intercollegiate athletics, the maple leaf emerged as an often used element of an organization's sporting logo. By 1890, the Toronto Football Club sported white maple leafs on the left breast of their otherwise black team jerseys (*Dominion Illustrated*, December 27, 1890) and, early in the first decade of the twentieth century, the jerseys of the Irish Canadian Athletics Club of Toronto featured a large green maple leaf embossed with a golden harp. But, foremost in the evolution of the red maple leaf as part of a sporting logo is the case of the University of Toronto. In 1893, the first formal University of Toronto Athletic Directorate was formed. Its primary mandate was to regulate and control intercollegiate athletics at the venerable institution. Ten years later, in 1903, the Athletic Directorate established the logo design that would adorn its sporting attire, indeed identify the university's sporting enterprises in the century ahead – the 'University Arms' embossed on a red maple leaf surmounted on a large blue 'T' (Reed 1945, 29).

A tussle with Great Britain's Union Jack

The formation of the Canadian sports system of the nineteenth century was shaped by the dominant influences of British sports and its amateur ideology. The incipient nature of this extension from 'Mother England' increasingly came to play a role in the search for a distinct Canadian sporting identity that went hand in hand with an increasing emphasis on Canadian identity characterized and fuelled by the experiences of Canadian participation in the second Boer War (1899–1901). The military historian Jonathan Vance argues that:

the Boer War had an enormous, if mixed, impact on Canada's young military. On the one hand it strengthened tendencies towards autonomy. In the popular imagination, Canada was no longer a child in the Empire but had proven its maturity in battle. In fact, the more politicians and journalists talked about the war the more they elevated Canada's achievements, often at the expense of Britain. (2012, 27)

Likewise in the space of sports, whereby the early 1900s, Great Britain had lost its sporting dominance in at least two of its major amateur athletic endeavours – rugby (to New Zealand and South Africa) and track and field athletics (to the USA), international competitions came to take on greater importance in the political contest between nations across the world (Llewellyn 2012, 15–16). It was a theme that persisted for the entire twentieth century. Thus, in this era of expanding Canadian nationalism, the national symbol issue attracted renewed attention. The Union Jack continued to dominate much of Canada's iconography, most certainly surpassing the maple leaf itself in cultural visibility. What passed for the national flag followed this pattern that being a standard placing the Union Jack in the upper left quadrant, while a collage of the coats of arms of the then nine existing Canadian provinces was arranged in the centre of the remaining space. Nevertheless, it was in the realm of sports, specifically at the 1908 Olympic Games, that a genuinely Canadian single symbolic expression of national identity was presented to an international audience. Canada's first Olympic team, supported in large measure by federal, provincial and municipal government funds,[1] selected by regional and final national trials, organized and managed by a National Olympic Committee and promoted by the country's press as 'Canada's Olympians', came to be distinguished by the large red maple leaf emblem that adorned their athletic gear and their dress uniforms.

Cometh the maple leaf in red

One year following Sir Albert Henry George Grey's arrival in Canada in 1904 as the new Governor-General, Colonel John Hanbury-Williams, a Welsh-born, career British officer, arrived in the Dominion to take up duties as Lord Grey's Secretary of Military Affairs. A seasoned veteran of Great Britain's military affairs in Egypt, India and South Africa between 1878 and 1900, Hanbury-Williams served in the War Office in London from 1900 to late 1904 as private secretary to the Secretary of State for War, Sir John Broderick. In November 1904, Hanbury-Williams was appointed Lord Grey's Military Secretary. He arrived in Ottawa in early 1905 (Tenison 1995, 365–366). Known for his aristocratic bearing and diplomatic acumen, Hanbury-Williams related well to Governor-General Grey, who himself exhibited similar personal qualities (Obit, *Times of London*, October 21, 1946).

Contemporary to Hanbury-Williams' arrival in Canada, the British Olympic Association (BOA) was formed in England (Mallon and Buchanan 2000, 2–4). The accomplished and indefatigable William Henry Grenfell, who, within two years, was knighted by King Edward VII, headed the nascent BOA. Grenfell was henceforth known as Lord Desborough, Baron of Taplow. It was to the BOA that the International Olympic Committee (IOC) extended an invitation to organize the Games of the fourth Olympiad in 1908. The first order of business for the BOA was to deal with the IOC's invitation, which, after conferring with various amateur sporting groups in England, it accepted on 19 November 1906.[2] A further year passed while organizational details, especially those surrounding the issues of finance and a central competition stadium, were attended to in London. It was, of course, a fundamental necessity that as many athletes as possible from 'countries of the world', and even more importantly, 'nations of the Empire' be present in

London for the competitions. Accordingly, in the late summer of 1907, a message from the BOA arrived on Governor-General Grey's Ottawa desk in his office in the East Block of Parliament House requesting his assistance in ensuring Canadian participation in the London Games, set for the summer of 1908 (*Hamilton Herald*, August 17, 1907). Time was short. Much would have to be done in scarcely a year. In communication with the BOA, Lord Grey nominated his Military Secretary, Colonel Hanbury-Williams, 'to represent the British Olympic Committee in Canada for the purpose of selecting Canadian representatives to participate in the Olympic Games of 1908'.[3] Lord Grey's recommendation was accepted by the BOA. The first public Canadian notation of Hanbury-Williams' appointment appeared in early November 1907 (*Montreal Daily Star*, November 7, 1907). And so it came to be that John Hanbury-Williams, never an athlete himself, inherited the task of organizing Canada's first Olympic team.

Where to begin? There was no Canadian Olympic Committee, no models for team selection, no funds for supporting a team to London and, in effect, little precedent to fall back on. Complicating the dilemma was the fact that Canada's two most significant amateur sport-governing organizations were at war with each other over what the definition and practice of the word 'amateur' really meant. As detailed by Lansley (1971), Reid (1990) and Kidd (1996, 32–37), the issue between the two bodies, the Canadian Amateur Athletic Union (CAAU) and the Canadian Amateur Athletic Federation (CAAF), placed a threatening cloud over Canadian unity of purpose when it came to the qualification of athletes for a united international Olympic effort. The CAAU, Toronto-based, favoured a strict interpretation of the concept 'amateurism', the essence of which ruled that an amateur athlete who participated in a sporting contest in which professional athletes were involved, automatically became a professional himself, and, therefore, ineligible for amateur competition (i.e. 'tainted by association'). The CAAF, on the other hand, practised a more liberal application, one in which amateur athletes could participate in events featuring professionals and still retain their amateur status. For help in resolution, Hanbury-Williams needed informed counsel. He soon identified Philip Dansken Ross (P. D. Ross), owner–publisher of *The Ottawa Evening Journal*, as just such an 'informed' individual. Ross was both knowledgeable and influential in business, social and sporting environments of early twentieth-century Ottawa. His newspaper was a vigorous reporter of sporting events in the city of Ottawa and the province of Ontario, indeed sporting news from across Canada. Ross' *Evening Journal* easily outranked its nearest local competitor, the *Ottawa Citizen*, in the reporting of sports news. By 1907, at 49 years of age, the time of Hanbury-Williams's initial contact with him, Ross was one of the two original trustees of the Stanley Cup, the crowning symbol of Canadian ice hockey.[4] Ross was also well versed in sporting affairs associated with Toronto (Reed 1945, 89). Among his associates in Toronto were several of those who organized and participated in the athletic affairs of the University of Toronto, an institution that Ross ranked parallel in 'athletic excellence' with his own Alma Mater, Montreal's McGill University.

With the assistance of Ross, Hanbury-Williams was ready to address two immediately pressing concerns: (1) creating harmony between the estranged Amateur Athletic Federation of Canada (AAFC) and CAAU amateur sport factions and (2) enlarging his Olympic Committee. On the latter, Hanbury-Williams immediately named Ross as his first appointee. Then, he conferred with AAFC officials in Montreal (*Montreal Daily Star*, November 13, 1907). Subsequently, he delegated Ross to do the same with CAAU leaders in Toronto. Invitations were issued requesting representatives of each body to attend a joint meeting at Parliament House in Ottawa (*Ottawa Evening Journal*, November 30, 1907). At noon on Saturday, 30 November 1907, a group of 16 representatives, 8 each from the CAAU and the AAFC, respectively, were invited to a 'pleasant luncheon' hosted by Hanbury-Williams and Ross at the Rideau Club. F.L.C. Pereira from the Governor-General's office was also present in his role as secretary of the proceedings. That the luncheon was a critical prelude towards promotion of a spirit of good will and the establishment of a favourable climate for solving a difficult problem is underscored by the *Evening Journal's* account of the affair:

> ... the delegates from the two fighting governing bodies mingled together, apparently the best of friends, and it is believed that those little differences that existed between the two bodies have been swept away by this friendly intercourse and that in the future a broader view will be taken by both sides on any question that may arise. The luncheon proved a pleasant affair, and the delegates walked over to the East Block for the conference in a body. (*Ottawa Evening Journal*, December 2, 1907)

Shortly after 2:00, following the luncheon, the delegates convened in Lord Grey's impressive office suite in the Parliament Building precinct. There followed one of the most important meetings in the history of Canadian sport. Hanbury-Williams' opening statement, reported by the *Ottawa Evening Journal*, captured the tone for the meeting:

> Gentlemen – We are met here today to have, I hope, an amiable discussion. Let us avoid, if possible, the wrangles and tangles of the past and look upon this matter from a broad point of view. This is a big country and we have to have big minds and big views to settle difficult points. We want, if we can, to leave the past – to leave what affects individual cases and look to the future. Pray do not believe that I am a comfortable and easy optimist about the future. We are now only on the fringe of an undertaking which if successful may be of great value to the boyhood and manhood of Canada. The task we have is a very difficult one – I recognize that. Plenty of people tell me so, but it is no use being afraid of it or being discouraged. I recognize that we may be up against many more difficulties, even if we are successful today. I am aware too that there are other bodies whose representatives will have to be called to our councils. We must not let the public think that we here are the only people who propose to run this business. There are other societies to be considered, but we have to do one bit of work at a time, and you gentlemen assembled here now are the representatives of two great conflicting elements in the world of sport in Canada. Mr. Ross and I both feel that if we can come to some understanding today, even if it be the temporary hoisting of a flag of truce, we shall have done something and it is time that something was done. Of course we shall be better pleased if the flag is run up to the top and left there – only to be replaced by one which bears the *emblem of one united body – one*, if I may use an eccentric expression, *great sporting Maple Leaf.* [Italics ours] (*Ottawa Evening Journal*, December 2, 1907)

Hanbury-Williams' eloquent expressions, 'emblem of one united body' and 'great sporting Maple Leaf', were entirely his own literary creations for what resulted in the 1908 Canadian Olympic team standard. And, his expressions stand as the first in a series of ensuing enunciations in the months following that tied the maple leaf to Canadian Olympic matters as a symbol of national identity.

Forging a symbol

In the months following Hanbury-Williams' pronouncement, there is little doubt that it was the maple leaf, and the maple leaf alone, that was envisioned by Canadian Olympic officials as the national symbol that would embellish their international sporting endeavours 'across the pond'. The Canadian press, too, embraced the idea of the maple leaf as the nation's logo relative to Olympic identification.

Two days after the historic Ottawa conference and Hanbury-Williams' first 'Maple Leaf' reference, a *Toronto Star* columnist further enhanced the concept of the maple leaf as a symbol of national identification in an international sporting context. Speculating on which Toronto-area athletes might qualify for the Games in England the following summer, he noted:

> ... We have Jack Tait, the West End Y.M.C.A.'s great little athlete – he is only 18 years old – and George Adams of Hamilton. Both are 'really' Canucks and both on form should be carrying the *Maple Leaf* shoulder to shoulder with the Irish Canadian pair of Toms. [Longboat and Coley] (*Toronto Star*, December 4, 1907)

In early February 1908, an even more sustained reference to the symbolic statement appeared in the *Star*. Extolling the virtues of the Olympic Games as a modern institution of noble worth, the *Star* reporter observed:

> One fine morning in the summer that is coming, a ship will steam out of the harbor of Montreal bearing on board a company of Canadians, our great men in athletics, setting out for the capital of the world *to bear the Maple Leaf* in a magnificent festival of athletics – the Olympic Games. Into this stadium in Old London will be gathered from the four corners of the earth the men of endurance, agility, strength, and speed. In the autumn they will return to their homelands and the victors will receive welcome, such as great men in the state in letters, in art, or industry, never get. [Italics ours] (*Toronto Star*, February 5, 1908)

Three months later, Hanbury-Williams once again revisited the *Maple Leaf* theme. Ruminating to the *Montreal Daily Star* on Canada's prospects for the upcoming Games, he uttered a further reference on the symbolism of the maple leaf emblem as representing the entire team:

> The governing bodies in both East and West have taken a firm grasp of the situation and are working with might and main. We expect the bearers of the *Maple Leaf* of Canada will make a very good showing when the events in the Stadium take place. (*Montreal Daily Star*, May 7, 1908)

In early June 1908, on the eve of the trials for selection to Canada's Olympic track and field team, Governor-General Earl Grey visited Toronto to take in some of the action he himself had initiated less than a year before with his appointment of Hanbury-Williams as head of the Canadian Olympic enterprise. Invited to an early morning rowing practice of the Olympic-bound Argonaut Club's rowing eight, Grey boarded a coaching launch to view the crew's performance. 'How did you like it', Grey was asked by a *Globe* reporter upon his return to shore. 'Very much, very much indeed', he responded, 'I hope they will be able to keep the maple leaf in front of the world' (*The Globe*, June 4, 1908).

In the context of this strengthening awareness of a specifically 'Canadian' national identity, the question of Olympic success from an imperial perspective received increased attention. Reporting on the results of the first marathon trials for Great Britain's Olympic team, well-known English champion long-distance runner A.B. George argued for a pan-Britannic Olympic team, one that would combine athletes from all nations comprising the Empire. In a special dispatch to the *Ottawa Evening Journal*, published in early April 1908, George argued against the demerits of a fractured imperial Olympic enterprise:

> Many sportsmen here consider that a big mistake has been made in dividing the forces of the British Empire for the Olympic Games. For the purpose of these, Canada, Australasia and South Africa are to be considered as separate nations and can each send teams, while Great Britain and Ireland can send another. It stands to reason that a united British Empire team would be stronger than a divided one, while from a sentimental and patriotic point of view it seems a pity. Canadians, Australians, South Africans and New Zealanders shame many residents of the British Isles when it comes to patriotism, and after the splendid way they rallied around the empire's flag on the South African battlefields, a division on the field of sport appears out of place. (*Ottawa Evening Journal*, April 8, 1908)

In the Canadian press, silence greeted George's 'imperialism cohesion' plea. As far as a survey of Canadian urban newspaper response is indicative (Toronto, Ottawa, Montreal), no supporting reaction greeted George's 'imperialism cohesion' idea.

On 6 June 1908, just before the start of the segment of the Olympic trials scheduled for Montreal, the *Daily Star* published a unique artistic/photographic display – a large panel featuring in silhouette likeness 16 athletes favoured to qualify for the Olympic team, each countenance superimposed on the outline of a maple leaf (*Montreal Daily Star*, June 6, 1908). Ironic, indeed, that athletes displayed in the press mounted on maple leafs would soon represent Canada in an international sporting competition themselves mounting the maple leaf emblem on their competition and dress uniforms. In the end, athletes from Nova Scotia, Quebec, Ontario, Manitoba, Alberta and British Columbia competed in sectional trials held across Canada (Halifax, Montreal, Toronto, Winnipeg, Calgary and Vancouver) for the right to compete in the final national trials held in Montreal and Toronto in early June 1908. In the final analysis, 37 athletes qualified for what came to be referred to as the 'Stadium Team'.

A final certification of Canada's accepted maple leaf logo presentation at the Olympic Games came from the very seat of authority on Canadian Olympic matters, Government House in Ottawa. Two letters sent to Pereira, 'Honorable Secretary' to the Canadian Olympic Committee, received in late June (1908) from L. C. Hoskins of the Argonaut Rowing Club in Toronto, merited a response. Hoskins' first letter, written on 27 June, enclosed a check for $398.54 as a contribution to the 'Olympic Fund' resulting from profits gained from an 'Assault-at-Arms' exhibition organized by the Club on 23 April. Hoskins' second letter, written on 30 June, queried Pereira on exactly what mark of identification (which Hoskins referred to as 'colours') should be worn by Argonaut rowers, who, in effect, had earned the right in earlier-held rowing trials to represent Canada at the Games in London. Responding on 2 July, Pereira offered thanks and 'high appreciation of the kindness of your Club in placing this large sum at the disposal of the Committee, and to congratulate you upon the splendid result obtained from the holding of the Assault'. In responding to Hoskins' query on 'colours', Pereira informed him that 'Mr. P. D. Ross suggests that it would be well, if possible, to add a maple leaf to the jerseys of the oarsmen'.[5] Hoskins passed along this advice to his superiors and Argonaut 'oarsmen' appeared on the Thames in London clad in blue and white horizontal-striped jerseys with a maple leaf sewed on the chest of each, unfortunately, in white rather than red. Secretary Pereira had neglected to specify the maple leaf's desired colour.

There is no doubt that press reception and acceptance of the 1908 Canadian Olympic team's embrace of the red maple leaf as a national identifier in international perspective came most strongly from Toronto newspapers. After all, Toronto and greater Ontario were, even then, the centres of developing Canadian neoliberal nationalism, disposed towards a greater sense of Canadian awareness represented by indigenous symbols (Champion 2010, 224). Was it not they, the 'Prussians of Confederation', who had played the major roles in the nation's historic Confederation quest in 1867? Montreal and greater Quebec, at best, were generally ambivalent on the subject. So, too, were Canada West and the Maritimes.

At the Games: the triumph of the maple leaf

Arriving in London, Canada's first Olympic team began to prepare for the athletic challenges awaiting it. As a tune-up, the track and field team competed in the British Amateur Athletics (track and field) Championships. Speculating on the soon-to-be contested Olympic Games sprint finals, and impressed by Canadian sprinter Bobby Kerr's performance in both the 100 and 200 metres at the British Championships held earlier, on 4 July, the *Daily Telegraph* commented:

> R. Kerr, the Canadian sprinter and five time champion of the Dominion... showed a clean pair of heels to all our short distance men. He won the 100 and the 200 yards races in surpassing style ... In all his four races, the two preliminaries and the two final heats, Kerr carried his white jersey emblazoned with the design of a maple leaf in red readily to the front. He is a sprint runner such as amateur athletics has seldom known. (As cited by *Montreal Daily Star*, July 18, 1908)

A little over a week later, the maple leaf emblem made a formidable international debut during the opening ceremonies of the Olympic Games. On the afternoon of Monday, 13 July 1908, a contingent of 32 Canadian athletes entered the Shepherd Bush Olympic Stadium and marched smartly to their assigned marshalling place on the infield of the recently constructed grand athletic stadium. Of the 18 nations represented in the proceedings that overcast summer afternoon, the Canadians made an especially strong visual impression. Their new uniforms, adorned with the red maple leaf emblazoned on the left breast of the dress sweaters, were the object of admiration by many of the 40,000 spectators present for the occasion. Grouped on the stadium infield behind their 'Canada' name standard and what, at the time, passed for the Canadian national flag, they witnessed the opening of the fourth Olympic Games by King Edward VII. A fanfare of trumpets from the Royal Guard followed the King's brief proclamation, then the national anthem 'God Save the King', during which the national flags of each Olympic team were dipped. Finally, a colourful parade by the national teams assembled wound its way around the stadium's running track, past the Royal Box, and out the exit (Figure 1).[6]

Figure 1. Colonel John Hanbury-Williams, ca. 1907.

Two weeks following the opening ceremonies, the *Brantford* (Ontario) *Exposition* published the reflections of William 'Billy' Wood, the premier long-distance runner and athletic pride of the 'Telephone City', Alexander Graham Bell's hometown. Wood described his enthusiastic impressions:

> I am sending with this letter two photos of your Brantford representative on the Canadian Olympic team, one in the regulation running costume, which all the Canadians wear, white knickers [shorts], white jerseys, with a large red maple leaf. It is a fine suit ... The reception suit [dress uniform], and also the one in which we paraded before the King is: white shoes, white trousers, white sweater jacket, with small red maple leaf on one side, with the word 'Canada' underneath, white collar and blue sailor tie, and white cap with a small red maple leaf on it, also with the word 'Canada' on it. We all attended Lord Strathcona's [Canadian High Commissioner to Great Britain] Dominion Day reception in a body, attired in this costume, and were the hit of the evening, being complimented time after time about our natty uniforms. And again everyone was proud of Canada. (*Brantford Exposition*, July 26, 1908)

Indeed, before the Games' opening ceremonies, another group photograph of the first Canadian Olympic team was taken – the largest single group of Canadian athletes who participated in the nation's first Olympic Games, 33 of the 37 individuals who competed in the track and field events, fencing, swimming and diving, gymnastics, wrestling and cycling. They were known as the 'Stadium Team' (Figure 2). John Howard Crocker, who wrote the final report of the Canadian Olympic team's appearance at the 1908 Games, similar to Wood, noted the visual impact of the Canadian team's uniforms:

> The Canadian Team, from the first day, took a prominent part and the Maple leaf was ever before the people helping to carry out those ideals hoped-for by the International Committee (IOC). In the opening day the team of thirty-five, dressed in neat cream white uniforms... marched before the King in a manner well pleasing to all.[7]

Following the conclusion of the Games, *The Times* of London pointedly remarked on the Canadian team and its colourful insignia (Figure 3):

> The Canadian Olympic Athletes furnish a good example of the combination of physical excellence with other qualifications which make athletics a higher thing than they may sometimes appear to be on the surface. The bearers of the red maple leaf have shown throughout these games a dogged pluck and a cheerfulness in the face of disappointment, which the representatives of none of the other nations have surpassed.[8]

Figure 2. Canada's 1908 Olympic Team, 'Maple Leaf Proud,' enters the Stadium.

Figure 3. The 32 member Canadian 'Marching Team' in Dress Uniforms – John Howard Crocker, Team Manager, pictured in Civilian dress suit.

Seated on Ground, left to right: William Sherring (athletics coach), Orville Elliott (gymnastics), Alan Keith (gymnastics), Percy Nobbs (fencing). Second row, left to right, squatting: Ed Cotter (marathon), seated: Bobby Kerr (sprints), Frank Lukeman (sprints), John Caffrey (marathon), John Howard Crocker (team manager), Ed Archibald (pole-vault, team captain and flag-bearer), George Lister (marathon), Jack Tait (1500 metres/marathon), kneeling: William Galbraith (steeplechase). Third row, standing, left to right: Fred McCarthy (cycling), William Anderson (cycling), Dave Beland (sprints), William Wood (marathon), J. G. MacDonald (jumps), Harry Lawson (marathon), Fred Simpson (marathon), George Barber (hurdles), Robert Zimmerman (swimming/diving), Robert Parkes (middle distance), Frank Savage (jumps/hurdles), Calvin Bricker (jumps), Harry Young (cycling), Walter Andrews (cycling). Back row, left to right: Norton Crowe (General Secretary-Canadian Olympic Committee), William Tait (athletics coach), Fred Meadows (distance runs/ marathon), William Goldsboro (marathon), George Goulding (marathon/walking), Donald Buddo (middle distance), Fred Noseworthy (marathon), Louis Sebert (sprints), John Fitzgerald (marathon), Aubert Coté (wrestling). Missing at the time of the photograph, but members of the team, were Connie Walsh (hammer-throw), Arthur Burn (marathon), Tom Longboat (marathon), and William Morton (cycling).

Following the conclusion of the Olympic competitions held in the great stadium, Canadian Olympians returned home to a joyous and celebrative welcome. Bobby Kerr, gold medallist in the 200-metre sprint and bronze medallist in the 100 metres proved to be Canada's star performer. The red maple leaf on the breast of his competitive jersey was a memorable identifier of his country in the greater international community of nations (Figure 4). Of Kerr's and Canada's athletics achievements, John Howard Crocker, the venerated Olympic team manager, told the *Toronto Star*:

Taking the field and track athletics only into consideration, and figuring first, second, and thirds, Canada ranks third in twenty-one nations ... We started out with several men we knew were not of championship caliber yet we kept the Maple Leaf well to the front. (*Toronto Star*, August 8, 1908)

Figure 4. The 1908 Canadian Olympic 'Stadium Team'.

Flag forward: the final triumph of the maple leaf

Months following the Canadian team's return home from the 1908 London Games, Governor-General Grey wrote to his appointed chief of Olympic matters, John Hanbury-Williams. One subject of discussion focused on Canada's flag of the future. Would it be a case where the Union Jack prevailed, or would the maple leaf, riding the crest of its Olympic 'coming out party', enter the stage in taking its place as the nation's national and international standard? 'My dear Hanbury', wrote Lord Grey:

> ... I am glad to see that Glazebrook [Arthur James Glazebrook, British-born, Toronto exchange broker, ardent Imperialist] has taken the flag as his own particular subject. When I was in Canada six years ago, I reported to Chamberlain [Joseph Chamberlin, British-born, father of 'the appeaser' Neville Chamberlin, former secretary of state for the colonies, also an ardent Imperialist] my views as to the necessity of putting some hook into the Union Jack, on which Canadian nationality might hang, but I did not receive any encouragement to persevere in my campaign. I did not see clearly at the time what the character of the hook should be, but I saw clearly enough and have never had a moment's doubt since, that a mark of some sort should be inserted in the Union Jack – or what my old friend Sir George Birdwood [George Christopher Molesworth Birdwood, Imperialist of the old school, involved in Far Eastern Indian Affairs] will insist upon calling the Union Flag – to enable every citizen of Greater Britain [Canadians?] to feel that he is directly represented in the flag. Ewart's [John Skirving Evart, Scottish-born, favored Canadian sovereignty following the Boer War] nine of diamonds, to represent the nine Provinces of Canada was of course a crude attempt to solve a petty problem. The five stars in the centre of the Union Jack, to represent the Self Governing States of the Empire was much better, but that cannot be adopted until Newfoundland becomes part of the Dominion. I am on the whole inclined to favor Doughty's [Arthur George Doughty, British-born, founder of the Public Archives of Canada, confirmed Canadian sovereigntist] suggestion of the small maple leaf. A device in the heart of the Union Jack has already received the approval of the King for the regimental colours of the Yeomanry and Infantry for the territorial forces. One thing, however, is clear to me and that it is desirable for the Canadians to make the first move in this direction and I shall be glad if you will pass to Glazebrook what I have said on the subject.[9]

Had not Lord Grey's fundamental challenge, 'it is desirable for the Canadians to make the first move in this direction', been effected? The international visibility of the Olympic spectacle, and its reporting in the Canadian press, served firmly to position the maple leaf emblem as a dominant signifier of Canadian national identity at home and abroad. And, as we shall learn, Canada's association with the Olympic Games provided a guiding stimulus to the man who, in effect, became the originator of the Canadian national flag with its distinctive red maple leaf design.

The issue of a Canadian national flag penetrated parliamentary proceedings in Ottawa as early as the mid-1920s. For years, what had passed for a national flag had aroused controversy in both public and private forums. Caught in this web of conflict were strong sentiments of British imperialism. In 1925, the Privy Council of Parliament struck a committee to research a design for a national flag; the committee never reached a decision. Two decades later, directly following World War II, Parliament appointed a similar committee. Design submissions were solicited from the public at large. More than 2600 were received but a recommendation never advanced beyond committee. The issue, though, continued to be raised in parliament on an almost annual basis, continually cast aside in the face of more pressing matters and political expediency. In early 1964, with Canada's 1967 centennial celebrations rapidly approaching, Liberal Party Prime Minister Lester Pearson revived the national flag issue. A Senate and House of Commons joint committee was established; design submissions were once again solicited (Stanley 1965).

An early respondent to the Joint Committee's call for submissions was George Francis Gillman Stanley, esteemed professor of history at the Royal Military College (RMC) in Kingston, Ontario. At the time, Stanley, a former Rhodes Scholar, was Dean of Arts at RMC. Writing to John Matheson, Member of Parliament and House of Commons Representative on the 'Flag Committee', Stanley submitted a recommendation for the national flag's design.[10] It was supported by a strong rationale underscored by simplicity and neutrality; the design sought to overcome connotations of ethnicity, religion and well-imbedded imperial arguments, each of which at one time or another had been implied by the various editions of Canadian flags prior to 1964. Stanley's flag design presented Canada's national colours, red and white (Stanley 1965, 31–33), and featured a bold rendition of a large red maple leaf centred in the flag's middle panel of white, itself set between two panels of red. On the morning of 15 December 1964, after 33 days of passionate and at times aroused parliamentary debate, documented by 252 speeches, Stanley's maple leaf flag design was approved by a 163 to 78 majority. Two months later, on 15 February 1965, the red and white maple leaf flag became the official flag of Canada (1965, 63–73).

There is no doubt that Stanley arrived at his flag design in full awareness and reminiscent appreciation of an episode in Canadian Olympic history. When he was 21 years of age, a student at the University of Alberta, he celebrated, along with the rest of Canada, Vancouver's Percy Williams' startling gold medal victories in both the 100 and 200 metres at the 1928 Olympics in Amsterdam. In 1994, in a lengthy reminiscence published in the *Moncton Times-Transcript*, Stanley, retired in nearby Sackville, still a celebrity at 87 years of age, was asked to comment on his inspirations in designing the national flag. He replied:

> As a boy, I was so impressed with a picture of Percy Williams winning the gold medal in the 1928 Olympics in Amsterdam. As he breasted the tape, you could see the large maple leaf on his jersey and there was no doubt that everyone knew it was Canada. (*Moncton Times-Transcript*, December 15, 1994)

Figure 5. The maple leaf before the world: Bobby Kerr wins the 200 meter gold medal.

In his now famous letter to Matheson setting forth his detailed design and rationale for a national flag, Stanley wrote:

> The traditional heraldic device or emblem of Canada is the maple leaf ... This emblem has official sanction by its inclusion in two provincial coats of arms and in the official coat of arms of Canada. It has been used by Canadian troops in two world wars, and by Canadian Olympic Teams (including the colors red and white). It appears to have universal acceptance both in and outside Canada as a distinctive Canadian emblem.[11]

Indeed, it did project Canadian recognition, as Percy Williams demonstrated to the world in 1928, and as Canadian Olympic teams have consistently demonstrated from the moment of their first Olympic appearance in 1908 (Figure 5). For those proud 1908 'pioneer bearers' of the maple leaf, there is little doubt that each of them realized the significance of what their actions meant to a sustained pride. The sense of their pride, indeed the value of their 'Olympic experience', can be summed up no better than by the feelings expressed by the stadium team on the eve of its departure from England. Signed by the officers of the team's executive board, Ed Archibald, J.G. MacDonald and William Anderson, a handsomely embossed, deeply emotional testimony was presented to team manager John Howard Crocker (Figure 6). The historic document survives:

> The members of the Athletic Team representing Canada at the Olympic Games, London, desire to express to you our sincere thanks for the way in which you, as Manager, have attended to all the interests of our team. Although we have been unfortunate in not having made as good a showing as we expected, still we believe we have gained experience which will be invaluable to future athletes who may go to foreign shores to uphold the athletic honor of the maple leaf .... (Barney 2009, 142–143)

Concluding thoughts

'What if four-coloured flags fly over Johannesburg, and Kangaroos over Canberra, and Maple Leafs over Ottawa? The Union Jack floats beside every one of them', wrote the eminent Canadian historian Stephen Leacock in 1939 (as cited by Champion 2010, XI).

Figure 6. George Stanley's Inspiration: Percy Williams and his gold medal finish of the 100 meters, Amsterdam, 1928.

And yet, a generation following the official proclamation in 1964 of the red maple leaf as Canada's national symbol,

> a dwindling proportion of Canadians identify themselves with the Maple Leafs' century old predecessor, or even know what it looked like ... and if the intention [the flag and Maple Leaf symbol debate] was to sever modern Canada from much of its historical moorings, then the Maple Leaf has been a marked success. (Champion 2010, 4–5)

For the Games of the Fifth Olympiad in Stockholm, Sweden in 1912, the Canadian Olympic Committee reasserted the maple leaf as its team's identification logo, with but one modification – the word 'Canada' was embedded in the middle of the maple leaf, rather than below it. Succeeding generations of Canadian Olympians, including the

Figure 7. The 1908 Canadian Olympic team Executive Council.

Figure 8. The Newington Montage.

Olympic Winter Games athletes, have steadfastly borne the maple leaf on every Olympic occasion since.

We offer a punctuation mark to the central message of this work. In a most remarkable photomontage of the gold medallists of the epic 1908 Olympic Games, created some two months following the close of the great Olympic festival by the noted British graphic artist Robert Newington, Canada's Bobby Kerr, winner of the 200-metre sprint, arranged in the centre of the front rank of athletes, stands erect, clad in his maple leaf-emblazoned singlet, the telling symbol on his chest announcing to the world – 'Canada'. A new Canadian identity symbol had thus taken its place among the assembled logos and ensigns by which other of the world's great nations were recognized (Figure 7).

Finally, what had Lord Earl Grey made apparent in his post-1908 Olympic Games letter to Hanbury-Williams on the subject of a national flag and the symbols therein embraced? 'One thing, however, is clear to me', he emphatically stated, 'and that it is desirable for the Canadians to make the first move in this direction ...' Without doubt, as the events attached to the 1908 Olympic Games have only too well demonstrated, Canadians had made 'the first move in this direction' (Figure 8).

Disclosure statement

No potential conflict of interest was reported by the authors.

Notes

1. The final 'Government Funding' figure in support of the 1908 Canadian Olympic Team totalled $18,500–$15,000 from the Federal Government, $2000 from the Province of Ontario, $1000 from the Province of British Columbia and $500 from the City of Toronto. This revenue figure ($18,500) was complemented by $1025 in personal subscriptions, balanced against an expense total of $20,797.84. See P.D. Ross, 'Canadian Olympic Committee: Final Report of the

Honorary Treasurer and Statement of Receipts and Expenditures, 1908', Library and Archives Canada (hereafter LAC), Jack Davies Fonds, PAC, MG 30 C 164, Box 19 (COC-COA Olympic Games) File 3, COC Final Report.

2. See *The Fourth Olympiad, London, 1908 – Official Report* (London: The British Olympic Association, 1909), 23.

3. The origin of this historic notation in Canadian Olympic history was reported to members of the Canadian Amateur Athletic Union at its annual meeting some months following the London Games. See 'President's Address', Minutes of the 25th Annual Meeting of the CAAU, Toronto, November 9, 1908, 4.

4. Ross had been a first-class athlete in his university days at McGill in the late 1870s, where he excelled as a member of the rowing and football clubs, as well as participating in golf, hockey, rugby and lacrosse. In his post-university days, he played football, lacrosse and hockey at a superior level, founded several golf clubs. Many years later (1974 and 1976), he was posthumously inducted into the Canadian Sports Hall of Fame and the Hockey Hall of Fame; see Cain No. 262244, LAC, Philip Dansken Ross fonds.

5. See Secretary F.L.C. Pereira to L.C. Hoskins, Esq., 2 July 1908, Jack Davies Fonds, File 3, Box 164 (COC-COA Olympic Games), LAC.

6. The schedule for the Opening Ceremonies set by the Organizing Committee was rigidly followed. Fortunately for all – competitors, officials, spectators and Royal Party – a thunder shower occurring in the morning, threatened again in the afternoon, but 'held off' sufficiently that the opening ceremony festivities were completed without interruption. *The Fourth Olympiad, London, 1908 – Official Report*, 47–49.

7. See J.H. Crocker, *Report of the First Canadian Olympic Athletic Team, 1908* (submitted 20 August 1908), Crocker Collection, Special Collections and University Archives, D.B. Weldon Library, Western University, 3–4. Crocker's post-Games memory failed on his notation that 'thirty-five' athletes marched in the opening ceremonies parade. Both the photograph of the 'Marching Team' taken before the ceremonies and the photograph of the Canadian contingent shown marching in the stadium clearly show 32 uniformed athletes.

8. *The Times* (London), undated, cited by Crocker in his 'Report . . .', 4.

9. Sir Earl Grey to John Hanbury-Williams, 1 December 1908, Box 25, Canada 1908–1909: [File 1]: Grey File, File III: Correspondence Earl Grey, 1908–1909', LAC.

10. Stanley's letter to Matheson is a fundamental document in understanding the evolution of Canada's national flag. See G.F.G. Stanley to John Matheson, Esq., 23 March 1964, Alan Beddoe Papers, MG30, D252, vol. 9, LAC.

11. See Stanley to Matheson, 23 March 1964.

References

Barney, Robert K. 2009. "For the Athletic Honor of the Maple Leaf: The Photographic Identity of the 'Lost Olympians' – Canada's Olympic 'Stadium Team', London, England, 1908." *Olympika: The International Journal of Olympic Studies* 18: 137–148.

Baxter, Arthur Beverley. 1935. *Strange Street*. London: Hutchinson.

Beddoe, Alan B. 1981. *Beddoe's Canadian Heraldry*. Belleville: Mika.

Champion, C. P. 2010. *The Strange Demise of Canada*. Montreal: McGill-Queen's University Press.

Kidd, Bruce. 1996. *The Struggle for Canadian Sport*. Toronto: University of Toronto Press.

Lang, Spencer Norris. 2002. "Importing Professional Baseball: An Examination of the Guelph Maple Leafs and London Tecumsehs in Canadian Baseball's First Professional Era, 1871–1878." Master of Arts thesis, University of Western Ontario.

Lansley, Keith. 1971. "The Amateur Athletic Union of Canada and Changing Concepts of Amateurism." PhD diss., University of Alberta.

Llewellyn, Matthew P. 2012. *Rule Britannia: Nationalism, Identity and the Modern Olympic Games*. London: Routledge.

Mallon, Bill, and Ian Buchanan. 2000. *The 1908 Olympics: Results for All Competitors in All Events, with Commentary*. Jefferson, NC: McFarland Publishers.

Morrow, Don, and Kevin B. Wamsley. 2010. *Sport in Canada: A History*. Don Mills: Oxford University Press.

Reed, T. A. 1945. *The Blue and White: A Record of Fifty Years of Athletic Endeavor at the University of Toronto*. Toronto: University of Toronto Press.

Reid, Daniel B. 1990. "The Amateur Athletic Union of the United States and the Canadian Amateur Athletic Union – 1897 to 1914: A Study of International Sporting Relations." Unpublished Master of Arts Thesis, University of Western Ontario.

Stanley, George F. G. 1965. *The Story of Canada's Flag: A Historical Sketch*. Toronto: The Ryerson Press.

Tenison, Richard Hanbury. 1995. *The Hanbury's of Monmouthshire*. Printed by the National Library of Wales.

Thompson, Neville. 2013. *Canada and the End of the Imperial Dream*. Don Mills: Oxford University Press.

Vance, Jonathan F. 2012. *Maple Leaf Empire: Canada, Briton, and Two World Wars*. Don Mills: Oxford University Press.

'In our case, it seems obvious the British Organising Committee piped the tune': the campaign for recognition of 'Ireland' in the Olympic Movement, 1935–1956

Tom Hunt

Independent Scholar

> In the 22 years between 1935 and 1956, the Irish Olympic Council and its later variant the Olympic Council of Ireland engaged in a struggle with the International Olympic Committee (IOC) for the right to be recognized as Ireland in Olympic competition and to include Irish nationals regardless of their place of residence on the island on the team. After competing as Ireland in 1924, 1928 and 1932, the landscape changed significantly in 1935 when Ireland was rebranded as the Irish Free State and its selection was limited to the state's boundaries by the IOC. As a result, Ireland failed to compete in the 1936 Berlin Games and over the next two decades Irish Olympic officials engaged in a campaign for the right to select Irish nationals, regardless of where they resided in the island and to be recognized as Ireland for Olympic purposes. This had serious implications for Irish sport and had the potential to split the national federations on political boundary lines.

Ireland's decade of political revolution (followed by a calamitous Civil War) ended in 1922 with the establishment of the Irish Free State as a self-governing dominion within the British Empire having the same constitutional status as Canada. The establishment of the new state effectively completed the partition of Ireland as the Government of Ireland Act had already established the Northern Ireland state in 1920. Ireland was now divided into two political units: the twenty-six-county Irish Free State, a dominion of the British Empire and the six-county semi-autonomous Northern Ireland. This state, designed to possess a durable unionist majority, remained within the United Kingdom and included a significant nationalist minority whose allegiance was to the Irish Free State (English 2007, 235–345; Fanning 2013; Hopkinson 2004; McGarry 2010; Townshend 2014). The political solution that secured Irish independence meant that defining Irish nationality was particularly difficult. Citizenship was the key, if somewhat narrow, principle used to define nationality. The Constitution of the Irish Free State effective from 6 December 1922 conferred a limited Irish citizenship on all those ordinarily born in and resident on the island, including residents of Northern Ireland, when the constitution became operative (Daly 2001, 391). This citizenship was only effective within 'the limits of the Irish Free State'; for international purposes, Irish citizens, as natives of a Dominion, were British subjects. This position continued until Britain formally recognized Ireland's separate nationality in the 1948 British Nationality Act, an act which also acknowledged that the member states of the Commonwealth were free to enact their own legislation on nationality (Daly 2001, 388). With the exception of the Irish Football Association, partition did not extend to the management of Irish amateur sport, and governing bodies continued to

---

John Chisholm to R.M. Ritter, honorary secretary-treasurer, FINA, 25 November 1948 (Irish Olympic Council Official Report, 1949, 44).

organize sport on an all-Ireland basis. This work examines how the interested parties and, in particular, the International Olympic Committee (IOC) and the Irish Olympic Council dealt with the participatory circumstances created by the political settlement. The management of the situation provides an insight into the internal politics of the IOC, as well as the role Irish Olympic history played in the evolution of the Olympic Charter.

This is an undocumented episode of Ireland's Olympic history. The role played by the Olympic Games in the evolution of an Irish identity in post-independent Ireland has received little attention from historians. Kevin McCarthy's (2010) seminal work concentrates on the pre-1924 period as it unravels the role played by the Olympic Games in the evolution of a national identity in Ireland and in the emergence of Irish America as a major sporting and political force in the USA. Mike Cronin in *Sport and Nationalism in Ireland* (1999) explores sporting nationalism through the experience of Gaelic games and soccer as examples of mass spectator sport. While Cronin identifies 'the Olympic Games as the most longstanding and contentious arena for the expression of nationalism through sport', issue pertinent to Ireland's Olympic participation are not part of his agenda (Mike Cronin, *Sport and Nationalism in Ireland*, 1999, 62–66).

The election on 9 June 1922 of John James 'J.J.' Keane as the Irish representative of the IOC paved the way for Ireland's entry, as an independent entity, to the Olympic Movement. Keane's appointment was made without any consideration given to the political unit he represented as to do so would have introduced the dreaded political dimension to the discussion (McCarthy 2010, 305–314). Ireland, including competitors from Northern Ireland, competed in the 1924 and 1928 Olympic Games at Paris and Amsterdam; no competitors from Northern Ireland were selected on the eight-man team that competed in Los Angeles in 1932. In 1924, two leading officials of the BOA, Col Reginald John Kentish and the Rev Robert de Courcy-Laffan failed in their attempts to confine the Irish selection to the territory of the Irish Free State. The claim was successfully resisted by Keane (*Irish Times*, 1, 4 April 1924) and in doing so he identified one of the cardinal principles of Olympic eligibility: 'States or parts of a country are not recognised … The IOC is founded on the basis of nationalities' (*Sport*, 12 April 1924). The Olympics, Mike Cronin has written, 'functioned as definers of the nation for a newly independent Ireland'. 'The choice of who an athlete competed for (indeed, who they were allowed to compete for) defined who was included, and who was excluded, from the ideal of the nation and national identity' (Cronin, Doyle, O'Callaghan 2008, 1017). The challenge to include all competitors considered to be part of the Irish nation dominated Irish Olympic business between the mid-1930s and the early 1950s.

The 1932 Los Angeles Games were the last at which Ireland's right to compete as a thirty-two-county entity remained unchallenged until 1960. Ireland's presence in the southern Californian metropolis was a triumph for Eoin O'Duffy who as President of both the National Athletics and Cycling Association of Ireland (NACAI) and the Irish Olympic Council managed to persuade the International Amateur Athletic Federation (IAAF) from making a final decision on the wish of the Northern Ireland Amateur Athletic Association (NIAAA) to control athletics as an affiliate of the Amateur Athletic Association (AAA) in Northern Ireland (McGarry 2007, 152–154; Reynolds 2012, 30–33). The IAAF's constitution, however, was later amended at its Stockholm Congress in August 1934 to limit the jurisdiction of its member federations to the political boundaries of the country or nation they represented (IAAF 1934, 79). As a result, if the NACAI wished to remain within the international community it had no option but to limit its activities to the Irish Free State. This of course it refused to do, and its suspension from the IAAF in April 1935 was made permanent in May 1937 (Griffin 1990, 124–131). The NIAAA, in association with the AAA, now controlled athletics in Northern Ireland. In the Irish Free State, a new national federation was founded in April 1937 and was elected to full membership of the IAAF as the Amateur Athletic Union of Eire (AAUE) in March 1938 (Griffin, 142–145).

Etat Libre d'Irlande or Irlande

In the December 1934 issue of the *Bulletin Officiel* of the IOC the country was identified as *Etat Libre d'Irlande* rather than the normal *Irlande* (April 1934, 2). It was apparent that the IOC intended to adopt the IAAF model and confine the jurisdiction of National Olympic Committee's (NOCs) to political units. Irish officials were informed by A.C. Berdez, honorary secretary of the IOC, that in reality no change had been made; the approval by the IOC of a delegate to Ireland in 1922 'was a delegate to the new state, ratified by Treaty and to unavle (*sic*) [enable] the citizens of the Free State of Ireland taking part in the Games under their own flag'.[1] As a result, on 2 September 1935, the Irish Olympic Council's members unanimously decided not to compete in the 1936 Berlin Games as the Irish Free State (*Irish Independent*, 3 September 1935). There was no room for disagreement as the national federations responsible for managing amateur sport continued to do so on an all-Ireland basis.

The Irish question was discussed by the IOC Executive Board at its meeting of 2 June 1936 in Stockholm, and again a month later at the IOC's annual Session in Berlin. Olympic officials confirmed that athletes from Ulster (sic) were ineligible to represent the Irish Free State in Olympic competition.[2] The 1933 Charter regulations decreed that 'only those who are native of a country or naturalised subjects of that country, or of a state which is part of that country, are qualified to compete in Olympic Games under the colours of that country' (IOC 1933, 13). Unlike the IAAF, the IOC did not define a country. In fact, the Berlin decision represented a very narrow interpretation of the regulation and equated nationality with a political entity. In doing so the complexities of the Irish situation were ignored. The regulations were largely unchanged in the more detailed 1938 and 1946 editions; the replacement of 'native of a country' with 'nationals of a country' arguably created an opportunity for greater flexibility in defining eligibility (IOC 1938, 52, IOC 1946, 14).

The attempt to limit the Irish Olympic Council's jurisdiction took place when the Fianna Fáil government under the leadership of Eamon de Valera engaged in a policy of systematically expanding the boundaries of Irish independence. The Oath of Allegiance was abandoned (May 1933) and the Irish Nationality and Citizenship Act (1935) established a separate Irish citizenship, although Britain continued to insist that all persons born within the Irish Free State were British subjects. The state's constitutional relationship with Britain was redefined. All reference to the king and governor-general were removed from the 1922 constitution, although the External Relations Act (1936) was used to preserve the most tenuous of connections with the British Commonwealth. The king was 'authorised to, act on behalf of *Saorstát Éireann* [Irish Free State]' in the appointment of diplomatic representatives and in the conclusion of international agreements when advised by the Executive Council [of the Irish Free State]. The process culminated on 29 December 1937 when *Bunreacht na hÉireann* (Constitution of Ireland) became operative and established an Irish republic in all but name (Kelly 2013, 52–59). Under Article 4, the state was renamed as '*Éire*, or, in the English language, *Ireland*'; the national territory was defined as 'the whole island of Ireland, its islands and territorial seas' and Article 2 recognised 'the entitlement and birthright of every person born on the island of Ireland, which includes its islands and seas, to be part of the Irish nation'. Article 9 was also important as it granted citizenship to any person who was a citizen of the Irish Free State immediately before the coming into operation of the new constitution (*Bunreacht na hÉireann* 2000, 4–10).

The new constitution provided the officers of the Irish Olympic Council with a legal framework to support their arguments; a copy of the document was immediately dispatched to A.G. Berdez, drawing his attention to Article 4 in particular with the request that the name Ireland be substituted for that of the Irish Free State in future Olympic publications. Berdez was also informed that the name *Éire* should not be used unless the Irish language was used, which was unlikely to happen in 'official correspondence for a long time yet'. In response, the IOC honorary secretary insisted that '*Etat Libre d'Irlande* to which J.J. Keane is the delegate of the IOC' would continue to appear in Olympic publications. Berdez chose to ignore the new reality. In describing Keane as a delegate to the *Etat Libre d'Irlande,* Berdez was 'acting in an impossible manner' because 'he cannot be the delegate to a country which does not exist' honorary secretary of the Irish Olympic Council, P.J. Kilcullen explained. He was advised in a manner that left no room for doubt that '*The use of the name "Etat Libre d'Irlande" must be discontinued since there is now no such country'*. Eventually in December 1938, the Irish Olympic Council officers were informed that in future Eire would be used to identify Ireland.[3] The architect of this decision was almost certainly Lord Aberdare, a member of the executive of the IOC since 1931. The decision coincided with the British government's decision to use Eire (without the accent) as the name of the independent Irish state, a decision which was confirmed in a statement issued on behalf of the British government on 30 December 1937. It was officially used in the Eire (Confirmation of Agreement) Act of 1938, which included a clause specifying that the territory known as the Irish Free State under earlier legislation 'shall be styled Eire' (Daly 2007, 77–78).

London calling

The position was unchanged when the Irish team travelled to the 1948 London Olympic Games. Early in 1948, Sigfrid Edström, the President of the IOC, confirmed that 'Competitors having Northern Ireland status can only represent Great Britain and Northern Ireland'. He was intimately familiar with the issues involved, as he was President of the IAAF when the NACAI was suspended from membership. Edström was the chief organizer of the 1912 Olympics in Stockholm and had used the occasion to establish the IAAF (Guttmann 2002, 75). Irish officials were only prepared to regard the Edström decision as an *ex-parte* one, as they were not given an opportunity to present their case. A lengthy written appeal followed, in which the council's president Eamon Broy outlined how the implementation of the ruling would undermine the authority covering all-Ireland sport vested in the Irish Olympic Council and would interfere with the agreements between the national federations and their governing bodies 'as it restricts their sphere of influence or authority'. The decision allowed another 'nation to encroach on the Irish Olympic Council's authority, particularly in regard to All-Ireland Associations'.[4] After considering the matter and consulting with J.J. Keane, Edström 'finally' confirmed his earlier decision. Irish officials now placed their faith in Rule 16 of the General Rules applicable to the Olympic Games. This specified that in the event of 'a claim dealing with the amateur status or nationality of a competitor, the International Federation involved shall decide upon the claim' (IOC 1946, 20).

Regardless of the implications of Rule 16, the IOC position was clear. The Irish team would compete as Eire, its territory was defined by its political boundaries and athletes from Northern Ireland were ineligible to represent Eire. None of this was acceptable to the Irish Olympic Council and the dichotomy produced a tension-filled and controversial two weeks throughout the duration of the London Games. Competitors from 11 national federations were included on the Irish team. Three federations, the Irish Amateur Boxing Association (IABA), the Irish Amateur Swimming Association (IASA) and the Irish Amateur Rowing Union (IARU) included athletes from Northern Ireland in their selection and faced potential disqualification before they entered the ring, pool or boat. The athletes of the AAUE represented a national federation affiliated to the IAAF, but their entry was not sanctioned by the Irish Olympic Council, while the IARU had yet to affiliate to its international federation, an essential prerequisite for Olympic participation.

On 29 July 1948, the practical implications of the dispute were unveiled as the nations assembled outside Wembley Stadium to prepare for the protocol-laden Parade of Nations segment of the Opening Ceremony. The position of the Irish team in the parade and the title under which they would participate became the subject of a heated confrontation between British and Irish officials. The general instructions decreed that countries would enter the stadium 'in alphabetical order according to English spelling' and this was explained to officials on the eve of the Opening Ceremony (Lord Burghley, ed 1951, 204– 205). Irish officials were informed of their requirement to march as Eire between Egypt and Finland and not as Ireland when they arrived at the stadium. Intense discussions took place and faced with the ultimatum of marching as Eire or not at all, pragmatism triumphed over principle and the decision was made to parade but under protest (Hampton 2008, 87; Irish Olympic Council 1949, 9–11).

The two Northern Ireland swimmers, Ernest McCartney, the greatest Irish freestyle swimmer of the day, and his heir apparent, William Fitzell Jones, were declared ineligible to represent Eire; the decision was appealed to the Fédération International De Natation (FINA) Congress held on the eve of the Opening Ceremony. Irish officials argued that the Belfast-born McCartney and Jones from Holywood, County Down, were eligible as they held Irish citizenship and that the terms of Rule 16 empowered FINA to adjudicate on the matter. However, FINA accepted the primacy of the IOC and rejected the Irish appeal. A subsequent appeal to the IOC was also rejected. As a result, the two Dublin swimmers, Patrick Kavanagh and Stuart Kramm were withdrawn 'to preserve the essential unity of Irish swimming', a move which fuelled unfounded rumours that the entire Irish team was to be withdrawn (Hampton 2008, 158–159; Irish Olympic Council 1949, 40–44).

Fortunately, from the Irish perspective, two international federations – the *Association International de Boxe Amateur* (AIBA) and the *Fédération International des Sociétiés d'Aviron* (FISA) – 'apparently, winked at the mandate issued by the International Olympic Committee' (*Irish Times*, 25 October 1948). As a result, two Belfast boxers, Willie Barnes and Hugh O'Hagan, competed without any objections. FISA and its secretary Gaston Mullegg also ignored Edström's instructions and Ireland competed in Henley with a crew that included Belfast rower Danny Taylor. They did so identified as Ireland in the *Official Programme*, the only Irish competitors to be so designated in official documentation in 1948 (5 August 1948, 15; Irish Olympic Council 1949, 36–39).

Preventing the athletes who were members of the AAUE from competing in London was also part of the agenda of Irish Olympic Council officials. The 10 athletes in London were *personae non gratae* as far as the officials were concerned. They had broken rank and undermined the claim for the recognition of Ireland as a thirty-two-county unit in sport and have been written out of the official Irish Olympic record. Their names or performances are not recorded in the council's *Official Report* which explained that it was not possible for the Irish Olympic Council to be represented in London because the national controlling body for all-Ireland athletics was suspended by the IAAF. The report records that 'The sponsoring of an Association with twenty-six-county status by the British Organising Committee, not approved by the Irish Olympic Council was the greatest piece of effrontery within our knowledge and on a par with their best tradition' (Irish Olympic Council 1949, 10–19). Despite their incomplete entry forms the athletes were always likely to compete in the Games. The main London power brokers were familiar with their situation and had strong associations with the IAAF in addition to their Olympic responsibilities. In addition to Edström, the two key London figures Lord Burghley (Chairman of the Organising Committee) and E.J. Holt (Director of Organisation) were president and honorary secretary, respectively, of the IAAF. Despite the presence of their friends in high places, they were only cleared to compete by an IOC decision. Speaking on the issue, American Avery Brundage pointed out that 'we cannot violate our own rules', but his belief that the dispute was politically motivated provided the IOC with sufficient reason to act. Edström also supported their inclusion but cautioned that such a decision was in breach of IOC rules. The proposal was eventually unanimously approved in Session with Brundage emphasizing that the decision was an exceptional one and not designed to create a precedent.[5] The 10 athletes then competed without distinction, with the notable exception of Jimmy Reardon in the 400 m, who was unfortunate not to reach the final.

Return to the debating chamber

The central issues were re-introduced to the international debating chambers shortly after the conclusion of the London Games. In January 1949, FINA contacted the IOC with a request that the 'whole Irish controversy' be thoroughly discussed and clarified at the Rome Session; clarification of Rule 16 was also sought.[6] The *Fédération International d'Escrime* (FIE) also contacted IOC headquarters seeking clarification on the legality of newly founded fencing clubs in Northern Ireland affiliating to the English fencing federation. IOC Chancellor Otto Mayer, obviously briefed on recent political events on the island, advised the President of the FIE, Jacques Coutrot, to postpone any decision until after a decision was made in Rome. 'The decision we shall take on this affair', he informed Edström, 'as the South made recently a proclamation that they are a republic and the North had a vote in favour of the Crown of England'.[7]

These requests reassured Edström of the importance of his long-term belief of confining the jurisdiction of national federations to their political boundaries. He regretted 'that so many federations have recognised Northern Ireland to be from a sporting point of view a part of the whole of Ireland. The IAAF never did that mistake'. IOC rules, he mistakenly believed, made it impossible to have 'British subjects competing for the republic of Eire'. That these British subjects were also Irish nationals and therefore eligible to represent Ireland in Olympic competition was ignored by the president. The matter was a late inclusion on the agenda for a meeting between the members of the IOC Executive Board and representatives of the international federations in Lausanne.[8] Edström informed those present of the wording of the resolution he intended to propose at Rome. There was no discussion or objections, which Edström chose to interpret as a vote of unanimous approval. Following from this meeting, the IOC members at the Rome Session on 28 April 1949 decided that athletes from Northern Ireland were required to affiliate to national federations in Great Britain and those from the south 'shall join the national federations of Eire'.[9] The removal of Rule 16 in Rome also brought about a significant shift in the balance of power between the IOC and the international federations. In the 1950 Charter, the IOC as 'the arbiter in the last resort on all questions concerning the Olympic movement' was recognized (IOC 1950, 7).

The Rome decision had potentially catastrophic implications for Irish sport. Irish athletics at this time was mismanaged by three federations. The sphere of influence of the

AAUE, affiliated to the IAAF, was confined to the Dublin region; the NIAAA in association with the AAA managed athletics in Northern Ireland with its main power base in the Belfast region. The suspended NACAI operated on an all-Ireland basis and catered for the majority of athletes and clubs active in Ireland. As a result of this tripartite division, less than 20% of Irish competitors in cycling and athletics were eligible for international competition. The IOC's Rome decision had the potential to precipitate a similar split in other national federations. The scenario that the Irish Olympic Council had worked to avoid since the mid-1930s had now apparently become a reality. In the notification received by John Chisholm, honorary secretary of the Irish Olympic Council, an attempt was made to justify the decision based on contemporary political developments in Ireland; the decision was taken 'after the political statuts (sic) of your country has been vey clearly determined'. This was a reference to the ill-conceived Republic of Ireland Act which came into operation on Easter Monday, 1949. This removed Ireland from the British Commonwealth and declared that the description of the state would be the Republic of Ireland. The official name of the state remained unchanged as Ireland or *Éire* in the Irish language (Kelly 2013, 127–130). A general election in Northern Ireland was also held in February 1949, which was to all intents and purposes a referendum on partition in which anti-partition candidates were soundly beaten by unionists (Buckland 1981, 81). In response, the British government passed the Ireland Act which recognized the Republic of Ireland, but also guaranteed the position of Northern Ireland 'or any part thereof' within the United Kingdom and effectively gave Ulster unionists a veto over Irish unity (Kelly 2013 134–138).

Irish Olympic Council officials reacted with predictable anger to the decisions taken at Rome and promised to fight the decision 'tooth and nail'. John Chisholm immediately informed Otto Mayer that the IOC did not have the power to 'hand over to British Sports associations the authority held by Irish sports associations over Northern Ireland athletes'; the decision represented a departure from Olympic rules and was illegal and 'therefore not binding'; it was 'evidently inspired by British Field and Track interests to endeavour to disrupt the all-Ireland control in other sports'; the move was 'likely to cause dissension and disunity in spheres where they have not existed so far' and Irish officials were given no opportunity to present their case at the meetings.[10]

Chisholm continued with another epistle to Otto Mayer in June 1949, in which he found it 'difficult to express and convey adequately the feelings of resentment and disappointment at the latest travesty perpetuated at Lausanne and Rome'. The decision was unacceptable because it was 'intrinsically wrong; it is illegal on various grounds ... and because it is just an effort to negative the national interests and legal rights of this country in matters of sport'. He requested what he termed the 'illegal direction' from the Rome meeting be cancelled at the earliest possible occasion, and that the rule of international law, as well as the Olympic Statutes and Rules be allowed to 'operate freely and properly' in the case of Ireland. An appeal to the 'Court of International Justice' was threatened where the 'principles of justice, law and equity' would prevail.[11] Chisholm's protestations had no immediate impact. In July, Edström informed Mayer that 'we cannot give in' and the decision was publicized in the IOC *Bulletin* No. 15.[12]

This decision also had obvious implications for the international federations. Support for the Irish position again came from the AIBA. Its executive committee unanimously decided in Oslo, in June 1949, that boxers from Northern Ireland were free to decide whether they wished to represent Great Britain or Ireland.[13] Lt-Col Russell, secretary-treasurer of the AIBA, contacted Mayer and requested that the matter be re-examined and expressed his concern about the impact the decision would have for the all-Ireland status of boxing. Although the IOC was now bound by the decision made in Rome, Russell argued that 'the international federations should be given an opportunity of expressing their views ... as it effects their own federations'. Russell also pointed out that the passport issue was more complicated than Mayer understood as 'citizens of Northern Ireland' were entitled to a British passport 'but were also entitled to one from the Irish Republic' and this entitled them to be included in the 'Irish Republic team at the Olympic Games'. Edström was surprised that Russell favoured 'these irregularities' and turned to his chief adviser Lord Burghley for support. He wondered if Burghley 'could have a talk' with the boxing official about the question.[14]

Irish Olympic Council officials also began a more comprehensive and nuanced campaign to introduce their arguments to a global audience. The council's honorary treasurer Patrick Carroll prepared a memorandum which was completed after advice from Conor Cruise O'Brien at the Department of External Affairs. Printed in French, Spanish and English, it was circulated to all NOCs, international federations and IOC members. Carroll analysed the eligibility of Irish nationals to represent Ireland regardless of where they resided under the applicable Olympic rules and statutes, the applicable Irish Constitutional Law and the structure of the controlling bodies of Irish sport (Irish Olympic Council Memorandum, 3–7). The test of nationality as the eligibility requirement for competitors at the time a competitor was entered for any particular Games was emphasized. The Rome direction was 'wrong and *ultra vires*', Carroll argued, and infringed on Irish nationality laws. The right of any Irishman to represent his country, Ireland, was based on positive law and clearly defined rights of nationality and Irish citizenship. The fundamental of the argument was that persons born in Northern Ireland were citizens of Ireland. The Constitution of the Irish Free State became operative on 6 December 1922, and on the following day the Northern Ireland Government exercised the right enshrined in the Anglo-Irish Treaty to contract out of its jurisdiction. These dates were central in defining citizenship as defined by Article 3 of the Constitution which conferred citizenship on every person domiciled in the area of jurisdiction of the Irish Free State on 6 December who was born in Ireland, or either of whose parents was born in its area of jurisdiction. This position was supported by case law which confirmed that the Constitution of the Irish Free State extended to Ireland in its entirety on its introduction (Daly 2001, 377–378; Irish Olympic Council 1949, 3–6). *Bunreacht na hÉireann* also conferred Irish citizenship on people who were citizens of the Irish Free State when it was introduced. The Irish Nationality and Citizenship Acts of 1935 and 1937 also regulated the acquisition by birth of Irish citizenship.

The memorandum also explained the institutional structure of Irish sport. All the important amateur sporting bodies in Ireland, with the exception of athletics, consisted of single national federations and managed their sport on an all-Ireland basis. This was accepted by the relevant international federations. The Rome directive, Carroll argued, 'assumed an unwarranted authority over International Federations which the International Olympic Committee does not possess'. The memorandum concluded with an appeal for support to have the Rome directive 'cancelled at the earliest opportunity' and pointed out that 'its implementation would cause disruption, disharmony and deterioration in the sports concerned which have operated happily and smoothly on an all-Ireland basis'(Irish Olympic Council 1949 Memorandum, 3–7).

Attempts to have the matter placed on the agenda for the Copenhagen Session were rejected. In his memorandum Carroll pointed out that in the 1937 Constitution the name of the state in the English language was Ireland and the IOC 'persistently refuses to call this State by its proper name when using the English language ...' Certification from the

Department of External Affairs to support the claim was provided prior to the Copenhagen meeting. This confirmed that under Article 4 of the Constitution of Ireland the name of the state was Ireland in the English language.[15] The IOC again investigated the matter which involved nothing more than seeking the advice of Lord Burghley who enquired 'in official quarters as to the proper name of the country'.[16] He informed Mayer and Edström that the official British designation was The Irish Republic, or, if pressed, The Republic of Ireland. Burghley explained that it was 'quiet certain' that they cannot be called Ireland 'when the six counties of Northern Ireland have nothing whatever to do with them and are part of the United Kingdom'. As 'a happy compromise' he suggested The Irish Republic. Burghley's advice was accepted and as a result the Irish Olympic Council was offered the choice of using either title for Olympic purposes.[17] Burghley's position faithfully reflected British government protocol on the issue which was developed after the passing of the Ireland Act. The use of Eire was discontinued and the preference was that the use of the 'Republic of Ireland' should be reserved for joint declarations between the two countries. The frequent use of the term would give offence to Northern Ireland and therefore it was important that when possible the term 'Irish Republic' should be used. Delegates to international conferences were instructed specifically to avoid referring to Ireland (Daly 2007, 84–86).

'Our "terrible" Irish friends are writing again'

Patrick Carroll, a high-ranking police officer and trained barrister, succeeded John Chisholm as honorary secretary of the Irish Olympic Council in 1950 and now became the lead advocate of the Irish case. He first made contact with Mayer by letter on 11 August 1950 and expressed his council's disappointment at the failure of the IOC to accept the advice of the Irish Olympic Council which was 'correct in law and in fact'. The name Ireland was validated by the Constitution of 1937 and 'so recognised in various international undertakings' in which the country participates. Carroll again drew Mayer's attention to 'the most important aspect of the situation as far as the Six Counties are concerned'. Residents there were Irish citizens and if some wished to represent Ireland in a future Olympic Games they would be nominated and supported by the Irish council 'in accordance with the Olympic Rules which operate on a nationality basis'. Irish officials had no interest in selecting any Irish resident 'who claims to be a British subject' and they had every reason to believe 'that our attitude in this matter has the support of our colleagues in Great Britain'.[18] The IOC Executive Board meeting in Lausanne on 28–29 August 1950 finally accepted the Irish position on the nationality issue but decided to stick to the 'status quo', and to use either Eire or the Republic of Ireland to identify the country'.[19] Mayer informed Patrick Carroll that 'we quite agree with your point of vue (sic) when you say that residents of Northern Ireland having the Irish Nationality and by this way being Irishmen may represent Ireland in any future Olympic Games'.[20] This was a most significant advance for the Irish Olympic Council and conceded one of its two objectives This position has remained unchanged since then; at the 2012 London Games 5 competitors from Northern Ireland represented Great Britain winning two silver and a bronze medal, while 13 represented Ireland winning two bronze medals.

Irish officials refused to accept the nomenclature decision as final, but opted for the Republic of Ireland 'as the only designation left which has any legal significance'. Proposals to allow the International Court at The Hague decide the issue was predictably and correctly rejected by Sigfrid Edström, who pointed out that 'we make our own rules and regulations, over which they have no authority'. Once again Lord Burghley was requested to study the question in order to make a 'final decision'.[21] The Vienna Session confirmed the use of the name Republic of Ireland.

'We shall never finish with those Irish people'

The Anglo-centric nature of the decision-making process that operated at the highest levels of the Olympic Movement during the Edström presidency is clear from the management of the Irish issues. Information received from the British Foreign Office was accepted; the official documentation of the Irish Department of External Affairs was rejected. Patrick Carroll and Otto Mayer then began a new round of correspondence on the decision to use the Republic of Ireland as the official title for Ireland. On 13 August, Carroll expressed 'the strongest disapproval of the methods which influenced and guided the decision'. A decision based on a report from Lord Burghley, formulated on information he received at the British Foreign Office, was 'an insult to this independent country' and was completely rejected. It was a political decision that breached a fundamental principle of the Olympic Charter which disallowed discrimination against any country on political grounds. The Irish Olympic Council was forbidden from using the proper name of the country, Ireland 'because Great Britain and the British Foreign Office, from political motives and considerations, has succeeded in influencing the International Olympic Committee to deny us our national rights and aspirations'. The IOC decision ignored the practice of several international institutions, including the Council of Europe. Carroll made it quiet clear that 'the just claim' in Olympic matters would continue to be pressed until Ireland was given 'the same right that these international bodies now accord us with the full approval of all their members'. He requested a further consideration of the council's views by the IOC.[22]

Edström continued to congratulate himself on the fact that the IOC were not going to repeat the mistakes other international organizations made by using the Ireland designation 'thereby including Northern Ireland within their field of activity'.[23] Burghley assured Mayer of the validity of the IOC decision: it had 'nothing to do with any machination of the British Foreign Office, but is a simple statement of fact'. 'The IOC deals only in political boundaries and the Irish Republic and Northern Ireland were completely separate countries and no amount of words or other fog can alter this situation'. However, Burghley was now prepared to accept the citizenship decision as a workable solution provided that it was made clear that someone born and residing in Northern Ireland was 'not entitled to compete for the Irish Republic merely because they are prepared to issue him with a passport'.[24] The Oslo Session of 12 February 1952 again confirmed the use of Republic of Ireland.

At the 1952 Helsinki Games neither nomenclature nor nationalities were contested issues, and bantamweight boxer John McNally from Belfast won Ireland's first boxing medal in Olympic competition. Ireland's failure to select any track-and-field contestants and some of the fencers nominated by their national federation caused problems. The AAUE again received the support of Lord Burghley and E.J. Holt; the IAAF officials appealed the non-selection to Sigfrid Edström, who ordered the Helsinki organizing committee to accept the entries in what was a clear breach of Olympic regulations which specified that 'Only National Olympic Committees can enter competitors in the Olympic Games' (IOC, 1949, 20).

The Irish Olympic Council underwent a radical transformation during the Helsinki cycle. Two significant changes took place at officer level. Patrick Carroll moved to the honorary secretary's chair and, in what was a great surprise, Lord Killanin, was appointed the council's President and brought a new sophistication and steely resolve to the manner in which Ireland's Olympic business was conducted (Killanin, 1983, 23–28). The council was also belatedly reconstituted as the Olympic Council of Ireland (OCI), and its membership was confined to national federations who were members of their international federations and who controlled their sport on a thirty-two-county basis. This excluded both the NACAI and the AAUE from membership and enabled the council to engage in its business in an atmosphere free of the rancour of the politics of sport.[25] The change of title also brought the OCI directly into line with government policy on the issue. In 1951, Fianna Fáil returned to power and insisted on re-establishing Ireland, as the title specified in the constitution, as the only officially acceptable name for the state. The Government Information Bureau issued a directive in 1953 which remained in force for several years, setting out the nomenclature requirements. In simple terms, Ireland was to be used whenever the name of the state was mentioned in an English language document, even when the reference was to the area of the twenty-six counties. The use of the expression Republic of Ireland or Irish Republic was to be avoided. The directive also advised the use of the term 'Six Counties' as far as possible; the expression Northern Ireland was to be used only in an unavoidable legal contexts (Daly 2007, 83). Two significant elections took place in 1952 which proved important in reaching a solution to the nomenclature issue. On the opening day of the Oslo Session, Lord Killanin, was elected a member of the IOC and replaced the inactive J.J. Keane.[26] Ironically Killanin owed his appointment to the recommendation of Lord Burghley who mistakenly believed that 'his views on Irish questions would not be to stir up continual trouble but rather as far as possible, to "let sleeping dogs lie"'.[27] At the Helsinki Session on 16 July, Avery Brundage was elected President of the IOC when he defeated Burghley, who also lost out in the vice-presidential election.[28]

'I suppose Holt is behind all this'

Brundage placed a high priority on achieving a solution to the Ireland issue. On 2 September 1952, he contacted Lord Killanin and expressed the 'hope that you can find an answer to this question'.[29] This signalled an end to the Anglo-centric approach to reaching a settlement. The issue returned to the agenda in 1955 when Lord Killanin received the official invitation, addressed to the Olympic Council of Eire, to compete in the Melbourne Games. Rather than present this at an OCI meeting and initiate a new round of public controversy, Killanin contacted Lewis Luxton, an IOC member in Australia and requested that the invitation be re-issued. The Irish Olympic attaché in Australia, John Mulrooney, also visited the offices of the Melbourne organizing committee and spoke to its CEO Lt General Bill Bridgeford and E.J. Holt, who was now based in Melbourne as technical adviser to the organizing committee. Bridgeford was willing to make any necessary changes but Holt insisted on the use of Eire. On 29 November 1954, Lewis Luxton informed Killanin that the Irish team would be called the Republic of Ireland, as this was the title used in IOC material and 'probably a completely correct attitude' Killanin conceded. Holt was responsible for this insistence and claimed credit for the hard-line attitude. He explained to Burghley that he had 'dug his heels in on this point' and explained the situation 'clearly and fully' to Luxton. In a letter of protest to Luxton, Killanin correctly surmised, 'I suppose Holt is behind all this'.[30]

Lord Killanin contacted Avery Brundage on 5 November 1955 and justified the use of Ireland using the standard legal and constitutional arguments previously used by Irish officials. However, on this occasion the emphasis was placed on the international situation rather than on domestic constitutionality. Killanin explained that the *twenty-six-county state* [author's italics] was recognized as Ireland by all international organizations including the Council of Europe, UNESCO, the Red Cross, FAO and 'only the IOC of international organisations seem to have decided otherwise'. International sports' organizations with the exception of IAAF and FIFA also used the Ireland designation. The Commonwealth position was explained using evidence from a perceptive speech given by Lester Pearson in the Canadian House of Commons, who pointed out that the passing of the Republic of Ireland Act of 1949 did not change the name of the state 'which was established by the Constitution, and which could only be changed by constitutional amendment'.[31]

Killanin also suggested that the issue was one on which Brundage could give a personal ruling. This was a not so subtle prompt to Brundage that he might engage with the autocratic dimension of his personality. Killanin concluded by offering a simple formula of words that would resolve the matter. 'The omission of the words "Republic of" in the *Bulletin* was all that is required to regulate the position'.[32] Killanin made it clear that the issue was a non-political one; it was a matter of using the legally correct nomenclature for the twenty-six-county state. Lord Killanin had provided Brundage with the assurance that the matter was non-political and the solution he requested in September 1952. He also provided him with the methodology to implement it.

Brundage took immediate action and issued a personal ruling on the matter. On 15 November 1955, he informed Lewis Luxton that Lord Killanin wanted 'his country listed under its proper name and I doubt if anyone can have a legitimate objection'. This official name was Ireland and Brundage explained that 'This does not involve the 26 Counties argument which has plagued us for so long'. On 12 December, Brundage instructed Otto Mayer that the name Ireland was to be used in official Olympic publications. Lewis Luxton, in turn, informed Killanin that Ireland would be used to identify the Irish team at the Opening and Closing ceremonies and 'this is perfectly justifiable, regardless of any political arguments that there might be, because all countries names will be set out in English and not their own language'.[33] The invitation was then reissued to the Olympic Committee of Ireland. As far as Holt was concerned, Brundage was 'entirely in the wrong and not abiding by the decision of the IOC formerly agreed upon'.[34]

'I though I had better tell you what they are up to'

Officials at the British Embassy in Dublin informed officers at the Commonwealth Relations Office (CRO) in London of the latest developments.[35] Lord Burghley was contacted for clarification but he was unaware of the latest development, an indication of the extent to which networks of influence had changed within the higher echelons of the IOC during the early stages of the Brundage presidency. The old Edström–Mayer–Burghley triumvirate, in which Lord Burghley played a central role, was dismantled. He immediately contacted Avery Brundage to inform him of what 'the Irish are up to' and again outlined British opposition to the change, an opposition that was 'upheld always in the past by the I.O.C. and the I.A.A.F'. He was aware of no circumstances that had altered that position.[36] In his reply of 21 April 1956, Brundage explained the changed circumstances 'according to our colleague Lord Killanin'. 'In the circumstances, I do not see how we can avoid accepting and listing the country in our English publications as Ireland'.[37]

Burghley contacted Eric G. Le Tocq, an official at the CRO, for guidance on the use of the name Ireland. It is clear that Burghley was a lone ranger where this issue was concerned and was not acting on behalf of the Foreign Office or the CRO. He was advised that 'it was often difficult to prevail upon international organisations to designate a State by any other than the name that State itself put forward'. Le Tocq's chief concern was to ensure that the UK team included Northern Ireland athletes, provided they reached the required standard. 'We should never allow ourselves to be manoeuvred into the position of forcing a resident of Northern Ireland to compete with the Irish team or not at all'. Le Tocq also mentioned that he was certain that any nationalist from Northern Ireland who objected to competing in the UK colours could 'manage to get himself into the Republican team if he tried'.[38]

Avery Brundage, at this stage, was concerned about the implications of this dispute for the 1956 Melbourne Games and its potential to undermine Olympic rules. The fact that no country called Ireland was affiliated to the IAAF was a concern and he made it absolutely clear to the interested parties that a repeat of the Helsinki situation would not be tolerated: 'We have spent a great deal of time getting our rules in order and they must be enforced or we will all appear ridiculous'. Entries in Melbourne would only be accepted provided they were countersigned by both the NOC and the national federation.[39]

Burghley in his response once again explained how Ireland was divided into 'two distinct and separate countries' as the 'principle seems to be ungrasped'. As a result of 'ever mounting political pressure Eire has endeavoured to absorb Northern Ireland'. This time, he wore his IAAF president's evening dress and pointed out that 'we [the IAAF] obviously must have some say as to who competes'. The Olympic Games were the world championships of the IAAF, therefore it was 'quite impossible … to break our rules and allow runners to compete in the colours of a country which we do not recognise as existing and is not affiliated'. However, if the IOC insisted on bowing to political pressure and affiliated Ireland then they 'can only compete in the athletic events as Eire'.[40] In private correspondence with Brundage, Burghley played the loyalty card: British interested parties had been 'Hardly done by' over the Ireland affair. The decision should not have been taken 'without consulting the representatives of the IOC to the other interested party, namely Lord Luke, Lord Aberdare' and of course Burghley himself. 'To give way to political pressure, which is all that it is from Eire without this consultation, I think you will agree on second thoughts, is not quite fair to your other colleagues', he pleaded.[41]

Endgame

A coalition of British athletic interests then planned to ensure that if the OCI competed in the Melbourne as Ireland it would be unable to do so in track-and-field. The British Amateur Athletic Board (BAAB) involved itself in the debate. Jack Crump, honorary secretary, protested to Donald Pain (secretary-treasurer of the IAAF) and to Sandy Duncan (secretary general of the BOA). Crump pointed out that 'under no circumstances' could the BAAB 'agree to any athletes from the jurisdiction of the Northern Ireland AAA, or being eligible for that Body being included in a joint team representing Ireland or Eire'. Harold Abrahams suggested to Sandy Duncan that 'the idea that Ireland was being represented as a unit in athletics should be strongly resisted' and the 'use of the word "Ireland" unqualified is open to the strongest possible objections'. Therefore, on 25 September 1956, Donald Pain who succeeded Holt as secretary of the IAAF in a private and confidential letter, contacted E.J. Holt and pointed out that the IAAF

> must take an absolutely strong line on this Irish question. These are our World Championships and they must be in accordance with our rules. Therefore I am asking you officially on behalf

of the IAAF to insist on the competitors from Eire being described in the programme as 'Eire' and not Ireland.

He concluded by noting that 'Avery Brundage has been completely stupid over the Irish question: rushing in where angels fear to thread'. The motive for the change was 'purely political and it smells badly'.[42]

Brundage placed the matter on the agenda for an 'urgent' executive meeting held in Lausanne on 3 October 1956 'to settle certain important questions' before the Melbourne Games.[43] Lord Killanin arrived in Lausanne armed with a detailed memorandum which set out the Irish constitutional, diplomatic protocol, and international custom and practice case for the recognition of the title Ireland. Since Killanin's representation to Brundage in November 1955, the country was admitted to the United Nations as Ireland, 'with no protest whatsoever from Britain or Australia'. As a result of the 'unique' complications arising from Irish and British citizenship laws, many Irish people, including Killanin himself, were 'British subjects by birth and Irish citizens'. Killanin made it clear that there was no compulsion on athletes 'to compete under a flag which is repugnant to them' and concluded by explaining that it would be constitutionally impossible to send a team to Melbourne to compete under any other name. It would be correct to call Ireland *Éire* if all countries were identified using their national language or correct to use the Republic of Ireland if countries were designated using the form of government in place The use of either term to describe Ireland was in direct contravention of the IOC rules as *Éire* is neither French nor English but the Gaelic name for Ireland.[44] Killanin's arguments convinced the executive members present. The minute of the meeting simply records that 'it is finally decided to maintain the status-quo' and that Lord Burghley demanded that 'his strong protest against this decision be entered in the minutes of the meeting'.[45] Ireland's place in the 1956 Melbourne Games was secured.

After 20 years of diplomatic manoeuvring the issue was quickly settled. However, Lord Burghley, as President of the IAAF, insisted on the implementation of the federation's policy for the Melbourne Games. Burghley immediately notified Holt of the IOC's decision 'that they [the Irish] will take part in the parade as Ireland'. He reminded Holt that as the athletics programme was the responsibility of the IAAF, 'they must appear as Eire as we have no such country as Ireland affiliated'.[46] At the Melbourne Session on 21 November 1956, Brundage ruled once again that Ireland was the correct identity and advised the IAAF to settle the matter before the next Games and suggested that Burghley and Killanin should meet and 'endeavour to settle the old and troublesome question once and for all'.[47] Burghley was not for turning and Irish track-and-field competitors Ronnie Delany, Maeve Kyle and Eamonn Kinsella were identified as athletes from Eire in athletics literature and in the daily programme; Great Britain and Northern Ireland was used to identify British athletes in all Olympic material associated with the Melbourne Games and for the only time in Olympic history, Great Britain and Northern Ireland was used on the standard to identify the British team in the Parade of Nations in the Opening Ceremony.

The OCI's 21-year campaign reached a successful conclusion in Lausanne in 1956. The charge was constantly made by Lord Burghley that it was a politically inspired campaign. Although the anti-partition agenda of the OCI officials coincided with that of successive Irish governments, they received neither prompting nor financial support for their campaign. During the most intense period of international debate between 1948 and 1950 when the Irish Olympic Council was most vulnerable, relationships between the ministers of the Inter-Party government (1948–1951) and Irish Olympic officials were fractured. The government provided no financial support for the London Games and an attempt by the officials to leverage support for the campaign for Ireland recognition was rejected.[48] The leaders of the Olympic Movement in Ireland were men of strong nationalist sentiment (Eamon Broy, for example, was a double-agent within the Dublin Metropolitan Police and a key figure in Michael Collins' intelligence network during the War of Independence [1919–1921] and acted as Collins' private secretary during the Anglo-Irish Treaty negotiations in London), but their primary interest was to preserve the unity of the national governing bodies that controlled sport on an all-island basis and to ensure that Irish nationals who resided in Northern Ireland were eligible to represent Ireland in Olympic competition. John Bowman has written that 'The Irish self-evidently formed a single nation was the most central tenet of Irish nationalism'. Nationalist leaders such as Eamon de Valera were firmly opposed to any 'two nations' theories and refused to countenance the ethnic differences between the inhabitants south and north of the border (Bowman, 1982, 300–301). Irish Olympic officials compromised on the all-inclusive view of what constituted the Irish nation. Irish citizens who were also British subjects were free to represent Great Britain if they so wished and the officials had no interest in staking a claim for their allegiance. The Irish campaign was constructed within a legal framework that embraced Irish law and constitutional exactitude, Olympic rules and regulations and international custom and practice in the context of an unfamiliar landscape for the examination of Anglo-Irish national issues. These were normally conducted within the context of Irish and British diplomatic channels; Irish Olympic officials introduced these issues to an international stage. On this stage, as we have seen, Lord Burghley was ambassadorial in representing the position of successive British governments as it related to nomenclature issues and Northern Ireland. His insistence that the Irish Olympic officials were engaged in a politically motivated campaign implied that his decision making was free of political values. The reality was far different and Burghley's pathway across the landscape of Olympic diplomacy was a very inconsistent one. His stance on the problems created by the German question was blatantly political and the polar opposite to his standard arguments on the Irish issues.[49] His support for the Olympic merger of the German Democratic Republic and the Federal Republic of Germany ignored the political boundaries involved and provided an opportunity for German nationals to compete together, an opportunity he resolutely opposed in the case of Irish nationals resident in Northern Ireland (Guttmann, 2002, 94).

The manner in which the IOC allowed Irish competitors who had not been entered by the OCI to compete in London and Helsinki focussed attention on the IOC's cavalier attitude to complying with the regulations of the Olympic Charter. The right of NOCs to enter competitors in the Games was breached in London by a decision made in Session on 29 July 1948 and in Helsinki by an instruction from Sigfrid Edström. This flexibility had no place in the Brundage regime and the authority of NOCs in matters of entry was strictly implemented. This was tested at the Mexico Games when the Australian Olympic Federation (AOF) refused to enter a water polo team despite the fact that FINA had decided that the team was qualified to compete without having to contest elimination rounds. The Australian Swimming Union successfully appealed the exclusion decision to FINA but the AOF confirmed its original decision. The water polo team travelled to Mexico and three days before the Opening Ceremony, FINA demanded another hearing. Avery Brundage, conscious of the Edström's Helsinki decision and determined to uphold the rules of the Olympic Movement, issued a statement to all the interested parties explaining that only the AOF was entitled to decide whether the water polo competed or not. He informed the FINA's Australian president Bill Phillips and the president of the

THE BRITISH WORLD AND THE FIVE RINGS

Mexico organizing committee that the water polo team was not to compete. An important marker in the IOC's establishing complete control of the Olympic Games had been laid down by Brundage (Gordon 1994, 271–273).

Acknowledgements

The author thanks Matthew Llewellyn and Erik Nielsen and the anonymous reviewers for their helpful comments on this article.

Disclosure statement

No potential conflict of interest was reported by the author.

Notes

1. Olympics Studies Centre Historical Archive (OSCHA), Lausanne. D-RMO1-Irlan/002, A.C. Berdez to P.J. Kilcullen, 14 May 1935.
2. OSCHA, IOC Meeting Minutes – DVD 1: Executive Board (henceforth IOCEB) 1921–1969, Stockholm, minute of 2 June 1936; IOC Meeting Minutes – DVD 1: IOC Session Minutes (henceforth IOCSM), Berlin Session, 31 July 1936, p. 1.
3. OSCHA, D-RMOI-Irlan/002, Kilcullen to Berdez, 24 January 1938, 8 February 1938; Berdez to Kilcullen, 4, 23, 25 February 1938, 24 May 1938.
4. OSCHA, D-RMOI, Irlan/002, Baillet-Latour to Aberdale, 20 June 1939; Broy to Edström, 18 March 1948.
5. IOCSM, London, 29 July 1948, pp. 14–15.
6. OSCHA, Corr. President (January–April) 1949, Mayer to Edström, 4 January 1949.
7. OSCHA, D-RMOI-Irlan/002, SD2, Corr. 1945–1949, O'Connor to Coutrot, 24 January 1949; Mayer to Edström, 19 February 1949.
8. OSCHA, Corr. President 1949, Edström to Mayer, 22, 25 February 1949
9. IOCSM, Rome, 24–29 April 1949, p. 11. Also Mayer to Chisholm, 3 May 1949.
10. OSCHA, D-RMOI/Irlan/002, Chisholm to Mayer 26, 28 April 1949.
11. OSCHA, D-RMOI/Irlan/002, Chisholm to Mayer, 10 June 1949.
12. OSCHA, Corr. President (May–September) 1949, Edström to Mayer, 22 June 1949, 23 July 1949.
13. National Archives Ireland (NAI), Dublin, TSCH/3/S11053 C, Patrick O'Carroll to Conor Cruise O'Brien at Department of Foreign Affairs, 11 July 1949.
14. OSCHA, Corr. President, Edström to Mayer, undated.
15. OSCHA, D-RMOI/Irlan/002, Russell to Mayer, 8, 15 July 1949; Mayer to Russell, 12 July 1949; Edström to Mayer, undated; Chisholm to Mayer, 3 May 1950.
16. British Olympic Association (BOA), IOC/ADM/8/1, Meyer to Chisholm, 26 May 1950.
17. OSCHA, D-RMOIIrl/002, Chisholm to Mayer, 26 May 1950; Burgley to Mayer, 31 May 1950; Burghley to Edström, 12 June 1950; Mayer to Chisholm, 21, 29 June 1950.
18. OSCHA,DRMOI/Irlan/002 Ibid., Carroll to Mayer, 11 August 1950.
19. IOCEB, 28–29 August 1950, p. 8.
20. OSCHA, D-RMOI-Irl/002, Mayer to Carroll, 2 September 1950.
21. OSCHA, ED 119, MER Burghley, David (M of Ex), SD1, Corr. 1933–1951, Burghley to Mayer, 22 January 1951.
22. OSCHA, D-RMOI-Irl/002, Carroll to Mayer, 13 August 1951, 21, 30 June 1950.
23. OSCHA, DT. Edstr Corr, Edstrom to Mayer, 18 August 1951.
24. OSCHA, MER Burghley, David, Corr. 1933–1951, Burghley to Mayer, 21 September 1951.
25. IrOCo, minutes of 26 June 1951, 26 July 1951, 26 June 1952.
26. IOCSM, Oslo Session, 12–13 February 1952, p. 1.
27. OSCHA, Burghley to Edström, 11 October 1951.
28. IOCSM, Helsinki Session, 16 July, 1952, p. 4
29. OSCHA, CIO Pt. Killa. Corr. SD1, Corr. 1952–1959, Brundage to Killanin, 2 September 1952.
30. BOA/IOC/ADM/8/2, Holt to Burghley, 22 May 1956.
31. OSCHA. CIO Pt KIlla. Corr, Killanin to Brundage, 5 November 1955.

THE BRITISH WORLD AND THE FIVE RINGS

32. OSCHA, Killanin to Brundage, 5 November 1955.
33. OSCHA, Brundage to Lewis Luxton, 15 November 1955; Killanin to Mayer, 6 December 1955; Mayer to Killanin, 12 December 1955.
34. BOA/IOC/ADM/8/2, Holt to Burghley. 22 May 1956.
35. National Archives (UK), London, DO 35/5435, C462369. E.G. Le Tocq to A.G.R. Rouse, 17 April 1956.
36. OSCHA, D-RMO1-Irl/002, SD5, Corr, 1955–1959, Burghley to Brundage, 6 April 1956.
37. BOA/IOC/ADM/8/2, Brundage to Burghley, 21 April 1956.
38. NA (UK), DO 35/5435, C462369. Minute of telephone conversation between Le Tocq and Burghley, 2 May 1956.
39. BOA/IOC/ADM/8/2, Brundage to Holt, 23 August 1956.
40. NA (UK), DO 35/5435, C462369. Burghley to Brundage, 7 September 1956. Copies of this letter were sent to Donald Pain (IAAF), the CRO offices, Otto Mayer, M. Massard and Prince Axel.
41. BOA/IOC/ADM/8/2.Burgley to Brundage, 7 September 1956.
42. BOA/IOC/ADM/8/2, Crump to Pain, Crump to Duncan, 7 September 1956; Abrahams to Duncan, 14 September 1956; Pain to Holt, 25 September 1956.
43. IOCEB, minute, 3–4 October 1956, Lausanne, p. 5.
44. NA (UK), DO 35/5435, C462369, Memorandum from Lord Killanin, member of the IOC regarding the name of Ireland in relation to the IOC.
45. IOCEB, minute, 3–4 October 1956, p. 5.
46. BOA/IOC/ADM/8/2, Burghley to Holt, 5 October 1956
47. IOCSM, 19–21 November 1952, p. 11.
48. NAI., see TSCH/3/S11053 C, Athletics and General Physical Training: Proposals for Promoting Revival, 1948–1952.
49. OSCHA, DT. Edstr Corr, Burghley to Edström, 5 June 1951

References

Bowman, John. 1982. *De Valera and the Ulster Question, 1917–1973*. Oxford: Clarendon Press.
Buckland, Patrick. 1981. *A History of Northern Ireland*. Dublin: Gill & Macmillan.
Bunreacht na hÉireann. 2000. Dublin: Government Publications.
Cronin, Mike. 1999. *Sport and Nationalism in Ireland, Gaelic Games, Soccer and Irish Identity Since 1884*. Dublin: Four Courts Press.
Cronin, Mike, David Doyle, and Liam O'Callaghan. 2008. "Foreign Fields and Foreigners on the Field: Irish Sport Inclusion and Assimilation." *International Journal of the History of Sport* 25 (8): 1010–1030.
Daly, Mary E. 2001. "Irish Nationality and Citizenship since 1922." *Irish Historical Studies* XXXII (27): 377–410.
Daly, Mary E. 2007. "The Irish Free State/Éire/Republic of Ireland/Ireland: A Country by Any Other Name." *Journal of British Studies* 46 (1): 72–90.
English, Richard. 2007. *Irish Freedom: The History of Nationalism in Ireland*. London: Pan Books.
Fanning, Ronan. 2013. *Fatal Path, British Government and Irish Revolution 1910–1922*. London: Faber and Faber.
Gordon, Harry. 1994. *Australia and the Olympic Games*. St. Lucia: University of South Australia Press.
Griffin, Padraig. 1990. *The Politics of Irish Athletics, 1850–1990*. Ballinamore, County Leitrim: Marathon.
Guttmann, Allen. 2002. *Olympics: A History of the Modern Games*. 2nd ed. Champagne: University of Illinois Press.
Hampton, Janie. 2008. *The Austerity Olympics: When the Games Came to London in 1948*. London: Aurum Press.
Hopkinson, Michael. 2004. *Green against Green, the Irish Civil War*. Dublin: Gill & Macmillan.
IAAF. 1934. *Handbook of the International Amateur Athletic Federation 1932–34*. Vesterås: IAAF.
IOC. 1933. *The International Olympic Committee and the Modern Olympic Games*. Lausanne: IOC.
IOC. 1938. *Olympic Rules, Citius, Altius, Fortius*. Berlin: IOC.
IOC. 1946. *Olympic Rules, Citius, Altius, Fortius*. Lausanne: IOC.
IOC. 1948. *Official Programme, Thursday 5 August 1948, Rowing at Henley-on-Thames*.

IOC. 1949. *Olympic Rules, Citius, Altius, Fortius*. Lausanne: IOC.

IOC. 1950. *The International Olympic Committee and the Modern Olympic Games. Citius, Altius, Fortius*. Lausanne: IOC.

Irish Olympic Council. 1949. *Official Report on Ireland's Participation, XIVth Olympiad, London, July–August 1948*. Dublin: Irish Olympic Council.

Irish Olympic Council. 1949. *Memorandum of Irish Olympic Council Concerning the Direction of International Olympic Committee to International Sports Federation on Question of Ireland Affiliations*. Dublin: Irish Olympic Council.

Kelly, Stephen. 2013. *Fianna Fáil, Partition Ireland and Northern Ireland 1926–71*. Dublin: Irish Academic Press.

Killanin, Lord. 1983. *My Olympic Years*. London: Secker and Warburg.

Lord Burghley, ed. 1951. *The Official Report of the Organising Committee for the XIV Olympiad*. London: The Organising Committee for the XIV Olympiad.

McCarthy, Kevin. 2010. *Gold, Silver and Green: the Irish Olympic Journey, 1896–1924*. Cork: Cork University Press.

McGarry, Fearghal. 2007. *Eoin O'Duffy: A Self-Made Hero*. Oxford: Oxford University Press.

McGarry, Fearghal. 2010. *The Rising, Ireland: Easter 1916*. Oxford: Oxford University Press.

Mike. 1999. *Sport and Nationalism in Ireland, Gaelic Games, Soccer and Irish Identity Since 1884*. Dublin: Four Courts Press.

Reynolds, Pearse. 2012. "'A First Class Split': Political Conflict in Irish Athletics, 1924–40." *History Ireland* 20 (4): 30–33.

Townshend, Charles. 2014. *The Republic: The Fight for Irish Independence*. London: Penguin Books.

Rhodesia and the Olympic Games: representations of masculinity, war and Empire, 1965–1980

Andrew Novak

Department of Criminology, Law and Society, George Mason University, Fairfax, VA, USA

> White-settler-ruled Rhodesia faced isolation from international sporting competition after its unilateral declaration of independence in 1965, including from the Olympic Games. Sport reflected the qualities of white Rhodesian society, including its gendered and racialized norms. Rhodesia inherited its sporting ethic from Great Britain, and the British influence on Rhodesian sport remained indelible even as anti-British sentiment flared in the white community as Britain worked to exclude Rhodesia from international sport. This work highlights the irony that Rhodesia adhered to Imperial British social norms on the playing field while trying to assert an independent and anti-British national identity.

In November 1965, Rhodesia's small population of white settlers declared a unilateral declaration of independence (UDI) from Great Britain. For the next 15 years, the territory faced political and economic isolation, including expulsion from major international sporting competition, as a guerrilla war raged against African nationalists (O'Meara 1979, 18–19, 27–28). The scattered and insecure white minority, surrounded by a far larger African population, increased racial segregation in the franchise, education, civil service, health care, and social services (O'Meara 1979, 23–24; Summers 1994, 269–271). However, racial segregation was never total, and pockets of multiracial sport and leisure activities survived (Novak 2012, 861–862). As white settlers in Rhodesia were a small and diverse group, national symbols helped to manufacture a white Rhodesian identity, including the cult of founder Cecil Rhodes and the early Pioneers. Sport increasingly became such a symbol, especially after the Second World War and the increasing transience of the white community due to emigration and immigration. Rhodesian isolation from international sport after UDI, including its expulsion from the Olympic Movement, caused social frustration for the white community. Britain's role ensuring Rhodesian exclusion from competition contributed to anti-British sentiment in a very British colony.

British sport diffused widely to the world because the British Empire saw the 'civilizing' value of sport among colonial subjects. As elsewhere in Africa, sport culture diffused from colonists and white settlers to African police and soldiers as part of their fitness regimen and to children in missionary schools (Guttmann 1994, 64). The colonial state sought to win the hearts, minds and bodies of their Imperial subjects as a way to spread middle-class values. However, sport also served as a tool of resistance by those same subjects, including among working-class men or men of colour, although the exclusion of women persisted even as sport became less exclusive on the basis of race and economic status (McDevitt 2004, 139–140). In Rhodesia, cricket and rugby became the iconic sports of the white community, while soccer remained a preserve of largely African control even after Rhodesia's expulsion from FIFA, the world governing body of association football, in 1969.

The Imperial origins of sport reflected the racial divide in broader Rhodesian society, and the white state controlled access to sporting opportunities for black populations, including international competition. Prevailing gender norms during the colonial period also impacted sporting opportunities for women. Rhodesia was a highly gendered and militarized society. Even when women achieved significant political accomplishments, they did so on the state's terms. In 1919, married women acquired the right to vote if they met property requirements either individually or through their husbands, effectively limiting the franchise to white women (Lowry 1997, 268). In 1920, Ethel Tawse Jollie became the first woman on the Legislative Council and the first female parliamentarian anywhere in the British Empire (Lowry 1997, 269). Women's bodies, however, remained controlled in Rhodesia through, for instance, limited access to contraception and the prohibition of white women's sexual relations with black men (Mason, 1962, 246–247; Pape 1990, 700; Kaler 2003). Imperial racial and gender norms persisted in Rhodesia long after independence came to former colonies elsewhere in Africa.

Rhodesia's increasing participation in international sporting events in the 1950s was abruptly halted by UDI. Now there was added impetus: facing isolation in sport provided opportunities for political recognition to the Rhodesian Front government under Prime Minister Ian Smith. Although Rhodesia sent two athletes to compete in the Amsterdam Olympics in 1928, they did not participate as part of a national team. Not until the Rome Olympics in 1960 did the colony compete as part of the Federation of Rhodesia and Nyasaland, an amalgamated colony composed of colonial Zambia, colonial Zimbabwe and colonial Malawi. After the dissolution of the Federation in 1963, Southern Rhodesia competed as a separate team in the 1964 Tokyo Games. While Rhodesia attempted to send athletes to the Mexico City Olympics in 1968 after UDI, pressure by the British government and protest by African governments forced the team to withdraw (Little 2005, 47). The permanent expulsion of South Africa from the Olympic Movement in 1970 as a result of apartheid made Rhodesia's presence increasingly untenable. Although Rhodesia sent a racially integrated team to the 1972 Munich Olympics, a threatened boycott by African countries and their allies led to Rhodesia's expulsion shortly before the opening ceremony. While the executive committee of the International Olympic Committee (IOC) bitterly protested Rhodesia's exclusion as a violation of the sacrosanct separation between politics and sport, the changing realities of the Olympic Movement – including pressure to include principles of human rights – led to Rhodesia's permanent expulsion from the Olympics in 1975 (Novak 2006, 1378–1383; Smith 2008).

A gendered history of sport and racial discrimination in colonial Rhodesia

On the fringes of the British Empire, sport helped to socialize a small and scattered white community and build a national identity. White Rhodesian society bordered on the sports obsessed, especially as international links deepened. 'Like other colonial societies, which used sporting achievements to define and enhance national self-esteem, the Rhodesians deified their heroes and relied upon their national teams to restore or sustain national morale', Godwin and Hancock (1995, 38) wrote. Rogers and Frantz (1973, 274) called white Rhodesians a 'sports-minded people'. Rhodesia's increasing sporting isolation after UDI had the consequence of deepening dependence on South African sport, where racial segregation on the playing field had become common. The two most important sports in Rhodesia were cricket and rugby, which were also the two most intertwined with South

African sport and the most highly gendered and racially segregated sports in Rhodesia. Rhodesia could still compete in the South African Currie Cup competition after UDI, but was increasingly excluded from international competition in sports that women and black athletes played, such as athletics, soccer and swimming (Rogers and Frantz 1973). In addition, '[t]he shared patriarchal assumptions of European and African cultures curtailed sporting opportunities for African women' (Alegi 2010, 4). The country's sporting obsession thus took on gendered and racialized qualities.

Even pre-modern sports in the earliest days of the colony of Southern Rhodesia reflected Imperial gender norms. In his analysis of hunting in colonial Southern Rhodesia, Mackenzie (1987, 176–179) writes that hunting was 'the supreme expression of Victorian manliness, an activity with an ideology closely identified with contemporary militarism and imperialism'. Prominent white hunters in Rhodesia were glorified in British popular culture, and tales of their exploits were reprinted in children's books, traveler's stories and magazines. Pre-modern sports like hunting adapted poorly to the process of urbanization and industrial development (Mackenzie 1987, 179–81, 189). Modern sport, rationalized to ensure equality of competition among participants, conceived of aiming at a standard-size target rather than a moving animal, but gender exclusion persisted after the transition from pre-modern to modern sport (Guttmann 1978, 42).

The Rhodesian colonial state served as the gatekeeper for sporting opportunities for black men. While sport was critical for introducing Africans to Imperial notions of masculinity and order, the white government feared the violence that could accompany uncontrolled sporting events, as in boxing. In the 1930s, African boxers appropriated the European sport on their own terms, eliciting a strong reaction by the white urban residents who believed that boxing made African domestic servants more 'aggressive' and contributed to urban violence (Ranger 1987, 196–197, 203). By contrast, soccer remained a preserve of African autonomy and tended to attract more elite players, while boxing remained working class. Soccer served as one of the few avenues available to achieving social mobility and higher status in the colonial period. Consequently, soccer spilled into political activism, including football strikes in Bulawayo, Rhodesia, in the late 1940s when the City Council attempted to assert control over the leisure activities of a burgeoning African urban population (Stuart 1996, 170–171, 174, 177). 'African administration of football was demonstrably sophisticated and created an effective, parallel football system to rival the European one', and by the early 1960s black players were selected for the Rhodesian national team. In 1963, an African team won the Austin Cup, the heretofore white Rhodesian cup competition, and, in 1965, a racially integrated soccer apparatus joined FIFA, allowing Rhodesia to compete in a single World Cup qualifying match in 1969 (Giulianotti 2004, 85–86). As in other areas of Rhodesian life, racial segregation gradually loosened in the late 1950s and early 1960s, until prematurely halted and reversed by UDI after 1965.

Rugby in particular was an arena that reinforced white Rhodesian nationalism and gender relations as the pre-eminent 'man's game'. Players exhibited their 'maleness' on the playing field, while male spectators celebrated a collective manhood (Grundlingh 1996, 197–198). Although colonial teams, including Afrikaners in South Africa, appropriated rugby as a symbol of nationalism separate and apart from British identity, the 'maleness' of the sport transcended nationality (Grundlingh 1996, 200). In sport, South Africa was the 'role model during a formative stage that laid the foundations for Rhodesia's position in the modern era' (Winch 2008, 601). Cricket and rugby in particular drew the small and scattered white population together, promoting racial and masculine power (Winch 2008, 583). The white Rhodesian population was transient, and a majority of the white population was born outside of the country for the duration of colonial rule (Lowry 1997, 264). Rugby and cricket served as essential ingredients for the manufacture and replication of white Rhodesian (male) identity.

As Mager (2010, 7) writes in her study of the sociology of beer drinking in South Africa, rugby was a constituent element of the Imperialist ideal of 'muscular Christianity', introduced in all-boy schools in the late nineteenth century and embraced by the Afrikaner establishment by the 1920s. A similar process of socialization was at work in Rhodesia. Mager (2010, 7–9) describes this male-centred culture of mass spectator rugby as a form of 'deep play' for white South Africans, acquiring a cultural power akin to that of religion in which men affirmed deeply held, shared beliefs and the desire for the validation of others. Like other masculine rituals such as military conscription or beer drinking, rugby defined not only the boundaries of what it meant to be male but also femininity by opposition, for instance as trophy girlfriends of sports players. Similarly, like conversion to Christianity and Western education, colonial Boy Scouting reinforced Imperial gender norms by introducing African communities to Western social values that defined manliness as physical courage, patriotism, stoicism and chivalry. In Rhodesia, where Scouting remained racially divided until the end of the 1950s, African scouts protested the amalgamation of the colony into the Federation of Rhodesia and Nyasaland and boycotted celebrations for Queen Elizabeth's coronation ceremony in 1954 (Parsons 2004, 7, 18, 210–213). Despite its Imperial origins and agenda, Scouting, like sport, became a site of contested control.

Sport also reinforced Imperial gender norms when it was spread by colonial armed services. Many commentators have emphasized the importance of colonial African police and military forces in popularizing organized sport such as rugby and football (Guttmann 1994, 65; Merritt and Nauright 1998, 55; Alegi 2010, 8). Conway (2012, 6, 14, 24) has linked masculinity, sport and military service in the South African context, noting that rituals such as military conscription or rugby are based on a culturally constructed gender binary that valorizes masculinity in relation to femininity. Sporting boycotts on South Africa and Rhodesia contributed to the white community's perception of isolation and encouraged celebratory nationalism when competition did take place (Conway 2012, 73). Sport was a primary means by which male bodies were shaped and prepared for military service; the conflation of sport and war reinforced an ideal of the male body as militarized through competitive activity and muscularity (Conway 2012, 71–74).

In colonial Rhodesia, sporting opportunities attracted energetic young men to the police force and to the military, emphasized in police training as a means to promote teamwork, fitness and character. As Stapleton (2011, 108, 112, 114) writes, sport was among the first leisure activities that allowed African policemen to interact with European policemen, and in the early 1960s the first multiracial sports competitions took place in athletics, boxing, football and golf among the Rhodesian forces of the British South African Police. During the protracted counter-insurgency campaign of the 1970s, volleyball became popular among members of the Rhodesian African Rifles because it could be played in bush camps with minimal equipment and space. Following Zimbabwe's independence in 1980, British soldiers overseeing the integration of the Rhodesian security services with the former insurgency forces organized volleyball and football games among the former combatants in order to reduce tension and promote reconciliation (Stapleton 2011, 115).

As with the Rhodesian police and military, officials with the Native Affairs Department, which governed the vast rural expanses of African communally held property known as the native reserves, also used sport for socialization and contact on the fringes of white settlement. William Taberer, appointed as Chief Native Commissioner of Mashonaland in 1902, was an internationally renowned cricket and rugby player, competing for both Rhodesia and South Africa. Taberer was said to recruit new members for the Native Affairs Department based on their athletic ability and saw that they were stationed in Salisbury at the appropriate season to benefit Mashonaland's sports teams (Maclean 1974, 165–167). Just like policing and military service, rural government administration was a man's world. White women often lived lonely lives in rural areas, and the foundation of women's clubs (often called Women's Institutes) provided social opportunities for women comparable to sport competition for men (Maclean 1974, 197–198).

These aggressive, masculine sporting rituals were not static, and they evolved as social conditions changed. While cricket and rugby remained important in wartime Rhodesia, sport suffered due to universal white male conscription and white emigration in the 1970s (Godwin and Hancock 1995, 296). In September 1979, the death in combat of the full back of the Zimbabwe-Rhodesian national rugby team during an incursion into Mozambique led to a poignant memorial (and a thrilling victory) in the subsequent South African Currie Cup competition. Only a short time before, the rugby player had been denied an exemption from the draft (Godwin and Hancock 1995, 259). Another sportsman, polo player Basil Kearns, was killed in an ambush in April 1979 when he was returning to Salisbury to act as a Shona language interpreter for the 1979 Zimbabwe-Rhodesia elections (Byrom 1980, 38–39). Although sport and military service reinforced one another, at times they seemed in conflict. The militarization of Rhodesia accentuated prevailing gender norms in the broader society, but the boundaries were constantly shifting.

International sport and Rhodesian identity

The late 1950s and early 1960s proved to be a formative time for Rhodesian sport, as the country's teams were introduced to international competition separate from Britain and South Africa for the first time. 'In an age of nationalist fervour, successes in war and sport most publicly demonstrated the relative prowess and vigour of a nation's manhood', Nauright writes with respect to rugby tours of Britain by colonial teams in the early 1900s (1996, 123). The defeat of British teams to New Zealand's All Blacks and South Africa's Springboks in 1905 and 1906 represented the success of the 'hardened' colonial male and the decline of the British race at home (Nauright 1996, 134). Although white Rhodesians likewise believed that British civilization was in decline, British heritage lay at the root of settler culture and comprised the country's virtual raison d'être, including the cult of Cecil Rhodes, the symbols of the country's police and armed forces, and the Rhodesian contribution on behalf of Britain in World War Two. Even after UDI when anti-British sentiment flared, 'the British imperial character of White Rhodesia ... remained indelible' (Lowry 2007, 178). Rhodesians could hate Britain and still be obsessed with it.

The heterogeneity and transience of white Rhodesians required constant construction and reconstruction of a national identity, which in turn reinforced racial and gender exclusions. Racial discrimination persisted in Rhodesian sport not because of state intervention as in South Africa, where a ministry of sport policed segregation on the playing field, but rather as a by-product of the organization of Rhodesian sport around private athletic clubs (Novak 2012, 859). Where sport was organized around business and mining interests or by police or military forces, athletic teams and events made significant progress towards racial integration during the 1950s. This trend was halted by the rightward shift of the white electorate in the mid-1960s, culminating in UDI. Public swimming pools and public elementary school athletic facilities, however, became segregated by law (Novak 2012, 859–860).

Sport became fused to the Rhodesian national myth upon the colony's founding when the Pioneer Column that raised the Union Jack at Fort Salisbury in 1890 counted among its members several prominent cricket players and soon organized the country's first tournaments (Winch 1983, 1). The person of Cecil Rhodes, an avid sportsman, contributed to this fusion of sport and the white Rhodesian 'myth', as Rhodes bequeathed to the country many of its national symbols. Tanser's (1974, 83, 95) history of the capital city Salisbury, Rhodesia (today Harare, Zimbabwe), indicates that the first recorded cricket match occurred at Fort Salisbury between police and civilians on 12 September 1891, though unrecorded matches likely occurred before this. In April 1892, the first barmaids arrived, although several women already lived in Salisbury engaged in commercial sex work. Even in the earliest days of sport in the colony of Southern Rhodesia, women's roles in the masculine rituals of sport were related to alcohol and sex.

By the mid-1950s, Southern Rhodesia experienced a thaw in social relations. Amalgamated with colonial Zambia and Malawi as the Federation of Rhodesia and Nyasaland, the influence of the white community in Southern Rhodesia was diluted to some degree. Reformist Prime Minister Garfield Todd made incremental moves towards majority rule in Southern Rhodesia, including strong support for African education, until he was replaced as prime minister by the more moderate Edward Whitehead in 1958. Although Whitehead's government began implementing draconian security legislation, a trend accelerated after the conservative Rhodesian Front won the parliamentary elections in 1962, Whitehead himself professed a commitment to racial integration (Denoon and Nyeko 1972, 180; Nelson 1975, 140; Wood 2004, 17). Like other areas of social relations, sport reflected this incremental progress towards racial integration in the 1950s and a reversal towards racial segregation the early and mid-1960s. Advances in African education, for instance, were halted by 1964 as a result of budget cuts by Smith's Rhodesian Front government (Nelson 1975, 141). A study of public attitudes towards multiracial sport in the late 1950s indicated sentiments favouring racial integration in sporting competition, but not integration of the social sides of sports clubs. Attitudes appeared to favour the creation of separate private sports clubs for the black Rhodesian population. However, the authors discerned 'a considerable shift in thinking and practice' as a result of the integration of some social facilities. Attitudes regarding the integration of swimming pools, however, were much more negative due to a concern for hygiene (Rogers and Frantz 1973, 275, 280–281).

Examples of this thaw in social relations on the playing field during the late 1950s and early 1960s were subtle, but consistent. In 1958, parents of white schoolchildren voted in favour of a football match against a 'coloured' (or mixed race) team from a different school (*Rhodesia Herald*, March 20, 1958, 13). Southern Rhodesia also began to host mixed-race matches in boxing, in which one of the competitors was South African and therefore could not compete in interracial sport within South Africa due to apartheid controls (*Rhodesia Herald*, March 6, 1958, 22, April 11, 1958, 26). Beginning in the early 1960s, the boxing control board had African members to govern professional boxing in the country (*Herald*, June 2, 1982, 6). The Rhodesian newspapers also began to cover non-white sporting events as well as women's sports in the sports pages for the first time, if briefly (see, e.g., *Rhodesia Herald*, May 12, 1958, 16, April 9, 1958, 20). Rhodesia also began to chafe under South African sport governance when its athletes were not chosen for South African teams; the country was beginning to assert an independent sporting identity.

The openings in Rhodesian sport in the late 1950s and early 1960s began to close by the time of UDI and Rhodesia's embattled international relations. One consequence of sporting isolation was that it made Rhodesia even more dependent on South Africa, where sport segregation was deeply entrenched after the installation of apartheid in 1948 and its expansion to sports facilities in the mid-1950s. Where Rhodesian sport was heavily intertwined with or governed by South African sport, Rhodesian sport followed South African racial controls. Cricket, rugby and field hockey were paradigmatic examples (Novak 2012, 858). While Rhodesian teams competing in South Africa tended to defer to 'local custom' by sending racially segregated teams well into the 1970s, in 1971 a Rhodesian weightlifting team boycotted a South African event when its multiracial team was denied entry (Little 2009, 532).[1] Rhodesia even agreed to host South African multiracial competitions when apartheid barred the contest from taking place in South Africa.[2] Rhodesia's sport relations with South Africa were ambiguous as to racial discrimination. In 1971, a Rhodesian school hockey team made headlines when it chose a Rhodesian of South Asian descent to tour South Africa, which would have made him the first non-white Rhodesian athlete ever sent to South Africa as part of a predominantly white team (*Rhodesia Herald*, June 18, 1971). In part, this was the result of the increasing integration of private sports clubs in Rhodesia during the later UDI period. In 1973, the Rhodesian Stragglers, a cricket team in Salisbury, cancelled a match with the Aurora Cricket Club in Pietermaritzburg, South Africa, as it was a racially integrated club composed of white players and players of mixed-race and South Asian descent. The Stragglers may have had difficulty obtaining entry visas for the match as a result of bureaucratic intimidation by the apartheid government (Merritt 2009, 274–275, 283). In this way, racial discrimination in Rhodesian sport waned in the decade before UDI as political attitudes liberalized, waxed during the 1960s as attitudes grew more conservative, and gradually waned again during the 1970s.

The sporting sphere remained a site of contested control throughout the UDI period, allowing black Rhodesians to achieve significant progress on the playing field. Soccer star George Shaya, who began playing as a child with an improvised ball in the African township of Harare, was named Rhodesian Soccer Star of the Year five times, and was selected as a finalist for Rhodesian Sportsman of the Year in 1976. In 1969, at the age of 21, he competed for Rhodesia's ill-fated soccer World Cup team in the only international game Rhodesia played before its expulsion from FIFA, losing to Australia (Byrom 1980, 166, 168). Schoolteacher Cyprian Tseriwa competed in the 10,000 metre for the Federation of Rhodesia and Nyasaland at the Rome Olympics in 1960. In addition, Mathias Kanda and Robson Mrombe competed in the marathon for Southern Rhodesia at the 1964 Tokyo Games. The ill-fated team selected for Mexico City in 1968 included Kanda and Bernard Dzoma in the 5000-metre race. Finally, in 1972, Rhodesia's Munich-bound Olympic team included at least six African athletes, including Artwell Mandaza, the unofficial world record holder in the 100-metre race (Novak 2006, 1374, 1377–1378). Unlike South Africa, which had never sent a non-white athlete to the Olympics, Rhodesia's Olympic teams were always racially integrated.

Relations with Britain and the IOC

Unlike individual athletes, who could travel abroad for sport competition if they carried a non-Rhodesian passport, nationally representative sports teams were increasingly defined to be representatives of the Rhodesian Front regime after UDI and therefore in violation of United Nations (UN) travel sanctions (Little 2009, 531). The embargo of Rhodesian passports impacted the ability of athletes to travel abroad. Rhodesia's famous cricket star Colin Bland, who competed for South Africa's Springboks, was denied entry into Great Britain in 1968 as a result of his passport. However, most white Rhodesians had some form of dual citizenship (typically British or South African) and could travel freely on the passports of these other countries; this allowed individual athletes and club teams to tour even after UDI (Little 2011, 199). The British government and many African counterparts pressured international sport federations to exclude Rhodesia, but with varying levels of success depending on the sport and their political influence.

White Rhodesians singled out the Labour Party and its leader Harold Wilson as particular objects for scorn after the imposition of sanctions, and Great Britain's treatment of athletes in general and Rhodesia's Olympic team in particular reflected a broader British foreign policy that favoured the Commonwealth (especially African allies) and sought to isolate Rhodesia. Wilson's government therefore encouraged an African boycott of the Mexico City Olympics in 1968 and protested the entry of Rhodesian athletes and sports teams into friendly nations (Novak 2013, 27–28, 36). The British government was particularly concerned about the propaganda victory that the Rhodesian Front would enjoy if a Rhodesian team were invited to Mexico City. 'If Rhodesia sent a team, including coloured athletes, to Mexico to compete as a separate nationality, then Mr. Smith could feel he had again succeeded in smacking us in the face', observed one Foreign and Commonwealth Office (FCO) official.[3] The Secretary of State recommended lobbying Commonwealth governments in order to 'internationalize' the problem of Rhodesian participation.

Wilson's surprising loss to Conservative Edward Heath in 1970 reoriented British foreign policy towards Europe. Under Heath, Great Britain no longer protested tours by Rhodesian teams in third countries, although Rhodesian athletes were still restricted from entering the UK. Heath's government pledged not to interfere with Rhodesian entry into West Germany for the 1972 Munich Olympics, and even offered to provide British passports to the athletes as they were, after all, colonial subjects (Novak 2013, 28–29, 36–37). In late 1971, the British government seemed on the verge of a breakthrough in British–Rhodesian relations, negotiating a framework for ending UDI. Relations seemed to thaw as Britain voted against a UN General Assembly resolution in December 1971 seeking exclusion of Rhodesia from the Olympics, indicating that the issuance of an invitation to Rhodesia did not imply recognition of the regime (Resolution 2796, 26th Session, 10 December 1971).

The shift from a Labour government hostile to the participation of Rhodesia to a more agnostic Conservative one reflected changing British perceptions of its former Empire. The merger of the Foreign Office and the Commonwealth Relations Office in 1968 ensured that British relations with Europe remained at the top of the country's foreign policy agenda. The importance of British relations with its former African colonies was deemphasized. The rhetoric of the British government in addressing Rhodesian Olympic participation reflected this shift. Under Wilson's Labour government, the FCO dismissed the idea that Rhodesian sport was less segregated than South African sport, stating that discrimination was 'not the point'. Rather, Britain's objection was recognition of an illegal regime. By contrast, to Heath's Conservative government, the fact that sport in Rhodesia was not segregated by law was a critical distinguishing factor from South Africa. Officials noted that the Rhodesian case involved 'different considerations' from the South African one and even suggesting that Britain use multiracial sport in Rhodesia as a tactic to prevent an African boycott of the Munich Olympics (Novak 2013, 38).

For the continent of Africa, however, a boycott of Rhodesian participation at the Munich Olympics was linked to the continent's opposition to imperialism and South African apartheid. According to the International Campaign against Racism in Sport, the racial discrimination practised in recreation and sport in Rhodesia violated the Olympic Charter. The Campaign called on all sportsmen opposed to racism, especially black and Asian sportsmen, to refuse to participate in any event in which the 'Rhodesian racist regime' participated, making reference to the 'other' German Olympics in Berlin in 1936, the 'great racist festival of sport'.[4] As the list of African countries threatening to boycott lengthened, especially Kenya and Ethiopia, favourites in track and field, African newspapers called for solidarity with black Rhodesians and condemned the multiracial Rhodesian team as 'calculated racism' (see *Daily Times*, August 18, 1972; *New Nigerian*, August 22, 1972). The boycott of Rhodesia was the peak of African unity on the IOC, and the bloc held together for another Olympic cycle when 33 Caribbean and African nations walked out of the 1976 Montreal Olympics as a result of the presence of New Zealand, the most flagrant violator of rugby sanctions on South Africa. The boycotts of the 1980 Moscow Games and the 1984 Los Angeles Games, however, divided the African bloc and ended the use of the Olympic boycott as a political tool (Soldatow 1980, 140; Cheffers 1992, 74).

No issue went directly to the heart of Rhodesian national legitimacy more than the controversy over Rhodesian passports and Olympic identity cards. In 1971, the IOC brokered a compromise pleased no one, allowing Rhodesia to compete in a time warp as the British colony of Southern Rhodesia (Olympic code RHS), as it had in Tokyo in 1964. On the medal stand, 'God Save the Queen' would play as the national anthem under the pre-UDI flag incorporating a Union Jack. Rhodesia's immediate acceptance of the so-called 'Tokyo conditions' created a firestorm in domestic Rhodesian politics (Strack 1978, 229; Novak 2013, 33). Rhodesia's right-wing perceived the 'Tokyo conditions' as essentially reversing Rhodesian independence, particularly after 1970 when Rhodesia became a Republic and adopted a new constitution, flag and anthem. In Munich, the British government even permitted the IOC to stamp the Olympic identity cards of the Rhodesian team with 'British subjects'. The cards served as official travel documents for Olympic athletes in lieu of passports and visas, and the Olympic team entered West Germany without incident.[5]

Although the willingness of the Rhodesian Front government to tolerate considerable symbolic compromises surprised the IOC, the isolated regime probably did seek to acquire some soft legitimacy from competition in the Olympic Games. After Rhodesia's exclusion from the 1972 Olympics, Smith sent a letter to outgoing IOC President Avery Brundage, a strong proponent of Rhodesian participation in Munich. Smith thanked Brundage on behalf of 'all in this world who believe in maintaining standards of morality and decency'. He praised the 'growing determination' to oppose the 'permissive society with its double standards'. Smith stated that although he was an enthusiastic sportsman, he was convinced that politics had no place in sport.[6] Smith's letter reinforced the notion that participation in non-political amateur sport was part of a broader notion of 'civilized society', with its Imperial and racial undertones. Four years earlier, in 1968, Smith had called the Rhodesian invitation to Mexico City a 'wonderful breakthrough for Rhodesia', and fundraising advertisements by the Rhodesian National Olympic Committee (NOC) called Smith 'Olympic Supporter No. 1' (*Rhodesia Herald*, February 10, 1968; Little 2005, 52). The expulsion of Rhodesia from the Olympic Games reinforced a widely held view among white Rhodesians that they were the victims of a double standard, punished in amateur sport, one area in which the country had a fairly decent record of multiracial cooperation (Strack 1978, 229).

Women and the Rhodesian Olympic Team

Women's sports diffused throughout the British Empire just as boys' and men's sports did. Impromptu matches led to clubs, and then competition among clubs led to regional, national and finally international organizations. Girls and women who had attended school in England brought sports with them throughout the British Empire (Guttmann 1991, 108). The Olympic Games was a gendered institution since its founding in Athens in 1896, and the founder Baron Pierre de Coubertin initially sought to have women excluded from competition. Women's golf and tennis appeared at the Paris Olympics in 1900; not until 1928 in Amsterdam after de Coubertin had retired were track and field and team gymnastics added to the Olympic programme (Guttmann 1991, 163–164). Indeed, the exclusionary tendencies of the IOC against women and working-class athletes encouraged the development of socialist models of sport competition such as the International Workers' Olympic Games between 1925 and 1937, which pressured the IOC to begin a slow (and incomplete) movement to a more democratic structure (Lynskyj 2013, 54–55). Women's sport became, like multiracial sport and opposition to apartheid, a tool of resistance to Imperial conceptions of sport that accompanied the spread of the British Empire.

Although sports remained a man's world, several white women achieved regional and even international fame on the playing field, contributing to the notion that gender norms in sport were not static. Golfer Gabrielle Tomlinson won the Rhodesian title 13 times between 1948 and 1968, although sanctions limited her international competition. She became the first woman to win the Quail's Trophy from the Rhodesia Golf Union in 1974, reflecting an increased openness on the playing field in the later UDI period (Byrom 1980, 28, 30). In squash, Gay Erskine was the Rhodesian champion 14 times between 1963 and 1977, among the top 10 players in the world at the peak of her career. As Rhodesia's squash organization was affiliated to the South African one, unlike golf, Erskine also participated in the South African squash circuit. In 1973, she became the only woman to become Rhodesian Sportsman of the Year during the UDI period, an honour previously won by only one other woman: Margot Boileau in hockey in 1956 (Byrom 1980, 102–103, 105). Among women field hockey players, Anthea Stewart stood out among a highly successful crowd, and she was on Zimbabwe's 1980 Olympic team where the country won the first Olympic gold medal ever given for women's field hockey, perhaps as a result of soft competition due to the US boycott (Byrom 1980, 111, 113). The Rhodesian tennis pair of Patricia Pretorius and Brenda Kirk won the 1972 Federation Cup in international women's tennis; they competed for South Africa, where they had emigrated to avoid travel restrictions on Rhodesian passports (Byrom 1980, 122, 124–126). Lucie Olver also achieved international acclaim in women's lawn bowls.

In addition to a number of prominent sportswomen, Rhodesia also claimed several high-level women sport administrators. In 1973, the IOC launched a study to determine the role of women in leadership positions within international sporting organizations as a result of criticism that arose at the 1973 Olympic Congress. The resulting 1974 report revealed that in the International Amateur Athletic Federation, Rhodesia was one of only four countries (the others being Belize, Haiti and Malawi) to have a female secretary general, E. Gillman. No national athletic association had a woman as president, and female vice-presidents and board members were rare. The secretary general of Rhodesia's archery federation was also a woman, M. Potter (IOC 1974, 402, 413). Compared to cricket and rugby, however, sports in which women excelled, such as squash, tennis, golf and hockey, were comparatively small potatoes. They were also among the most racially segregated.

According to the IOC commission of enquiry that toured Rhodesia in 1974, not a single multiracial team existed in women's field hockey anywhere in the country except at the University of Rhodesia. The commission also found that tennis, another sport in which white women excelled, was almost entirely segregated (IOC Investigating Report, 23 October 1974).

The influences of the British culture on Rhodesian sport were evident not only in the racial make-up of the Rhodesian Olympic team, but in its gender composition as well. In 1960, 13-year old Dottie Sutcliffe competed for the Federation of Rhodesia and Nyasaland in Rome, competing in freestyle swimming and backstroke events (*Bulawayo Chronicle*, July 4, 1960). Sutcliffe's participation was overshadowed by another female Rhodesian swimmer, Natalie Steward of Bulawayo, who won silver and bronze medals when she competed for Great Britain (*Bulawayo Chronicle*, August 30, 1960, 1). Despite Rhodesian efforts to assert an independent sporting identity separate from Great Britain or South Africa, especially after UDI in 1965, the country claimed among its own sportsmen and women those who competed abroad.

Media coverage of the Rhodesian Olympic teams referred to the female members of the team in gendered terms, often as the wives of sportsmen who introduced them to sports. Only one woman was chosen for the 1968 Rhodesian Olympic team: South African-born Joan Mitchell, a mother of four, who was to compete in small-bore shooting. According to an article in the *Sunday Mail* (July 28, 1968), Mitchell's husband competed in the sport and she decided to start a small-bore club with several local housewives in 1957 by holding raffles and bingo sessions. As Cheffers (1972, 144) writes, Myra Fowler, a schoolgirl, narrowly missed qualifying for the 1968 Olympic team in pentathlon. Two white women did travel to Munich to compete for Rhodesia in 1972: 15-year-old Christine Meal in freestyle swimming and 17-year-old Jean Fowlds in sprinting, the only female member of the 10-member-strong track and field team. After Rhodesia's ouster from competition just days before the opening ceremonies, the Rhodesian team members were allowed to remain in the Olympic Village and attend the events in which they participated. One international newspaper interviewed Meal and Fowlds after the team's expulsion, commenting that Meal was 'hiding her sadness behind a shopping bag and a smile' (*Saratoga Herald-Tribune*, August 24, 1972, E1). Despite success on the playing field, media characterizations of women's sport perpetuated familiar gender stereotypes.

No African women were ever selected for any of the Rhodesian Olympic teams chosen between 1960 and 1972, although all included African men. A letter to the editor of the *Rhodesia Herald* criticized the president of the Rhodesian Amateur Athletics Union for stating that sport in Rhodesia was completely multiracial: 'an African girl, who attends a private school near Marandellas and who recently broke the junior inter-schools high jump record, is debarred ... not only from taking part in [an athletic meeting], but also from attending as a spectator' (*Rhodesia Herald*, April 16, 1971). Because of reduced opportunities for training and competition, women's sports for black athletes remained underdeveloped for the duration of UDI. In an unpublished history, familiar gender stereotypes characterized African women's sport in the country. 'By custom, African women are retiring and have not been so forthcoming in sport as their menfolk' (Kennedy 1970, 3–4). The first woman to take part in a multiracial event was recorded a schoolgirl named M. Dowa, who won the 100 yard national championship in 1959, followed by M. Muchenwa who won the javelin championship in 1961. Not until 1970 did an African woman win a national championship when Njekwa Kwabisa won the 400- and 800-metre championships. In assessing black Rhodesian women's performances in long-distance running, the study wondered 'whether they will compete after leaving school or whether,

THE BRITISH WORLD AND THE FIVE RINGS

like so many European girls, will disappear from the track to marry' (Kennedy 1970). Kwabisa, who was 14 years old according to news reports, was excluded from training for the 1972 Olympic team 'for her own good', and, as the only African girl in the group, would have been 'out of her depth' in Munich due to her age (*Rhodesia Herald*, May 25, 1971). The unpublished study concluded that African women would likely perform their best at longer distance races.

Women also successfully competed on Rhodesia's Paralympic and disability sport teams, despite the charity-driven and institutional nature of disability services in the colonial period and the organization of disability sport around private sports clubs (Devlieger 1995; *The Zimbabwean*, May 14, 2010). One of the first athletes in the Stoke Mandeville Games in the UK, the precursor to the Paralympics, immigrated to Rhodesia in 1957. The athlete, Margaret Harriman, won numerous medals at the first Paralympic Games in Rome in 1960 representing the only African team at the Games. Later, disability athletes like Lynn Gilchrist and Sandra James continued Rhodesia's extremely successful Paralympic streak in Tokyo in 1964, Tel Aviv in 1968, and Heidelberg in 1972 and at the Empire and Commonwealth Games in Perth, Australia, in 1962. Because of the comparatively high entry costs to disability sport and the skeletal nature of disability services in Rhodesia, disability sport was virtually entirely composed of white athletes and Rhodesia never sent a multiracial disability athletic team to an international sporting event during UDI (Novak 2008, 50–54; Little 2011, 198; Novak 2014, 50). Unlike the Olympics, however, the Paralympics were founded on a radically integrative alternative to Imperial sport and seen as medical or humanitarian in nature by the British government (see Howe 2008, 23–24; Brittain 2011, 1167).

Conclusion

The isolation of Rhodesia from international sports was a paradox, as exclusion occurred earlier in sports that were the most multiracial, while cricket and rugby proved far more difficult. Rhodesia's isolation from international competition may actually have *increased* sporting segregation as it made the country's sports teams more dependent on South African competition. Rhodesia inherited its sporting obsession from Great Britain, fuelling its quest to assert a national sporting identity on the international stage, yet Great Britain was perhaps the greatest obstacle to Rhodesian international competition, by preventing Rhodesian athletes from entering and embargoing Rhodesian passports. Rhodesia's exclusion from the Olympic Games was the most dramatic clash of these ironies, particularly because, unlike South Africa, Rhodesia's Olympic teams were multiracial. Yet, racial discrimination *did* exist in Rhodesian sport because of the decentralized organization of sport around private clubs and because of secondary discrimination in schools, public swimming pools and sporting venues.

Rhodesia inherited an Imperial conception of sport from Britain, one that conceived of sport in a gendered, racially exclusionary manner, even long after such conceptions had eroded elsewhere in the (former) Empire. Some African and women athletes were nonetheless able to overcome these barriers, but they were the exception and not the rule. The effects of racial discrimination in Rhodesian sport were still visible in independent Zimbabwe, especially in cricket and rugby, where white players continued to dominate in the national team well into the post-colonial period. The Zimbabwean sports that were previously the most intertwined with South African sport, such as cricket and rugby, suffered from a lack of competition with South African athletes for the remainder of the apartheid era. After independence, the sports pages of Zimbabwe's newspapers were filled with articles of games against Uganda and Tanzania, rather than against South Africa or Australia. The importance of international sporting contacts for showcasing the national team and providing legitimacy for the government are also still visible: in 2003, England refused to play cricket in Zimbabwe as part of the Cricket World Cup, because of political opposition to the deteriorating state of affairs in President Robert Mugabe's Zimbabwe after the 2002 elections (Dabscheck 2005, 62–64).

The expulsion of Rhodesia from the Olympic Games was more than a historically contingent artefact: it was a founding episode of the movement to incorporate principles of human rights in sport competition. The most immediate consequence of the Rhodesian expulsion from the Olympics was that it held the African bloc of NOCs together for another cycle. The African boycott of the 1976 Montreal Olympics over New Zealand's presence has long perplexed observers; New Zealand was the most flagrant violator of cricket and rugby sanctions on South Africa, but these were not Olympic sports (Mzali 1976, 463–465). To the African NOCs, however, cricket and rugby were two of the most important symbols of South Africa's apartheid establishment, just as they were in Rhodesia. The financial loss of the Montreal Olympics caused Canada to strenuously work to prevent a boycott of the 1978 Commonwealth Games in Edmonton, Alberta, as African countries made up nearly half the participants. Canada negotiated a consensus document among Australia, Great Britain and New Zealand to sever sporting relations with South Africa: the Gleneagles Agreement, which led to South Africa's final expulsion from cricket and rugby (Novak 2013, 47). In 1981, the Olympic Charter was revised to state that the practice of sport was a human right and fair play required non-discrimination, principles originally reflected in the Gleneagles Agreement. It was a visible repudiation of the Imperial myth of sport, and, in this, the Rhodesian case study was a formative event and not simply a historically contingent footnote.

Disclosure statement

No potential conflict of interest was reported by the author.

Notes

1. See also, Untitled Clipping, October 1971, British National Archives, FCO 7/672.
2. Letter, Hennings to Young, 28 January 1968, FCO 25/549. The memorandum in question questioned Rhodesia's offer to host the world welterweight boxing championship between a black American Curtis Cokes and a white South African Willie Ludick.
3. Note, A.D. Brighty to Faber, 13 February 1968, FCO 36/317.
4. Circular, Protest Against Racism in the Olympic Games, International Campaign against Racism in Sport, July 1972, Avery Brundage Papers, University of Illinois.
5. West Germany was not yet a member of the UN (it did not join until 1973), and so it was not formally bound to accept UN sanctions on Rhodesia. However, the country pledged to comply in a note sent to the secretary general when the sanctions were first installed (Novak 2006, 1380, 1386, n. 48, 2013, 34).
6. Letter, Ian Smith to Avery Brundage, 30 October 1972, Avery Brundage Papers, University of Illinois.

References

Alegi, Peter. 2010. *African Soccerscapes: How a Continent Changed the World's Game*. Athens: Ohio University Press.
Brittain, Ian. 2011. "South Africa, Apartheid and the Paralympic Games." *Sport in Society* 14 (9): 1165–1181.

Byrom, Glen. 1980. *Rhodesian Sports Profiles, 1907–1979*. Bulawayo: Books of Zimbabwe.

Cheffers, John. 1972. *A Wilderness of Spite: Rhodesia Denied*. New York: Vantage.

Cheffers, John. 1992. *Shallow Were the Giants*. Dubuque, IA: Brown and Benchmark.

Conway, Daniel. 2012. *Masculinities, Militarisation, and the End Conscription Campaign: War Resistance in Apartheid South Africa*. New York: Manchester University Press.

Dabscheck, Braham. 2005. "Out on a No Ball: Industrial Relations in Zimbabwean Cricket." *Sporting Traditions* 22 (1): 57–79.

Denoon, Donald, and Balam Nyeko. 1972. *Southern Africa since 1800*. New York: Praeger.

Devlieger, P. 1995. "From Self-Help to Charity in Disability Service: The Jairos Jiri Association in Zimbabwe." *Disability & Society* 10 (1): 39–48.

Giulianotti, Richard. 2004. "Between Colonialism, Independence and Globalization: Football in Zimbabwe." In *Football in Africa: Conflict, Conciliation and Community*, edited by Gary Armstrong and Richard Giulianotti, 80–102. New York: Palgrave Macmillan.

Godwin, Peter, and Ian Hancock. 1995. *'Rhodesians Never Die': The Impact of War and Political Change on White Rhodesia, c. 1970–1980*. Harare: Baobab Books.

Grundlingh, Albert. 1996. "Playing for Power? Rugby, Afrikaner Nationalism and Masculinity in South Africa, c. 1900–1970." In *Making Men: Rugby and Nationalist Identity*, edited by John Nauright and Timothy J. L. Chandler, 181–204. Portland, OR: Frank Cass.

Guttmann, Allen. 1978. *From Ritual to Record: The Nature of Modern Sports*. New York: Columbia University Press.

Guttmann, Allen. 1991. *Women's Sports: A History*. New York: Columbia University Press.

Guttmann, Allen. 1994. *Games and Empires: Modern Sports and Cultural Imperialism*. New York: Columbia University Press.

Howe, P. D. 2008. *The Cultural Politics of the Paralympic Movement: Through an Anthropological Lens*. New York: Routledge.

IOC (International Olympic Committee). 1974. "Women in the World's Sport Organizations." *Olympic Review*, September–October, 83–84.

Kaler, Amy. 2003. *Running after Pills: Politics, Gender, and Contraception in Colonial Zimbabwe*. Portsmouth, NH: Heinemann.

Kennedy, Philip W. 1970. "Rhodesian Track and Field 1970." Unpublished paper, Avery Brundage Papers, University of Illinois.

Little, Charles. 2005. "Preventing 'a Wonderful Breakthrough for Rhodesia': The British Government and the Exclusion of Rhodesia from the 1968 Mexico Olympics." *Olympika* 7: 47–68.

Little, Charles. 2009. "Rebellion, Race and Rhodesia: International Cricketing Relations with Rhodesia during UDI." *Sport in Society* 12 (4): 523–536.

Little, Charles. 2011. "The Sports Boycott against Rhodesia Reconsidered." *Sport in Society* 14 (2): 193–207.

Lowry, Donal. 1997. "'White Woman's Country': Ethel Tawse Jollie and the Making of White Rhodesia." *Journal of Southern African Studies* 23 (2): 259–281.

Lowry, Donal. 2007. "The Impact of Anti-Communism on White Rhodesian Political Culture, ca. 1920s–1980." *Cold War History* 7 (2): 169–194.

Lynskyj, Helen Jefferson. 2013. *Gender Politics and the Olympic Industry*. New York: Palgrave Macmillan.

Mackenzie, John M. 1987. "Hunting in Eastern and Central Africa in the Late Nineteenth Century, with Special Reference to Zimbabwe." In *Sport in Africa: Essays in Social History*, edited by William J. Baker and J. A. Mangan, 172–195. Teaneck, NJ: Holmes and Meier.

Maclean, Joy. 1974. *The Guardians: A Story of Rhodesia's Outposts and the Men and Women Who Served in Them*. Bulawayo: Books of Rhodesia.

Mager, Anne Kelk. 2010. *Beer, Sociability, and Masculinity in South Africa*. Bloomington: Indiana University Press.

Mason, Philip. 1962. *The Birth of a Dilemma: The Conquest and Settlement of Rhodesia*. London: Oxford University Press.

McDevitt, Patrick F. 2004. *May the Best Man Win: Sport, Masculinity, and Nationalism in Great Britain and the Empire, 1880–1935*. New York: Palgrave Macmillan.

Merritt, Christopher. 2009. *Sport, Space and Segregation: Politics and Society in Pietermaritzburg*. Scottsville: University of KwaZulu-Natal Press.

Merritt, Christopher, and John Nauright. 1998. "South Africa." In *The Imperial Game: Cricket, Culture, and Society*, edited by Brian Stoddart and Keith A. Sandiford, 55–78. New York: Manchester University Press.

Mzali, Mohamed. 1976. "Mr. Mzali: I am Sorry About the Boycott of the Montreal Olympic Games." *Olympic Review* 107–108: 463–465.

Nauright, John. 1996. "Colonial Manhood and Imperial Race Virility: British Responses to Post-Boer War Colonial Rugby Tours." In *Making Men: Rugby and Nationalist Identity*, edited by John Nauright and Timothy J. L. Chandler, 121–139. Portland, OR: Frank Cass.

Nelson, Harold. 1975. *Area Handbook for Southern Rhodesia*. Washington, DC: American University Foreign Area Studies.

Novak, Andrew. 2006. "Rhodesia's 'Rebel and Racist' Olympic Team: Athletic Glory, National Legitimacy, and the Clash of Politics and Sport." *International Journal of the History of Sport* 23 (8): 1369–1388.

Novak, Andrew. 2008. "Politics and the Paralympic Games: Disability Sport in Rhodesia-Zimbabwe." *Journal of Olympic History* 16 (1): 47–55.

Novak, Andrew. 2012. "Sport and Racial Discrimination in Colonial Zimbabwe: A Reanalysis." *International Journal of the History of Sport* 29 (6): 850–867.

Novak, Andrew. 2013. "Averting an African Boycott: British Prime Minister Edward Heath and Rhodesian Participation in the Munich Olympics." *Britain and the World* 6 (1): 27–47. doi: 10.3366/brw.2013.0076.

Novak, Andrew. 2014. "Disability Sport in Sub-Saharan Africa: From Economic Development to Uneven Empowerment." *Disability and the Global South* 1 (1): 44–63.

O'Meara, Patrick. 1979. "Rhodesia/Zimbabwe: Guerrilla Warfare or Political Settlement?" In *Southern Africa: The Continuing Crisis*, edited by Gwendolen M. Carter and Patrick O'Meara, 18–56. Bloomington: Indiana University Press.

Pape, J. 1990. "Black and White: The 'Perils of Sex' in Colonial Zimbabwe." *Journal of Southern African Studies* 16: 699–720.

Parsons, Timothy H. 2004. *Race, Resistance, and the Boy Scout Movement in British Colonial Africa*. Athens: Ohio University Press.

Ranger, Terence. 1987. "Pugilism and Pathology: African Boxing and the Black Urban Experience in Southern Rhodesia." In *Sport in Africa: Essays in Social History*, edited by William J. Baker and J. A. Mangan, 196–212. Teaneck, NJ: Holmes and Meier.

Rogers, Cyril A., and C. Frantz. 1973. *Racial Themes in Southern Rhodesia: The Attitudes and Behavior of the White Population*. Port Washington, NY: Kennikat Press.

Smith, Maureen. 2008. "Examining 'The Rhodesian Affair': The IOC and African Politics in the 1970s." Proceedings of the International Symposium for Olympic Research.

Soldatow, Sasha. 1980. *Politics of the Olympics*. New South Wales: Cassell Press.

Stapleton, Timothy. 2011. *African Police and Soldiers in Colonial Zimbabwe, 1923–80*. Rochester, NY: University of Rochester Press.

Strack, Harry R. 1978. *Sanctions: The Case of Rhodesia*. Syracuse, NY: Syracuse University Press.

Stuart, Ossie. 1996. "Players, Workers, Protestors: Social Change and Soccer in Colonial Zimbabwe." In *Sport, Identity and Ethnicity*, edited by Jeremy MacClancy, 167–180. Oxford: Berg.

Summers, Carol. 1994. *From Civilization to Segregation: Social Ideals and Social Control in Southern Rhodesia, 1890–1934*. Athens: Ohio University Press.

Tanser, G. H. 1974. *A Scantling of Time: The Story of Salisbury, Rhodesia, 1890–1900*. Salisbury: Pioneer Head.

Winch, Jonty. 1983. *Cricket's Rich Heritage: A History of Rhodesian and Zimbabwean Cricket, 1890–1982*. Bulawayo: Books of Zimbabwe.

Winch, Jonty. 2008. "There Were a Fine Manly Lot of Fellows': Cricket, Rugby and Rhodesian Society during William Minton's Administration, 1896–1914." *Sport in History* 28 (4): 583–604.

Wood, J. R. T. 2004. *So Far and No Further: Rhodesia's Bid for Independence during the Retreat from Empire, 1959–65*. Victoria: Trafford.

The 'British World', other worlds, and the five rings: possibilities for trans-imperial histories and historical 'what ifs'

Mark Dyreson

Departments of Kinesiology and History, The Pennsylvania State University, University Park, PA, USA

> In the early 1890s an ardent British imperialist proposed a 'Pan-Britannic Olympics' that included not only the British Empire but the USA in a plan to use sport to unite the English-speaking peoples of the globe into a world-ruling coalition. While that proposal was eventually bested by the Baron Pierre de Coubertin's movement that created an even more inclusive modern Olympics, the sentiments of the 'Pan-Britannic' scheme became in embroiled in debates over the national and imperial uses of international sport. Pondering the role of Coubertin's Olympics in forging a variety of imperial and national identities within the British Empire while also employing speculative alternative histories reveals the complex transnational and trans-imperial dimensions of the Olympics in modern global history.

In the last decade of the nineteenth century, an obscure British imperialist envisioned that in the near future the 'many lands' of the globe might well be ruled by 'one people', the English-speaking denizens of imperial 'Greater Britain' and the United States (Cooper 1891a, 458). John Astley Cooper, an ardently imperial Briton who spent his childhood in Australia and his adolescence and adulthood in England, argued that in order to fully assume the duties of global command, these world-ruling 'one people' needed an institution to remind them of their common bonds and commingled interests (Llewellyn 2011; Mangan 1985; Moore 1988, 1991). Divided into a multitude of distinct polities and dispersed to the far corners of the earth, this heterogeneous band of English speakers could only meet their leadership duties if they remembered the essential Englishness that animated their many but related cultures, whether they had been born in the original homelands of the British Isles or in the far-flung realms of North America, Africa, Asia or the Antipodes (Cooper 1891a, 1891b, 1891c, 1895).

Cooper proposed that a 'Pan-Britannic Festival' composed of many cultural elements but grounded especially in sporting contests could serve as precisely the sort of institution that would make the twentieth-century world into a harmonious planet-wide civilization ruled by English speakers. Cooper manifested a remarkable devotion to philhellenism in his scheme. The Olympic festival of ancient Greece, or at least the *fin de siècle* Anglo-American interpretation of this cultural artefact, functioned as Cooper's fundamental template. In his scheme as the original Olympics had provided the 'one people' of 'many lands' that comprised ancient Greek civilization with regular reminders of their essential 'Greekness' and energized their leadership over a polyglot ancient world, so too would the Pan-Britannic Festival crystalize the essence of 'Englishness' (or, perhaps, 'Britishness') into an elixir that when consumed in quadrennial doses would stiffen the spines of the English-speaking leaders of a polyglot modern world (Cooper 1891a, 1891b, 1891c, 1895).

Cooper built his scheme in the pages of the leading British newspapers and magazines of the era. His design cultivated a lively debate that spanned several years. As the proposal matured, he dropped many of the artistic, scientific and technological aspects that had been portions of his original plan and focused on the sporting aspects, including the 'muscular Christian' spirit he thought would animate the broad Protestant evangelical sentiments to which he believed his 'one people' subscribed (Cooper 1891a, 1891b, 1891c, 1895). In spite of criticisms from various quarters within the British Empire he kept the emerging American Empire enfolded in his scheme. When a Canadian ally pleaded with Cooper to exclude the USA on the grounds that the 'greatest difficulty we in Canada have is to preserve our nationality intact from American aggression', Cooper insisted that his 'Olympic' plan must include every tribe from the English-speaking 'race'. Even the USA, which seemed to play the role of Sparta in the analogies of many adherents of Pan-Britannic dreams to England's Athens, had to be included for the project to work, Cooper (1895, 427–431) insisted.

In spite of the spell that philhellenism clearly cast over the enterprise, Cooper contended that his brainchild would not be a narrow exercise in antiquarianism but rather a thoroughly modern endeavour.

> With regard to the assertion that the proposed Britannic and English-speaking festival may in course of time prove to be the Olympian games – and, as such, a unifying force – of a larger world than the Greek, let me repudiate here once and for all the feeble insinuation and witless charge that we are trying to bring about a slavish and ridiculous imitation of the Greek institution. (Cooper 1895, 427)

While like the ancient Greek games the Pan-Britannic festival would feature athletics, Cooper explained that it would not merely reproduce antiquated events but promote modern track-and-field disciplines supplemented by copious doses of cricket and crew (Cooper 1891a, 1891b, 1891c, 1895).

In the short term it was not Cooper's Pan-Britannic Festival that ultimately created a thriving international sporting spectacle that drew sustenance from the ancient Greek model but the Baron Pierre de Coubertin's Olympic Games that began in Athens in 1896 – as the debate over Cooper's scheme in the Anglo-American world ground to an inconclusive finish. The French aristocrat's plan had, of course, the attraction of a much more inclusive target audience, incorporating not only the English-speaking 'race' but much of the rest of the West at the outset, with pretensions of drawing an even more inclusive set of international participants in the future (MacAloon 1981; Young 1996). Scholars have linked Cooper's plan with the emergence, nearly four decades later, of the British Empire Games, first held in Hamilton, Ontario, Canada, in 1930, which became, in 1954, the Commonwealth Games – events in which the USA played no role whatsoever (Gorman 2010; Moore 1991).

Ultimately, defining 'Britishness' and British identities in a renovated Olympic scheme ripe with rich 'symbolic and narrative-performing properties', as the Olympic scholars Erik Nielsen and Matthew P. Llewellyn (2015) have observed in the introduction to this collection, compelled Greater Britain to confront more than just the 'one people' from 'many lands' on whom Cooper had focused his unrealized Pan-Britannic dreams. These insightful essays remind readers, however, that Cooper's scheme was far from the mere pipe dream of a solitary imperialist. In fact, as these essays reveal, the mostly white 'settler nations' – Canada, Australia and New Zealand – that formed what scholars have dubbed the 'inner core' of the 'British World' (Buckner and Francis 2005) sometimes employed the Olympics in precisely the fashion that Cooper hoped that they would use his

Pan-Britannic festival, to create symbols and narratives for the invigoration and spread of British civilization across the modern globe (Nielsen and Llewellyn 2015).

Unlike Cooper's proposed Pan-Britannic games, the Olympics eventually required the 'British World' to confront other worlds in the struggle to maintain dominion. Indeed, as Nielsen and Llewellyn articulate, as 'arguably the most important sporting "nation" Britain had to accept the presence of outsiders into the world of sport, which they had previously dominated' (Nielsen and Llewellyn 2015). As the resistance of many Britons to the inclusion of the USA into Cooper's Pan-Britannic extravaganza betrays, however, acceptance of 'American World' and other nations and empires came neither quickly nor gracefully. In his masterful *Rule Britannia*, Llewellyn (2012) has demonstrated that beyond the ranks of a cohort of aristocratic imperialists who promoted the Olympics as a mechanism for reviving faith in the vitality of the Empire when many worried that British hegemony had greatly waned, the 'Home Nations' of the British Isles mostly ignored the games from the renaissance in the 1890s through the end of the Second World War, a half century in which even London's service as host in two Olympian spectacles could not kindle a deep public passion for the games.

While the Empire's metropole in the British Isles ran behind the rest of the world in catching Olympic fever for more than half century, the rest of 'British World', as the essays contained in this collection reveal, welcomed the games as mechanisms for negotiating the competing challenges of their national and imperial identities, as opportunities for the expression of local politics in both mounting challenges to and constructing embraces of 'Britishness', as stages for redefining and perpetuating ideologies of race and as occasions for negotiating power between peripheries and core. In focusing on these issues *The 'British World' and the Five Rings* opens the door for a new set of transnational, or, perhaps, trans-imperial studies of those themes in other 'worlds', the American, the French, the German, the Japanese, the Soviet and now the Chinese come to mind immediately. While in many ways quite distinct from the British Empire, each of these entities contained metropoles and peripheries, struggled with contesting notions of imperialism and nationalism, and constructed notions of racial and ethnic identities through sport. A contrast between the long war of Ireland to extricate its Olympic prospects from 'British World' and the similar struggle of Korea within that Japanese empire might well prove quite instructive (Ok 2007). French incorporations of colonial athletes onto national teams, such as the 1928 marathon victory of the Algerian Abdel El Oaufi for France, provide a rich vein of comparisons to British practices (Terret and Roger 2009). Comparisons of the multiple nationalisms within the Soviet orbit, Ukrainian, Belarussian, and Georgian versus Russian, to the multiple nationalisms within the home nations, Scottish, Welsh, and Cornish versus English, could prove instructive (Edelman 1993; Llewellyn 2012; Riordan 1977).

The contrast of 'British World' to 'American World' represents one of the most fertile potential lines of inquiry for illuminating these themes. Clearly, the construction in Olympic arenas of racial identities in the two states differed markedly. While in the late nineteenth century and early twentieth century the idea of race carried cultural and political designations as well as representing biological and evolutionary categories – hence Cooper's use of the 'Anglo-Saxon race' as contrasted to the employment of an 'African race' – in Olympian realms, American commentataries on race differed markedly from British viewpoints. The 'inner core' or 'white dominions' of the British Empire developed an abiding interest in using the Olympics to trumpet the prowess of Anglo-Saxonist 'whiteness' in imperial affairs, as several of the essays in this collection illumine (Barney and Heine 2015; Kohe 2015; Nielsen 2015).

Similar notions of Anglo-Saxon superiority certainly swirled about the USA during the early decades of the modern Olympic Movement. However, in the USA unbridled Anglo-Saxonism had to confront an Olympic reality in which a much broader 'whiteness' won the nation glory in the international contests. Athletes especially from Irish, but also from a multitude of other European, lineages garnered Olympic medals for the American team. The sheer weight of Olympic medals harvested by immigrants and their progeny for the USA made the 'melting pot' motif a central vehicle of interpretation of American sporting prowess, pushing to the side counter-arguments about Anglo-Saxon and later Nordic racial superiority (Dyreson 1998, 2001, 2009). In fact, the rabid Celtic nationalism that flourished in the USA helped to fuel Ireland's passionate resistance to incorporation into Great Britain's Olympic teams until independence altered the Olympic landscape (Dyreson 1998; Llewellyn 2012, 2015).

US teams also employed non-European athletes much earlier than 'British World' squads. As early as 1904 African Americans won Olympic medals for the USA. In 1908 at London – of all places – John Taylor became the first African American gold medallist. Persons of colour first appeared decades later on 'British World' squads. The first Afro-British medallist was the sprinter McDonald Bailey who in 1952 won a bronze medal in the 100-meters at Helsinki. Daley Thompson became the first black gold medallist for Great Britain in 1980 when he triumphed in the decathlon at Moscow, a feat he repeated at Los Angeles in 1984 (Cashmore 1983, 2014).

Among the nations of the 'white core', Canada fielded black Olympians much earlier. In 1928, middle-distance runner Phil Edwards became the first Afro-Canadian medallist with an 800-meter bronze medal (Humber 2014). In South Africa, some contemporary historical accounts claim that black South African participation began at the 1904 St Louis Olympic marathon when two members of the Tswana nation, Len Tau and John Mashiani, entered the race. The two runners, however, allegedly misidentified by the Americans as Zulus, were not representatives sent by South Africa but rather players in the popular Boer War re-enactment staged at the world's fair that also housed the Olympics (http://www.sahistory.org.za/topic/south-africa-and-olympic-games; accessed 10 September 2014). This claim, that the two Tswanas actually 'represented' South Africa, strain credulity. Nearly a century later at another American venue, Josiah Thugwane, a black South African, who actually represented the nation became the first black South African medallist when he ran to an unexpected marathon triumph in the 1996 Atlanta Olympic Games (http://www.sahistory.org.za/people/josiah-thugwane; accessed 10 September 2014). In the Antipodes, New Zealand's Valerie Adams (who has a Tongan mother) won gold medals in the shot put in 2008 in Beijing and 2012 in London (http://media.newzealand.com/en/story-ideas/new-zealand-sports-star-valerie-adams/; accessed 10 August 2014). Lisa Carrington (who has a Maori father) won a flat-water canoe gold medal in 2012 in London (http://www.stuff.co.nz/sport/olympics/other-sports/7462462/Small-but-strong-Carrington-lifts-nation; accessed 10 August 2014).

In Australia, Samantha Riley won Olympic swimming medals in 1992 at Barcelona and 1996 in Atlanta. Researching her family genealogy in 2001 she discovered aboriginal ancestors, making her the first indigenous person in her nation to earn an Olympic medal (http://corporate.olympics.com.au/athlete/samantha-riley; accessed 10 August 2014). In the minds of most Australians, however, Cathy Freeman's silver medal in the 400-meter dash in Atlanta in 1996 and gold medal in the same event at Sydney in 2000 represent the first individual medals won by an aboriginal Australian athlete at the Olympics (Nova Peris [field hockey player, runner and Senator for the Northern Territory in the 44th Australian parliament] won a gold medal as part of the Australian field hockey

THE BRITISH WORLD AND THE FIVE RINGS

team at Atlanta as well). Freeman's feats occurred before Riley discovered her ancestry and Freeman's well-known aboriginal identity shaped massive Australian discourses about racial barriers and social conditions in her home nation and around the world (Bruce and Wensing 2012).

This brief survey of Olympic 'firsts' by representatives of non-European groups competing for 'British World' and 'American World' teams should not be read as a celebration of American racial egalitarianism or a condemnation of British laggardness in regards to civil rights. In discourses over how 'manliness' (and after the Great War 'womanliness') and 'civilization' played out in Olympic arenas, Americans could in spite of the greater ethnic heterogeneity of their teams still use sport to reinforce the racial apparatus that promote white hegemony in their social structures (Bederman 1995; Hartmann 2003). Still, the early inclusion and larger numbers of non-white athletes on American Olympian teams made discourses about 'white settler' superiority more difficult to craft in the US cultural context. Instead, in 'American World' Olympic racial discourses tended to stress progress towards the ideal of equality at the expense of more complex, nuanced and accurate interpretations of race relations (Baker 1986; Wiggins 1997).

Interestingly, Pan-Britannic dreamer Cooper understood these varying 'racial' dynamics in the English-speaking world as early as the 1890s. To his fellow Angles and Saxons in the Empire who objected to sporting engagements with Americans on the grounds that the 'polyglot' nature of the USA stood as grounds for excluding it from the Anglo-Saxon fraternity of nations, Cooper proclaimed instead that the American 'fusion of races' melded a society still Anglo-Saxon at its essential core. While Cooper worried that the new Olympics, 'open to the whole world, to Fins [sic], Poles, Neopolitans, Greeks, and Frenchmen', might not effectively serve the interests of reinforcing a Pan-Britannic coalition to rule the globe, he was convinced that a USA inhabited by Finns and Poles, Russians and Italians, and Greeks and the French remained dominated by Anglo-Saxon institutions and sensibilities that made the multi-ethnic US part of the English-speaking tribe of 'one people' (Cooper 1895, 428–440).

Similar discourses about ethnic and national identities, as *The 'British World' and the Five Rings* demonstrates, eventually garnered attention in every realm of 'British World'. While Britain slowly warmed over the course of the last decade of the nineteenth century and the first five decades of the twentieth century to the prospect of the Olympics as a forum for the development of symbolic narratives of national identity, other domains within the 'British World' seized upon the Olympics as a crucial modern testing ground. Australia and Canada in particular gravitated to the Olympics at the beginning of the modern revival and have used them to locate their places not only within the Empire but also in broader international contexts (Barney and Heine 2015; Nielsen 2015). Other units of the Empire followed suit over the course of the twentieth century (Hunt 2015; Kohe 2015; Novak 2015).

Interestingly, while Britain ranks third in the overall historic Olympic medal count, behind only the USA and the now defunct Soviet Union (enhancing Britain's prospects of rising to number two since it is highly unlikely that Soviet Empire will reanimate) with 806 medals, the two less-populous dominions have won a combined 928 medals (480 for Australia and 448 for Canada). The rest of the 'inner core', New Zealand and South Africa, has also done quite well in Olympic contests, earning 100 and 76 medals, respectively. South Africa's total is quite respectable given that the global furore over apartheid led to a more than three decade ban from the Olympics between the Rome games of 1960 and the Barcelona games of 1992 (http://en.wikipedia.org/wiki/All-time_Olympic_Games_medal_table; accessed 10 August 2014). Most historic comparisons of medal counts by

THE BRITISH WORLD AND THE FIVE RINGS

British or American interpreters generally concentrate US superiority and UK inferiority. Since 1896, the USA has garnered 2681 medals to 806 for the UK, building over a bit more than a century an enormous lead of 1875 medals (http://en.wikipedia.org/wiki/All-time_ Olympic_Games_medal_table; accessed 10 August 2014).

Sometimes, however, if historians ponder 'what if' scenarios that did not happen, a very interesting set of alternative perspectives emerges. What if Cooper's scheme had borne more immediate fruit and the British Empire had been linked in a Pan-Britannic sporting allegiance before the emergence of Coubertin's Olympian alternative? What if that allegiance had sparked broader support in the motherland and the dominions for the creation of a Pan-Britannic team to compete in Coubertin's spectacle in order to challenge 'American World' and the other rising and falling empires of the early twentieth century? What if the multitude of nationalisms that roiled the so-called United Kingdom and its Empire had been satiated in the crucible of Pan-Britannic athletic wars and at Coubertin's Olympian temple the British came garbed in uniforms of 'British World'? Certainly these 'what if' scenarios, while implausible, were not necessarily impossible given the terrain on which Great Britain built its Olympic enterprise. Taking the roster of nations at Glasgow's 2014 Commonwealth Games as potential members of a 'British World' team that could have potentially survived into the twenty-first century provides a very different reading of 'national' athletic prowess of the course of modern Olympic history (http://www. glasgow2014.com/; accessed 22 August 2014).

Empowered by the 'white settler nations' strong performances over more than a century of Olympic contests and bolstered by the more recent rise to prominence in track-and-field events of former colonies such as Kenya and Jamaica, 'British World's historic medal haul rises to 2199 approaching the USA's commanding total and closing the overall gap between 'Greater' Britain and the USA from 1875 to 482. Indulging in an even more controversial 'what if', keeping Ireland in the orbit of 'British World', would add another 28 Olympic medals to the Empire's total and cut the American lead to 454 (http://en. wikipedia.org/wiki/All-time_Olympic_Games_medal_table; accessed 10 August 2014).

In such a 'what if' scenario it might not be China rising as the great rival to the USA for twenty-first-century Olympic superiority but the old British Empire's unified team of English-speaking peoples from around the world chasing the USA across the sands of history for 'all-time' Olympic supremacy. The 'nation' of nations that Nielsen and Llewellyn have posited as 'arguably the most important sporting "nation"', might well retain more of that patina into the current epoch (Nielsen and Llewellyn 2015). Were he still alive to see it that prospect might have warmed the heart of Cooper even as his dismay that an Olympics that would reinvigorate the bonds of an English-speaking 'one people' spread over 'many lands' had been lost in those historical sands to a much more multilingual and multicultural Olympic tradition. Instead, as the scholars who crafted these explorations for *The 'British' World and the Five Rings* demonstrate history moved through other channels.

Disclosure statement

No potential conflict of interest was reported by the author.

References

Baker, William J. 1986. *Jesse Owens: An American Life*. New York: Free Press.
Barney, Robert K., and Michael Heine. 2015. "'The Emblem of One United Body … One Great Sporting Maple Leaf': The Olympic Games and Canada's Quest for Self-Identity." *Sport in Society* 18 (7): 816–834. doi:10.1080/17430437.2014.990688.

Bederman, Gail. 1995. *Manliness & Civilization: A Cultural History of Gender and Race in the United States, 1880–1917*. Chicago: University of Chicago Press.

Bruce, Toni, and Emma Wensing. 2012. "The Olympics and Indigenous Peoples: Australia." In *The Palgrave Handbook of Olympic Studies*, edited by Helen Lenskyj and Stephen Wagg, 487–504. New York: Palgrave Macmillan.

Buckner, Phillip Alfred, and R. Douglas Francis. 2005. *Rediscovering the British World*. Calgary: University of Calgary Press.

Cashmore, Ernest. 1983. "Champions of Failure: Black Sportsmen." *Ethnic and Racial Studies* 6 (1): 90–102.

Cashmore, Ernest. 2014. *Black Sportsmen*. London: Routledge.

Cooper, J. Astley. 1891a. "Many Lands – One People. A Criticism and a Suggestion." *Greater Britain*, 15 July, 458–462.

Cooper, J. Astley. 1891b. "The Proposed Pan-Britannic or Pan-Anglian Contest and Festival." *The Times*, 30 October, 3.

Cooper, J. Astley. 1891c. "Sport as a British Bond of Union." *Greater Britain*, 5 August, 507.

Cooper, J. Astley. 1895. "Americans and the Pan-Britannic Movement." *The Nineteenth Century* 38 (September): 426–441.

Dyreson, Mark. 1998. *Making the American Team: Sport, Culture and the Olympic Experience*. Urbana: University of Illinois Press.

Dyreson, Mark. 2001. "American Ideas about Race and Olympic Races from the 1890s to the 1950s: Shattering Myths or Reinforcing Scientific Racism?" *Journal of Sport History* 28 (2): 173–215.

Dyreson, Mark. 2009. *Crafting Patriotism for Global Domination: America at the Olympic Games*. London: Routledge.

Edelman, Robert. 1993. *Serious Fun: A History of Spectator Sports in the USSR*. New York: Oxford University Press.

Gorman, Daniel. 2010. "Amateurism, Imperialism, Internationalism and the First British Empire Games." *International Journal of the History of Sport* 27 (4): 611–634.

Hartmann, Douglas. 2003. *Race, Culture, and the Revolt of the Black Athlete: The 1968 Olympic Protests and Their Aftermath*. Chicago: University of Chicago Press.

Humber, William. 2014. *A Sporting Chance: Achievements of African-Canadian Athletes*. Toronto: Natural Heritage Books.

Hunt, Tom. 2015. "'In Our Case, It Seems Obvious the British Organising Committee Piped the Tune': The Campaign for Recognition of 'Ireland' in the Olympic Movement." *Sport in Society* 18 (7): 835–852. doi:10.1080/17430437.2014.990689.

Kohe, Geoff. 2015. "(Dis)located Olympic Patriots: Sporting Connections, Administrative Communications and Imperial Ether in Interwar New Zealand." *Sport in Society* 18 (7): 800–815. doi:10.1080/17430437.2014.990686.

Llewellyn, Matthew P. 2011. "Prologue: An Indifferent Beginning." *International Journal of the History of Sport* 28 (5): 625–647.

Llewellyn, Matthew P. 2012. *Rule Britannia: Nationalism, Identity and the Modern Olympic Games*. London: Routledge.

Llewellyn, Matthew P. 2015. "For a 'United' Kingdom and a 'Greater' Britain: The British Olympic Association and the Limitations and Contestations of 'Britishness'." *Sport in Society* 18 (7): 765–782. doi:10.1080/17430437.2014.990687.

MacAloon, John. 1981. *This Great Symbol: Pierre de Coubertin and the Origins of the Modern Olympic Games*. Chicago: University of Chicago Press.

Mangan, J. A. 1985. *The Games Ethic and Imperialism: Aspects of the Diffusion of an Ideal*. New York: Viking.

Young, David C. 1996. *The Modern Olympics: A Struggle for Revival*. Baltimore: Johns Hopkins University Press.

Moore, Katharine. 1988. "The Pan-Britannic Festival: A Tangible but Forlorn Expression of Imperial Unity." In *Pleasure, Profit, Proselytism: British Culture at Home and Abroad, 1700–1914*, edited by JA Mangan, 144–162. London: Frank Cass.

Moore, Katharine. 1991. "A Neglected Imperialist: The Promotion of the British Empire in the Writing of John Astley Cooper." *International Journal of the History of Sport* 8 (2): 256–259.

Nielsen, Erik. 2015. "Flights to Empire: Australia's Imperial Engagement with the Olympic Games." *Sport in Society* 18 (7): 783–799. doi:10.1080/17430437.2014.991085.

Nielsen, Erik, and Matthew P. Llewellyn. 2015. "Prologue: Britain, Empire and the Olympic Experience." *Sport in Society* 18 (7): 759–764. doi:10.1080/17430437.2014.991086.

Novak, Andrew. 2015. "Rhodesia and the Olympic Games: Representations of Masculinity, War and Empire." *Sport in Society* 18 (7): 853–867. doi:10.1080/17430437.2014.990691.

Ok, Gwang. 2007. *The Transformation of Modern Korean Sport: Imperialism, Nationalism, Globalization*. Elizabeth, NJ: Hollym.

Riordan, James. 1977. *Sport in Soviet Society: Development of Sport and Physical Education in Russia and the USSR*. Cambridge: Cambridge University Press.

Terret, Theirry, and Anne Roger. 2009. "Managing Colonial Contradictions: French Attitudes toward El Ouafi's 1928 Olympic Victory." *Journal of Sport History* 36 (1): 3–18.

Wiggins, David K. 1997. *Glory Bound: Black Athletes in a White America*. Syracuse, NY: Syracuse University Press.

Index

Note: Page numbers in **bold** represent figures
Page numbers followed by 'n' refer to notes

Aboriginal people 29
Act of Union (1707) 9
Africa: boxers 97; domestic servants 97; sport culture 95–6; women 105
African race 112
Afro-British medallist 113
agency 26
Alderson, H.G. 35, 36, 37
Alexander, W.B. 25
Amateur Athletics Association (AAA) 27–8
Amateur Swimming Union of Australia (ASUA) 33
amateurism 29, 35, 36, 61; meaning of 63
American World 112, 114
Amos, H. 54n
Amsterdam Olympics (1928) 29, 31
Anglo-Saxon: fraternity 114; race 112; superiority 113
annexation of Wales with England (1536) 8–9
anti-British sentiments of Irish athletes 13
Antipodes 43, 113
Association International de Boxe Amateur (AIBA) 81
Athens Intercalated Games (1908), British team 11, **11**
athletes: Canada 66–8; Irish 12, 13; New Zealand 30; non-European in US 113; Pablo rejection as amateur 29; Shepherds Bush Olympic Stadium 67
Australasians, Indigenous 29
Australia 25–41; agency 26; Amateur Swimming Union of Australia (ASUA) 33; authoritarian nations 34–7; Dominions 38; history 25; and imperialism 25; and New Zealand 4; Olympic Games (1900–38) 25–41; Olympic Movement 26, 34, 35, 37; picking Olympic team 26–30; political culture 37; relationship with Britain 25; rugby union 25; specialization 29; swimming 33; swimming medals 113

authoritarian nations, Australian response 34–7
awareness, Canadian national identity 65

Barney, R.K., and Heine, M.H. 4, 58–76
Belich, J., recolonization 25–6
Berlin Games (1936) 36; British Empire team 17
Boer War (1899–1901), and Canada 61–2
Booth, D.G. 4
boxers 97
boxing, Irish Amateur Boxing Association (IABA) 81
Boy Scouting 98
boycotts, sporting 98
British Amateur Athletic Board (BAAB) 89
British Commonwealth of Nations 36, 83
British Conservative Party, party politics 3
British culture, influence on Rhodesian sport 105
British East Africa 34
British Empire 18; Canada in 59; and war 95–107
British Empire Games 30–4; *Morning Bulletin* 31
British Empire team 27; Berlin Games 17
British Olympic Association (BOA) 7–24; and Hanbury-Williams 62, 63
British Olympic team, Irish athletes in 12
British Organizing Committee 77–95
British team 10; Athens Intercalated Games (1908) 11, **11**; and Celtic nations 13; and Gaelic Union 13; making of 13–16
British World, concept 5
Britishness 3, 7–24, 29; Colley on 19; defining 111; Home-Nations 20; limitations and contestations 20–1; political forces 3; and World War I 20; and World War II 20
Brundage, A. 87, 89, 90
Bulletin Officiel (IOC) 79
Burghley, Lord D. 82, 89, 91

INDEX

Canada 4, 27, 113; amateur sport 61; at London Games (1908) 66; athletes 66–8; and Boer War (1899–1901) 61–2; in British Empire 59; Grey 62–5, 70–1, 74; Hanbury-Williams 62–5, **67**; imperial union 59; Maple Leaf 58–76; Marching Team 68, **69**, 75n; national flag, design submissions 71; national identity awareness 65; nationalism 62; Olympic track and field team 65; Olympic Winter Games host (2010) 58; press 71; self-identity 58–76; symbolism 59–61

Canadian Amateur Athletic Federation (CAAF) 63, 64

Canadian Amateur Athletic Union (CAAU) 63, 64

Canadian Olympic team (1908) 68, **68**; Executive Council **73**, 74

Carlton, J. (Jimmy) 31–2

Carroll, P. 84, 85, 86

Casement, Sir R. 15–16

Celtic nations 13

Charter regulations (1933) 79

Chisholm, J. 83

Christianity, Western Education 98

City of London 1, 2

Colley, L. 9, 19

Collins, M. 91

colonial contemplations, and cultural cringe 51–2

Commonwealth Games, Glasgow (2014) 115

Commonwealth Relations Office (CRO) 88; and Foreign Office merger 102

competitors 17

Conan Doyle, Sir A. 18

Conservative Party 10, 16

Constitution, of Irish Free State 77

Coombes, R. 26, 27, 28, 30, 33, 34, 37, 38, 54n

Cooper, J.A. 110, 111, 112, 114, 115; Pan-Britannic festival 34, 111

Cornwall 14

Coubertin, P. de 4, 8, 53n, 104

cricket 19, 95, 96, 97, 100–2, 106–7

Crocker, J.H. 68, **69**, 75n

Cronin, M. 78

Crump, J. 89

Cuff, L. 53n

cultural cringe, and colonial contemplations 51–2

culture: African sport 95–6; British 105

Daily Star 66

Davis Cup (1900) 10

decentering, British identity 7

Depression, The 45–6

Desborough, Lord W.H.G., Irish Home-Rule Movement 16, 17

diversity 2, 3

Dominions: Australia 38; nationalism 20; South Africa 19; white settlers 19

Duff, L. 31

Eastern European nations 37

Edström, P. 82, 84, 86

Edward VII, King 67–8

Empire team 17, 27

England: annexation of Wales with (1536) 8–9; Cornwall 14

Etate Libre d'Irelade 79–80

Evening Journal 63, 64

Expansion of England (Seeley) 17

expatriates 47; performance 48–9

External Relations Act (1936) 79

Fédération International des Sociétés d'Aviron (FISA) 81

Fédération International d'Escrime (FIE) 82

Fédération Internationale de Football Association (FIFA) 35

Fédération Internationale de Natation (FINA) 81, 91

fencing: *Fédération International d'Escrime* (FIE) 82; Northern Ireland 82

fencing clubs, Northern Ireland 82

field hockey 21n, 104

flags: Maple Leaf 58–76; Union Jack 61–2

football: FIFA 35; Scotland 9; United Kingdom 11; World Cup 15

Foreign and Commonwealth Office (FCO) 102

foreign policy, under Heath 102

fortification forces, New Zealand Olympic Committee (NZOC) 44–6

Frantz, C., and Rogers, C.A. 96–7

Gaelic Union 13

gender norms 96, 98

gendered history, sport 96–9

George III, King 12

Gladstone, W.E. 12

Glasgow, Commonwealth Games (2014) 115

global position, Great Britain 17

golfer 104

Gorman, D. 30

government, Rhodesian Front 103

Great Britain (GB): and Australia 25; global position 17; and International Olympic Committee 101–3; and New Zealand 45; Union Jack 61–2

Greece 35

Grey, Lord A.H.G. 62–5, 70–1, 74; letter to Hanbury-Williams 70

Hanbury-Williams, Governor-General Colonel J. 62–5, **67**; and British Olympic Association 62, 63; letter from Grey 70

Heath, E. 102

INDEX

Heine, M.H., and Barney, R.K. 4, 58–76
Hellenic Organizing Committee 12
Helsinki Games (1952) 86
historical what ifs, trans-imperial histories 110–17
hockey team, Rhodesia 101
Holt, E.J. 82, 89–90
Home-Nations 9–10; Britishness 20; United Kingdom 11
Honner, R. 28–9
Hunt, T. 5, 77

identity: British 7; decentering 7; nationalism 43; NZ sporting 51–2; Rhodesia 99–101
identity cards, Rhodesian passports 103
imperial powers, post-enlightenment 18
imperial union, Canada 59
imperialism 26, 43, 111; Australia 25; cohesion 65–6; nationalism 3
independence, Ireland 16
Indigenous Australasians 29
International Amateur Athletics Federation (IAAF) 81, 82, 83, 89–90
International Campaign against Racism in Sport 103
International Olympic Committee (IOC) 5, 78, 82, 89, 91, 96; *Bulletin Officiel* 79; and Great Britain 101–3; Olympic Charter 8
international sport, and Rhodesian identity 99–101
internationalism, peaceful 8
Ireland 12; *Etate Libre d'Irelade* 79–80; and Olympic Movement recognition 77–95; political revolution 77; sport 9; sporting independence 16
Irish Amateur Boxing Association (IABA) 81
Irish Amateur Rowing Union (IARU) 81
Irish athletes: anti-British sentiments of 13; in British Olympic team 12
Irish Free State 78, 79
Irish Home-Rule Movement 13, 16, 17
Irish Independent 13
Irish Nationality and Citizenship Act (1935), Oath of Allegiance 79
Irish Olympic Council 77, 78, 79, 83, 85, 86; *Official Report* 81
Irish Olympic team 15–16
Irish Republic 85
Irish Swimming Association (IASA) 81

Jollie, E.T. 96
Jones, W.F. 81
jus soli principle, subjecthood (citizenship) 18

Kerr, B. 66–7, 69; Maple Leaf 72, **72**
Killanin, Lord M.M. 87–8, 90
Kohe, G. 4

Labour Party (GB), and Rhodesia 102
Llewellyn, M.P. 2, 27, 28; and Nielson, E. 111, 112
London 66, 80–2; Commonwealth Relations Office (CRO) 88, 102
London Olympic Games: (1908) 16, 66, 67–8; (1948) 80
Los Angeles Games (1932) 78
Lovelock, J.E. 47–8, 49–51

McCartney, E. 81
Mager, A.K. 98
male population, New Zealand 45
maleness, players 97
Maple Leaf (Canada) 58–76; and Kerr 72, **72**; symbolism 59–61; triumph of 66–70
Maple Leaf Forever song (Muir) 60–1
married women 96
Marryatt, A. 44, 54n
masculinity 95–107
Mayer, O. 83, 86
Meaney, N. 25
medals 69, 113
media coverage, Rhodesian Olympic teams 105
Melbourne Games (1956) 89–90
melting pot motif, USA 113
Merrick, J.G. 20, 33–4
Moore, K. 30–1
Morning Bulletin (British Empire Games) 31
Muir, A., *Maple Leaf Forever* 60–1
Munich Olympic Games (1972) 102
Munster Express 16

National Cyclists Union (NCU) 27–8
National Olympic Committee (NOC) 12, 79, 91
nationalism 5, 20–1, 35–6; Canada 62; Dominions 20; identity 43; imperialism 3; non-British 19
Nationalist leaders 91
nationality, test of 84
New Zealand 30, 34, 42–57; and Australia 4; and Great Britain 45; male population 45; and Olympic Movement 53n; sporting connections 47–51; sporting identity 51–2
New Zealand Amateur Athletics Association (NZAAA) 54n
New Zealand Olympic Committee (NZOC) 42, 46–8, 52, 53n, 54n; fortification forces 44–6
Newington Montage 74, **74**
Nielson, E. 19; and Llewellyn, M.P. 111, 112
non-European athletes, USA 113
Norman, P. 25
norms, gender 96, 98
Northern Ireland: fencing clubs 82; swimmers 81
Novak, A. 5, 95–107

INDEX

Oath of Allegiance, Irish Nationality and Citizenship Act (1935) 79
O'Duffy, E. 78
Olympic Charter (IOC) 8
Olympic Council of Ireland (OCI) 87
Olympic Games: Amsterdam (1928) 29, 31; Berlin (1936) 17, 36; London (1908) 16, 66, 67–8; London (1948) 80; Los Angeles (1932) 78; Melbourne (1956) 89–90; Munich (1972) 102; Stockholm (1912) 18, 53n
Olympic Movement 38; Ireland 77–95, 91; and New Zealand 53n
Olympic Winter Games (2010), Canada 58
opening ceremonies 68, 75n
Ottawa Citizen Journal 63, 64, 65

Pablo, T. 29
Pain, D. 89–90
Pan-Britannic festival, and Cooper 34, 111
Pan-Britannic sporting alliance 115
party politics, British Conservative Party 3
passports, Rhodesia 101–2
patronage, Porritt 48–9
peaceful internationalism 8
per-modern sports 97
Pereira, F.L.C. 66
players, maleness 97
political forces, Britishness 3
political revolution, Ireland 77
polo 21n
popular culture 2
Porritt, A.E. 47–8, 49–51, 54n; (ex)patriotic performance 48–9; political patronage 48–9
post-enlightenment, imperial powers 18
protagonists 42

race: African 112; Anglo-Saxon 112
racial discrimination, Rhodesia 96–9
racial segregation 95
racism 103
recolonization, Belich 25–6
Referee 32
Rhodes, C. 100
Rhodesia 5, 95–107; hockey team 101; identity 99–101; identity and international sport 99–101; and Labour Party (GB) 102; racial discrimination 96–9; socialization 98; sport 101; sport and British culture influence 105; white hunters 97
Rhodesian Front, government 103
Rhodesian Olympic team: media coverage 105; women 104–6
Rhodesian passports 101–2; Olympic identity cards 103
rituals, sporting 99
Robinson, M.M. 30
Rogers, C.A., and Frantz, C. 96–7
Rome 83, 84

Rome direction 84
Ross, P.D. 66, 75n
rowing: *Fédération International des Sociétés d'Aviron* (FISA) 81; Irish Amateur Rowing Union (IARU) 81
Rowley, S. 27, 28
rugby 95–9, 101, 103, 104, 106–7; tours 99; Wales 9
rugby union 4, 10, 11, 14, 17, 19; Australia 25; Cornwall 14
Russell, Lt-Col R.H. 84

scholars 43
Scotland, football 9
selection procedures 33
self-identity, Canada 58–76
Shepherds Bush Olympic Stadium 67
Six Counties 87
Social Darwinism 18–19
social relations, Southern Rhodesia 100
socialization, Rhodesia 98
South Africa 20, 27, 97, 98; Dominions 19
South African Currie Cup 97
Southern Rhodesia, social relations 100
specialization 28, 29
sport: Africans 97; British 95; Coubertin 4; gender norms 98; gendered history 96–9; Ireland 9; Rhodesia 101; symbolism 95
sport culture, Africa 95–6
sporting boycotts 98
sporting connections, New Zealand 47–51
sporting identity, New Zealand 51–2
sporting independence, Ireland 16
sporting landscape, twentieth century 11
sporting rituals 99
sporting unification 16; *Munster Express* 16
sprinters 27, 31–2, 66–7
Stanley, G.F.G. 71, 72, **73**, 75n
Stapleton, T. 98
Star 65
Stewart, A. 104
Stockholm Games (1912) 18, 53n
subjecthood (citizenship), *jus soli* principle 18
superiority, Anglo-Saxon 113
Sutcliffe, D. 105
swimmers 81, 105
swimming: Australia 33; *Fédération Internationale de Natation* (FINA) 81, 91; Irish Swimming Association (IASA) 81; medals 113
Sydney Morning Herald 19, 31
Sydney Referee (Keartland) 19–20
symbolism: Canadian Maple Leaf 59–61; sport 95

tennis: Davis Cup (1900) 10; pairs 104
Times 68
Tomlinson, G. 104

INDEX

track and field team, Canada 65
trans-imperial histories, historical what ifs 110–17
twentieth century, sporting landscape 11

unification, sporting 16
Unilateral Declaration of Independence (UDI) 5, 95, 97
Union Jack, Great Britain 61–2
United Kingdom (UK) 7–24; football 11; Home-Nations 11
United States of America (USA) 35, 36, 113; melting pot motif 113; non-European athletes 113; teams 113

Vance, J. 61–2

Wales 9; annexation with England (1536) 8–9; Gaelic Union 13; National Eisteddfod 14; rugby 9

war, and Empire 95–107
War of Independence (1919–21) 91
Washminster mutation 37
West Australian 31
West Germany 102, 107n
Western Education, Christianity 98
white dominions 2; inner cores 112
white hunters, Rhodesia 97
white settlers, dominions 19
Whitehead, E. 100
Wilding, A. 53n
Williams, P. 72, **73**
Winter Games 74; Vancouver (2010) 58
women: African 105; married 96; Rhodesian Olympic Team 104–6
womens' sport 32
Wood, 'Billy' W. 68
World Cup football 15
World War I (1914–18) 20, 44
World War II (1939–45) 20; post- 7